An Uncommon Lectionary

An Uncommon Lectionary

Lectionary

A Companion to Common Lectionaries

John Beverley Butcher

The following have generously given permission to use their translations in this volume: *The Complete Gospels: Annotated Scholars Version,* ed. Robert J. Miller. Polebridge Press, 1992. Used by permission; *The Lost Gospel Q,* trans. Mark Powelson and Ray Riegert. Berkeley, CA: Ulysses Press, 1996. Used by permission; *The Jerusalem Bible,* copyright © 1966, 1967, and 1968, and *The New Jerusalem Bible,* copyright © 1985, by Darton Longman & Todd, Ltd., and Doubleday, a division of Random House, Inc. Reprinted by permission; *The Nag Hammadi Library in English,* ed. James M. Robinson. San Francisco: Harper & Row, 1977, 1988. Used by permission; *The New Revised Standard Version of the Bible,* copyright © 1989, and *The Revised Standard Version of the Bible,* copyright © 1946, 1953, 1971, by the Division of Christian Education of the National Council of Churches in the USA. Used by permission. All rights reserved; *New Testament Apocrypha,* ed. Wilhelm Schneemelcher and Edgar Hennecke. John Knox Press, 1991. Used by permission of Westminster John Knox Press; *The Odes of Solomon,* Willis Barnstone, translator; *Old Testament Pseudepigrapha,* ed James. M. Charlesworth. Garden City, NY: Doubleday, 1983. Used by permission; *The Tanakh, A New Translation of the Holy Scriptures according to the Traditional Hebrew Text.* Philadelphia and Jerusalem: Jewish Publication Society, 1985. Used by permission.

Cover: The Assembled Nag Hammadi Codices. Courtesy of the Institute for Antiquity and Christianity, Claremont, California. Used by permission.

An Uncommon Lectionary

Published in 2002 by Polebridge Press, P. O. Box 6144, Santa Rosa, California, 95406.

Copyright © 2002 by John Beverley Butcher

Library of Congress Cataloging-in-Publication Data

Butcher, John Beverley
    An uncommon lectionary : a companion to common lectionaries /
John Beverley Butcher.
    p. cm.
    Includes indexes.
    ISBN 0-944344-91-7
    1. Apocryphal Gospels--History and criticism. 2. Apocryphal books--Criticism, interpretation, etc. 3. Lectionaries. 4. Apocryphal books. 5. Bible--Liturgical lessons, English. I. Title.

BS2851 .B88 2002
229'.8--dc21   2002072266

Contents

Preface

Common lectionaries provide a three-year cycle of Sunday readings based on the Gospels of Matthew, Mark, Luke, and John. *An Uncommon Lectionary* adds one more year to make full use of all the Gospels beyond the familiar four.

In this lectionary, the Gospel translations are from the Scholar's Version as found in *The Complete Gospels*. Unless otherwise noted, *Q Gospel* readings are from the Mark Powelson and Ray Reigert version. *The Odes of Solomon* follow the translation by Willis Barnestone with editing by John Butcher.

In choosing from the various translations available, the editor has made several specific theological choices including the following: Kingdom of God, Kingdom of Heaven, and Kingdom of the Father are retained rather than "God's Imperial Rule." The problem is that almost any wording in English is inadequate. "Kingdom" may be out of style, but is "Imperial Rule" any improvement? In a world where imperial powers reign mightily over weaker nations, the connotations are, in my opinion, equally disturbing. I have retained the familiar phrasing.

Son of Man, is a major theological concept whose day is clearly yet to come. Masculine "Son" and masculine "Man" create a contemporary reaction, particularly among those of us who value equality of the sexes. Yet is the Scholars Version use of "Son of Adam" any improvement? The bright light in resolving this problem is provided by Dr. Karen King's translation of the underlying phrase as "Seed of True Humanity" and "Truly Human being" in the Gospel of Mary. With her insights in hand, can we go back into Thomas, Q, and the Synoptic Gospels and retranslate? As an interim solution I use "Son of Man" followed a by bracketed alternative: (Truly Human Being).

Bridal Chamber is another major theological issue and spiritual experience. I have retained Bridal Chamber rather than bridal suite as in the SV because, for me, the experience is not akin to entering a set of rooms or an apartment, but rather like going into that one, intimate place of Holy Union with the unfathomable Mystery.

Blessed is retained over words substituted like Congratulations, Fortunate, and Lucky.

This Uncommon Lectionary is one of the many fruits of the diligent research of Robert Funk, Robert J. Miller and the scholars of the Jesus Seminar who produced *The Complete Gospels*. Since 1989 I have been participating in the spring and fall meetings of the Westar Institute which have deepened my understanding of the formation of the Gospel tradition.

In developing this lectionary, I give special thanks to the readers of the manuscript: my wife Grace, Antonnette V. Graham, Tom and Barbara Hall, Dennis L. and Carol Maher, and Robert Funk. Char Matejovsky, COO of Polebridge Press has given careful attention to detail, particularly in the selection of headings and printing style, organization of a user friendly index, and inclusion of a glossary of terms and this preface. Special thanks go to Ron Cox for locating the photograph of the books of Nag Hammadi Library used on the cover.

Introduction

Our data base on Jesus and the early communities of faith has been expanded significantly because of recent discoveries. *An Uncommon Lectionary* is designed to assist priests, pastors, liturgical leaders, and congregations to make creative use of that expanded information. Our purpose is to help bring hidden Gospels and related documents into the open while moving toward full disclosure of Jesus and his message.

Jesus entered into a deep experience of the ultimate Source of life whom he addressed as "Father." From his own spiritual experience flowed an energized ministry of teaching and healing. Unfortunately, Jesus wrote nothing himself, or if he did we do not have it now. For us to obtain information, we must rely upon the people who continued to experience his presence with them, the communities of faith, and the itinerant teachers who kept him and his teachings alive.

Competent scholarly research reveals that the Gospel tradition has many layers, the first being Jesus' life and teachings. This was followed by the oral tradition, in which people passed on to others what they had heard. Next came the collecting of his sayings into written form. The earliest of these are the Gospel Q and the Gospel of Thomas, both in first edition about the year 50 CE. They are primary source material for the later narrative Gospels of Mark, Luke, Matthew, and John. For dating and development of the Gospels, see the chart," From John the Baptist to Nicea."

From John the Baptist to Nicea:
Stages in the development of the early Christian tradition

1–30 C.E.

John the Baptist
The precursor and mentor of Jesus
(died about 27 C.E.)

Jesus of Nazareth
Traveling sage and wonder-worker
(died about 30 C.E.)

30–60 C.E.

Paul of Tarsus
Chief founder of gentile Christianity
(letters written about 50-60 C.E.)

Sayings Gospel Q
(first edition, about 50 C.E.)

Gospel of Thomas
(first edition, about 70 C.E.)

60–80 C.E.

Signs Gospel
(eventually incorporated into John)

Gospel of Mark
The first narrative gospel
(first edition, about 70 C.E.)

Didache
First believers handbook
(first edition)

80–100 C.E.

Gospel of Matthew
Incorporating Mark and Q
(about 80 C.E.)

Gospel of Luke
Incorporating Mark and Q
(about 90 C.E.)

Dialogue of the Savior
(first edition, probably 50–100 C.E.)

Gospel of Peter
(first edition, probably 50–100 C.E.)

Egerton Gospel
(probably 50–100 C.E.)

Gospel of John
Incorporating the Signs Gospel
(about 90 C.E.)

Gospel of Mark
Canonical edition
(about 100 C.E.)

100–150 C.E.

Gospel of John
Third edition
(insertions and additions)

Secret Book of James
First edition
(found at Nag Hammadi)

Gospel of Mary

Jewish-Christian Gospels
(preserved in patristic quotations)

Didache
Second edition
(insertions and additions)

Gospel of Thomas
Second edition
(surviving edition)

*Surviving fragment of
Gospel of John*
(p52)

*Surviving fragments of
Egerton Gospel*
(PEgerton2 and PKöln255)

150–325 C.E.

*Emergence of four recognized
gospels*

*Emergence of an official collec-
tion of Christian writings* ("New
Testament")

*Christianity becomes a legal
religion* (313 C.E.)

Council of Nicea (325 C.E.)

First official creeds

*First surviving copies of
"Bibles"* (about 325–350 C.E.)

The Scholars of the Jesus Seminar have gathered all the presently known Gospels together into one convenient volume entitled *The Complete Gospels* where you will find a fresh translation, the Scholars Version, and very helpful introductory material.

Beyond the Holy Four

"Most who have sought to understand the words and deeds of Jesus and the traditions about him have confined their attention to the New Testament Gospels. Those texts are readily available and have been intensively studied. Many interested in Jesus were not even aware of the existence of other gospels, or if they knew of them, did not know where to find them. While scholars had access to these documents — they are called extracanonical gospels because they were not included among the so-called canonical gospels — and could study them in the original languages, the vast majority tended to dismiss them as unimportant, on the hasty assumption that all of them were fanciful elaborations based on the New Testament gospels, or at least came from a much later period. However, research in the last several decades has significantly broadened our understanding of the diversity and complexity of the early Jesus traditions. Scholars now find it necessary to turn to the extracanonical gospels to learn about the development of even the earliest Jesus traditions. These texts disclose to us how Christian communities gathered, arranged, modified, embellished, interpreted, and created traditions about the teachings and deeds of Jesus.

"All of the intracanonical and extracanonical texts in this volume are witnesses to early Jesus traditions. All of them contain traditions independent of the New Testament gospels.

"During the first few centuries after Jesus, most Christian communities, if they were fortunate enough to possess written gospels at all, contented themselves with one or more of the four major gospels. These predominant narratives eventually gained ecclesiastical approval in the fourth century with a ruling by the Greek-speaking hierarchy that the only gospels authorized for official use — belonging to the rule or norm of the church and therefore canonical — were the texts attributed to Matthew, Mark, Luke, and John.

However, in earlier centuries many Christians had cherished other gospels, which they sincerely believed to carry the revealed truths about Jesus.

It is only from the perspective of later centuries that these texts which nourished the faith of generations of Christians can be called extra-canonical.

The distinction between the canonical and extra-canonical gospels did not exist in the period of Christian origins, and therefore is not helpful for understanding the earliest centuries of Christianity in their rich diversity."

— from the Introduction to *The Complete Gospels*

Selected Readings Supporting the Gospel

An Uncommon Lectionary is Gospel driven. It also includes two supporting readings for each Sunday and Major Holy Day. The first of these will normally relate directly to the Gospel. As is the case with the four familiar Gospels, earlier scriptural passages on a similar theme often serve as precursors.

For example, just as Israel's passage through the waters of the Red Sea is their baptism as a people, so Jesus, as sign of the renewed Israel, is baptized in the Jordan River. Similarly, the Israelites spend 40 years in the wilderness and Jesus spends 40 days in the wilderness. The Exodus story of the feeding of the Israelites in the desert is echoed and developed in the Bread of Life theme in the Gospel of John. Paul is particularly clear in citing the parallels between the Israelites and Jesus in I Corinthians 10.

The so-called extra-canonical Gospels exhibit frequent thematic and symbolic parallels to the Hebrew Bible and other Holy Scriptures written prior to the time of Jesus. This lectionary normally provides a supporting reading for each of these Gospel readings.

In addition to the Book of the Acts of the Apostles, there are other early documents like the Didache that provide descriptions of early communities of faith. They enrich our understanding of what faith and life were like in the congregations. Sometimes they provide insights into the contexts in which Gospels are being written. Selections from these writings are included in the lectionary and normally used as a second reading before the Sunday Gospel.

At the back of this book you will find a Chart of Gospels and Readings that provides the citations for each Sunday and Major Holy Day. Next follows an Index of Holy Scripture.

What Did They Sing in the Early Church?

Have you ever wondered what the family and friends of Jesus sang when they met together in the days, weeks, months, and years following his death? Most of his original disciples were Jews, so their repertoire would have begun with the familiar collection of songs known as the Book of Psalms.

But since their experiences needed fresh expression, they began singing new songs. After a while, they took some of the oral singing tradition and began writing the words down. Unfortunately, since musical notation hadn't yet been invented, so we have only the words without the tunes. One of the priceless gifts to us is a collection songs known as the Odes of Solomon written ca. 100 CE.

King Solomon, reigning 976–936 BCE, lived a thousand years before the Odes of Solomon were written. Why, since he could not have possibly written them, is Solomon's name attached to this collection of songs? For the same reason his name was attached to the delightful erotic poetry we know as The Song of Solomon, and his father, King David, was associated with the Book of Psalms: new music gained greater and more immediate acceptance when it was attributed to the tradition of David and Solomon.

The situation is rather like that of Old King Cole, that merry old soul who called for his pipe, called for his bowl, and called for his fiddlers three. We remember King Cole, but who knows the names of his fiddlers? So who were the people who wrote the songs in the collection known as the Odes of Solomon? We know they belonged to an early community of faith, but their names are lost forever.

In a very real sense the One who deserves the most credit for their composition is the Spirit of the Resurrected Jesus who touches hearts and sets them free to express musically what they are feeling. There are forty-two Odes. The second one is missing, but we have all the others in fresh translation thanks to Willis Barnstone.

Now that the Odes of Solomon are once again available, composers are writing new music for them. First century texts are being sung again in the twenty-first. If you are a musician, might new tunes spring up in you? If "some of your best friends" are musicians, why not show them the Odes and ask if they feel the Spirit welling up in them to provide melodies or chants for these wondrous texts?

A Companion to the Common Lectionaries

What do people normally hear read and preached in churches and other communities of faith? Many congregations follow either a common lectionary or a denominational variation. Sunday propers are normally in a three year cycle: Year A focuses primarily on Matthew, Year B on Mark, and Year C on Luke. The Gospel of John is inserted into all three years. Thus the four Gospels of the conventional New Testament are well covered.

An Uncommon Lectionary is designed to be a companion, complement, and supplement to the common lectionaries by providing orderly arrangements of readings from Gospels other than the basic four.

This Lectionary provides one year of propers for Sundays and Major Holy Days in the familiar format of two Readings, Psalm, and Gospel:

The Gospel selection is the heart and center of the propers. Gospel material is arranged in harmony with the liturgical year.

The First Reading will normally be a selection from Holy Scripture on a theme that relates to the Gospel.

The Second Reading will normally be a reading "in course" from such early Church sources as the Didache, The Apostolic Tradition of Hippolytus, The Secret Book of James, and others.

The Psalm will draw from the Church's oldest songbook, The Odes of Solomon, plus psalms and songs found in the Wisdom literature, the Nag Hammadi Library and other early church sources. Asterisks (*) are provided as designated breaks for responsive readings or musical notation for chanting.

The liturgical year in this lectionary begins with the primary spiritual event in the life of Jesus: his Baptism by John in the Jordan River. Mark, the earliest narrative Gospel, opens with the ministry of John the Baptizer who is "calling for baptism and a change of heart that lead to forgiveness of sins." (Mark 1:4, SV)

According to Luke 3:23, Jesus was about thirty when he went to hear John preach. What might there have been in John's message that prompted Jesus to ask for baptism? And what might he have experienced during his baptism and the forty days in the wilderness that reportedly followed? Might the baptism in the Jordan and the time in desert comprise a story illustrating his enlightenment?

The evidence is clear that something profound happened within Jesus which provided direction and energy for a ministry of teaching and healing. Without Jesus' baptism, there might have been no ministry, no getting into trouble with the authorities, no crucifixion, no resurrection experiences, no church, no Christian religion, and no church history! The course of human civilization would have gone quite differently.

Because of the enormous value and tremendous implications of the baptism of the historic Jesus, *An Uncommon Lectionary* begins with this profound story. In harmony with most lectionaries in common use, the Baptism of Jesus is celebrated on the first Sunday after the Epiphany (January 6). Therefore this lectionary begins with the first Sunday after January 6.

Teachings ascribed to Jesus in the Gospel of Thomas are the main focus of Gospel readings in Epiphany and Lent. Passion narratives are from the Gospel of Peter. Easter season focuses on the Gospel of Mary (Magdalene). Pentecost season returns to the Gospel of Thomas and then the Q Gospel. It can be both refreshing and very thought provoking to hear Q speaking on its own. The Infancy Gospel of James provides readings for Pre-Christmas and Advent. The Twelve Days of Christmas make full use of the Infancy Gospel of Thomas.

As in any lectionary, the Epiphany Season is shorter when Easter is earlier; Epiphany is longer when Easter is later. Easter also affects the number of Sundays after Pentecost. Sundays after Pentecost will overlap with the Pre-Christmas Season and Advent providing a number of choices for creative liturgists.

Choices for Pastors, Priests, and other Leaders of Community Worship

An Uncommon Lectionary can be used in a variety of ways including the following:

• **As a "Year D" following years A, B, and C of lectionaries presently in use.** Clearly this would put the congregation out of step with others who choose to follow an unceasing round of A, B and C. But maybe one year in the sequence could be omitted in order to get back on track the following year. When considering varying from the accustomed pattern, one might entertain a paraphrase of Jesus: "The lectionary was made for people and not people for the lectionary."

• **At one of the Sunday Services while other services continue using familiar lectionaries.** This choice allows continuity with the conventional lectionary while offering the missing information at another service. Members of the congregation would then have a choice, even though the preacher might have to prepare two different sermons for some Sundays!

• **One Season at a time.** For example, you might choose to start with the Baptism of Jesus and the Sunday readings for Epiphany, then return to the familiar lectionary. Or you might choose to follow this lectionary just for Lent and Holy Week. Or you could begin with Easter Sunday by stating that during the Easter season people will have opportunity to hear more of other reported encounters with the Resurrected Jesus.

• **During a designated week day service.** This choice would probably be the easiest, but would reach a more limited number of people. Another option would be to explore *An Uncommon Lectionary* with a smaller group of people before introducing it to the entire congregation on Sunday mornings.

• **As a resource for preachers to weave into sermons.** At the very least, those who are responsible for leading worship might choose to familiarize themselves with the gospels and readings in this lectionary and select stories and quotations to weave into their sermons, Lenten series, and other teaching situations.

• **As a resource for communities and congregations that do not normally use a lectionary.** Some traditions rely entirely on their pastors to select what will be read and preached on Sunday mornings. The advantage of this approach is that the pastor has full reign and responsibility to select scripture according to his or her perception of the needs of the congregation. The disadvantage is that people in the congregation may hear only their pastor's favorite selections. Increasingly, pastors are finding lectionaries useful as a guide in making selections. *An Uncommon Lectionary* provides significant information often previously unknown and a host of new choices.

• **For individuals and families in their homes.** This lectionary is designed primarily for congregations, but individuals, couples, families, religious orders, and other intentional communities may find this resource enriching for their spiritual lives.

Whichever plan is chosen, the central purpose of this lectionary remains the same: to encourage people to make use of the fullness of the Gospel tradition and to enhance the vitality of worship and spiritual life now.

Introducing the Complete Gospels to the People

As I travel around the country offering seminars on *The Complete Gospels*, I find great interest and eagerness to hear about the long hidden Gospels. I have discovered that people who love Jesus and value Holy Scripture are quite receptive to the "new" information. They are often intrigued when they hear that there are more Gospels than the four offered by conventional Bibles.

I have also discovered that many people are already aware of some of these Gospels through books and informative television specials on early Christianity. I find, for example, that many people outside conventional religious groups are quite aware of the Gospel of Thomas.

Also of special interest is the Gospel of Mary, the only Gospel named for a woman. This exciting Gospel reports experiences of Mary Magdalene with the Resurrected Jesus and illustrates clearly the leadership role of women in the early church together with the predictable resistance from some males. Feminists and all who are seeking a more balanced presentation of the Gospel welcome the discovery of these priceless early documents. When that which was "lost" is now "found" there may well be great rejoicing. In short, I have discovered that there is a greater openness to *The Complete Gospels* than I had anticipated.

For anyone feeling a bit cautious in introducing these Gospels, I would respond by saying that I totally understand. I, too, was cautious and concerned that I might be opening up a Pandora's box. But I continued feeling the vibrant vitality of these Gospels and kept hearing from reliable scholars that these documents are indeed very early and close to the heart and spirit of Jesus, so what could I do? I knew I must speak about them even if someone might object. The echoing sound of "The Truth shall set you free", gave me the strength to persist in studying the documents myself and the courage to share them with my congregation. Having used them in preaching and teaching for nearly two decades in my own parish, I can report from personal experience that the risk is well worth it.

So how might a local pastor go about introducing *The Complete Gospels* and this lectionary to the people? One could begin by saying something like this, "The writer of the Gospel of John tells us that 'Jesus of course did many other things. If they were all to be recorded in detail, I doubt that the entire world would hold the books that would have to be written.' (John 21:25, SV)

Because of recent discoveries of early texts, we now have more Gospels available to us than ever before. They contain vital information that can deepen and enrich our faith. If I am to be a responsible pastor, I do not think I should withhold this information from you. Therefore, on ＿＿ we plan to begin using Gospels and accompanying readings following *An Uncommon Lectionary*. I invite you to explore these Gospels with me..."

Once you come to appreciate their great value, then you will find your own words and discover gentle and effective ways of introducing *The Complete Gospels* and this lectionary. It all begins with your own interest, investigation, and study. You might well decide to form a study group with people you believe are open and ready to explore all the Gospels. Seek, and you will find others who are interested in discovering the meaning and vitality of Gospels beyond the familiar four. When in doubt as to how to proceed, why not pray and ask, "Lord, what do You want me to do?"

Interpreting the Complete Gospels

As with any lectionary, the sermons preached from these texts will be determined in large measure by the perspective and understanding of the preacher on a given Sunday morning. There is no single interpretation. The further one gets into any text of Holy Scripture, the more illumination is shone upon others. The same preacher can deliver a sermon on the same text sometime later and have a rather different message. Whenever there has been a change of circumstances or a spurt of spiritual growth within the preacher, it is likely that a fresh message will spring from the same text. In considerable measure, the meaning is in the eye of the beholder. Jesus says that those who have eyes to see should take a close look! Consider one additional fact: the Good News has proved to have a powerful voice of its own; the Gospels have a persistent way of engaging people, and inviting their responses.

As an aid to the critical study of these texts, each preacher or teacher would do well to start by acquiring and using the following:

The Complete Gospels, Robert J. Miller, editor, Polebridge Press, Santa Rosa, California, 1994

The Nag Hammadi Library in English, third edition, James M. Robinson, ed., Harper & Row, San Francisco, California, 1988.

The Five Gospels, Robert W. Funk and Roy W. Hoover, Macmillan Publishing, New York, 1993.

Telling the Untold Stories, (Encounters with the Resurrected Jesus), John Beverley Butcher, Trinity Press International, Harrisburg, Pennsylvania, 2000.

Each interpreter will bring his or her own persistent questions to the Gospel text and might include some of the following:

What might be the origin and context of this story or teaching? Where does the energy in the story originate: with the Historical Jesus, the Resurrected Jesus, the Archetypal Jesus, or the friends and followers of Jesus? Is this story to be understood as historic, symbolic, or a blend of the two?

Most important, what does this passage really mean for us now? What might be some of the implications for our spiritual life, our relationships, and our daily living? Ultimately, how might these texts deepen our awareness of and encounter with the Holy Mystery whom some name God?

A Summary of Selection Criteria

An Uncommon Lectionary assumes that it will be used as a companion to the common lectionaries so that together they will provide all the available Gospel material on Jesus. It makes full use of all the Gospels beyond the familiar four.

Because this lectionary is Gospel driven, supporting readings are selected to be consistent with the Gospel.

Theologically, this lectionary is thoroughly incarnational, affirming a creation spirituality with the union of body and soul. It does not include material with serious mind-body splits.

This lectionary arranges Gospels and readings according to the normal sequence of the liturgical year with one exception: it begins with the Baptism of Jesus.

This lectionary reveals the diversity of faith and spiritual practice in early church traditions. The process is one of restoration, not innovation. We are reclaiming those parts of our tradition which have been ignored, lost, or hidden. Suppressed voices, like those of Mary Magdalene and other women leaders, are allowed to speak again.

The primary selection criteria springs from a desire for full disclosure of Jesus and the experience of early communities of faith.

Praying Your Way through the Uncommon Lectionary

I conclude this introduction with an adaptation of one of my favorite prayers from the Book of Common Prayer:

Blessed Lord, who has caused all holy Scriptures to be written for our learning: Open our minds and hearts to hear them, read them, mark them, learn them, and inwardly digest them, that we may embrace and hold fast the eternal life available to us now through Jesus the Anointed by the power of Your Holy Spirit. Amen.

John Beverley Butcher
San Francisco, California
Easter 2002

The Epiphany Season

An Uncommon Lectionary begins with the primary event in the life of Jesus, his Baptism by John in the Jordan River. Following ancient custom, his Baptism is celebrated on the first Sunday after the Epiphany on January 6.

The number of Sundays of Epiphany varies each year and they continue until the "Last Sunday of Epiphany" which comes immediately before Ash Wednesday. Always use the Last Sunday because it climaxes the season.

Epiphany 1 — The Baptism of Jesus
First Reading *Isaiah 40:1–8, Tanakh*

> Comfort, oh comfort My people,
> Says your God.
> Speak tenderly to Jerusalem,
> And declare to her
> That her term of service is over,
> That her iniquity is expiated;
> For she has received at the hand of the LORD
> Double for all her sins.
>
> A voice rings out:
> "Clear in the desert
> A road for the LORD!
> Level in the wilderness
> A highway for our God!

13

Let every valley be raised,
Every hill and mount made low.
Let the rugged ground become level
And the ridges become plain.
The Presence of the Lord shall appear
And all flesh, as one, shall behold —
For the LORD Himself has spoken."

A voice rings out: "Proclaim!"
Another asks, "What shall I proclaim?"
"All flesh is grass,
All its goodness like flowers of the field:
Grass withers, flowers fade
When the breath of the Lord blows on them.
Indeed, man is but grass:
Grass withers, flowers fade —
But the word of our God is always fulfilled!"

Second Reading *Mark 1:1–6 SV, Q 3:7–9, 16b–17, Robinson*

The good news of Jesus the Anointed begins with something Isaiah the prophet wrote:

Here is my messenger,
whom I send on ahead of you
to prepare your way!
A voice of someone shouting in the wilderness:
"Make ready the way of the Lord,
make his paths straight."

So, John the Baptizer appeared in the wilderness calling for baptism and a change of heart that lead to forgiveness of sins. And everyone from the Judean countryside and all the residents of Jerusalem streamed out to him and got baptized by him in the Jordan river, admitting their sins. And John wore a mantle made of camel hair and had a leather belt around his waist and lived on locusts and raw honey. . . .

He saw the crowds coming to be baptized: Snakes' litter! Who warned you to run from the impending rage? So bear fruit worthy of repentance, and do not presume to tell yourselves: We have as forefather Abraham! For I tell you: God can produce children for Abraham right out of these rocks! And the ax already lies at the root of the trees. So every tree not bearing healthy fruit is to be chopped down and thrown on the fire.

I baptize you in water, but the one to come after me is more powerful than I, whose sandals I am not fit to take off. He will baptize you in Holy Spirit and fire. His pitchfork is in his hand, and he will clear his threshing floor and gather the wheat into his granary, but the chaff he will burn on a fire that can never be put out.

Psalm *Ode 24*

The dove flies over the head of the Anointed One who is her
  head*
  She sings over him and her voice is heard.
The inhabitants are afraid and travelers shudder.*
  Birds take flight and all creeping things die in their holes.
Chasms open and close, seeking God as a woman in labor...*
  Chasms sink and are sealed by the Lord.
People perish in their old ways of thinking.*
  Everyone is imperfect and dies, saying nothing.
The Lord destroys the imagination of all who do not have
  truth.*
  They are weak in wisdom and are rejected, lacking truth.
The Lord discloses the Way and spreads grace in alien lands.*
  Those who understand know holiness. Hallelujah!

Gospel *Mark 1:9–13, SV, and Q 4:1–4, 9–12, 5–8, 13, Robinson*

During that same period Jesus came from Nazareth, Galilee, and was baptized in the Jordan by John. And just as he got up out of the water, he saw the skies torn open and the spirit coming down toward him like a dove. There was a voice from the skies: "You are my dear son in whom I delight."

And right away the spirit drives him out into the wilderness, where he remained for forty days, being put to the test by Satan. While he was living there among the wild animals, the heavenly messengers looked after him . . .

And the devil told him: If you are God's Son, order that these stones become loaves. And Jesus answered him: It is written: A person is not to live only from bread.

The devil took him along to Jerusalem and put him on the tip of the temple and told him: If you are God's Son, throw yourself down. For it is written: He will command his angels about you, and on their hands they will bear you, so that you do not strike your foot against a stone. And Jesus in reply told him: It is written: Do not put to the test the Lord your God.

And the devil took him along to a very high mountain and showed him all the kingdoms of the world and their splendor, and told him: All these I will give you, if you bow down before me. And in reply Jesus told him; It is written: Bow down to the Lord your God, and serve only him.

And the devil left him.

Note "You are my dear son in whom I delight" is William Tyndale's translation of 1534. SV reads, "You are my favored son — I fully approve of you."

Epiphany 2

First Reading *Deuteronomy 30:11–14, Tanakh*

Surely, this Instruction which I enjoin upon you this day is not too baffling for you nor is it beyond your reach. It is not in the heavens, that you should say, "Who among us can go up to the heavens and get it for us and impart it to us, that we may observe it?" Neither is it beyond the sea, that you should say, "Who among us can cross to the other side of the sea and get it for us and impart it to us, that we may observe it?" No, the thing is very close to you, in your mouth and in your heart, to observe it.

Second Reading *Gospel of Philip 70:34–71:4, 74:29–31, 77:8–15, NHL*

Jesus revealed himself at the Jordan: it was the fullness of the kingdom of heaven. He who was begotten before everything was begotten anew. He who was anointed was anointed anew. He who was redeemed in turn redeemed others . . .

As soon as Jesus went down into the water he came out laughing at everything of this world, not because he considers it a trifle, but because he is full of contempt for it . . .

By perfecting the water of Baptism, Jesus emptied it of death. Thus we do go down into the water, but we do not go down into death in order that we may not be poured out into the spirit of the world. When that spirit blows, it brings winter. When the Holy Spirit breathes, the summer comes.

Psalm *Sirach 51:13–18, NRSV*

While I was still young, before I went on my travels,*
    I sought wisdom openly in my prayer.
Before the temple I asked for her,*
    and I will search for her until the end.
From the first blossom to the ripening grape*
    my heart delighted in her.
My foot walked on the straight path;*
    from my youth I followed her steps.
I inclined my ear a little and received her,*
    and I found for myself much instruction.
I made progress in her;*
    to him who gives wisdom I will give glory.
For I resolved to live according to wisdom,*
    and I was zealous for the good, and I shall never be disappointed.

Gospel *Gospel of Thomas Prologue 1–5, SV*

These are the secret sayings that the living Jesus spoke and Didymos Judas Thomas recorded. And he said, "Whoever discovers the interpretation of these sayings will not taste death."

Jesus says, "Those who seek should not stop seeking until they find. When they find, they will be disturbed. When they are disturbed, they will marvel, and will rule over all, (and when they rule, they will rest.)

Jesus says, "If your leaders say to you, 'Look, the Father's imperial rule is in the sky,' then the birds of the sky will precede you. If they say to you, 'It is in the sea,' then the fish will proceed you. Rather, the Father's imperial rule is inside you and outside you. When you know yourselves, then you will be known, and you will understand that you are children of the living Father. But if you do not know yourselves, then you live in poverty, and you are the poverty."

Jesus says, "A person old in days won't hesitate to ask a little child seven days old about the place of life, and that person will live. For many of the first will be last, (and the last first) and will become a single one."

Jesus says, "Know what is in front of your face, and what is hidden from you will be disclosed to you. For there is nothing hidden that won't be revealed.

(There is nothing buried that won't be raised.)

Note Sections in parentheses are from a Greek fragment of the Gospel of Thomas.

Present Tense in Thomas The earliest extant fragments of the Gospel of Thomas are in Greek and use the present tense, "Jesus says . . ." The later Coptic version found at Nag Hammadi uses past tense, "Jesus said . . ."

In their 1998 translation of Thomas, Stephen J. Patterson, James M. Robinson, and Hans-Gebhard Bethge follow the Greek and use present tense throughout the Gospel of Thomas, with the exception of those brief conversations between Jesus and the disciples that are rendered in past tense.

This Lectionary uses the Scholars Version of Thomas with one exception: it follows the present tense, "Jesus says . . ." For those who have eyes to see and ears to hear, the teachings ascribed to Jesus are alive and vibrant in the present moment.

Epiphany 3

First Reading *Isaiah 64:1–3, Tanakh*

If You would but tear open the heavens and come down,
So that the mountains would quake before You —
As when fire kindles brushwood,
And fire makes water boil —
To make Your name known to Your adversaries
So that nations will tremble at Your Presence,
When You did wonders we dared not hope for,
You came down
And mountains quaked before You.
Such things had never been heard or noted.
No eye has seen them O God, but You,
Who act for those who trust in You.

Second Reading *Gospel of the Hebrews 3, SV*

The whole fountain of the holy spirit comes down on him. For the Lord is spirit and where the spirit is, there is freedom.

And it happened that when the Lord came up out of the water, the whole fountain of the holy spirit came down on him and rested on him. It said to him, "My Son, I was waiting for you in all the prophets, waiting for you to come so I could rest in you. For you are my rest; you are my first-begotten Son who rules forever."

Psalm *Ode 11:1–8*

My heart is cloven and a flower appears;*
    grace springs up and fruit from You, Lord.
You, the Highest One, split me with Your Holy Spirit,*
    expose my love for You and fill me with Your love.
Your splitting of my heart is my salvation*
    and I follow the way of Your peace, the way of truth.
From the beginning to the end I receive Your knowledge*
    and sit on the rock of truth where You place me.
Speaking waters come near my lips*
    from the vast fountain of You, Lord.
I drink and am drunk with the living water that never dies,*
    and my drunkenness gives me knowledge.
I turned off vanity, turned to You, my God,*
    and Your bounty makes me rich.
I throw off the madness of the earth,*
    I strip it from me and cast it away.

Gospel *Gospel of Thomas 8–11, 17, SV*

Jesus says, The *truly human being* is like a wise fisherman who cast his net into the sea and drew it up from the sea full of little fish. Among them the wise fisherman discovered a fine large fish. He threw all the little fish back into the sea, and easily chose the large fish. Anyone here with two good ears had better listen!"

Jesus says, "Look, the sower went out, took a handful of seeds, and scattered them. Some fell on the road, and the birds came and gathered them. Others fell on rock, and they didn't take root in the soil and didn't produce heads of grain. Others fell on thorns, and they choked the seeds and worms ate them.

And others fell on good soil, and it produced a good crop: it yielded sixty per measure and one hundred twenty per measure.

Jesus says, "I have cast fire upon the world, and look, I'm guarding it until it blazes."

Jesus says, "This heaven will pass away, and the one above it will pass away. The dead are not alive, and the living will die. During the days when you ate what is dead, you made it come alive. When you are in the light, what will you do? On the day when you were one, you became two. But when you become two, what will you do?"

Jesus says, "I will give you what no eye has seen, what no ear has heard, what no hand has touched, what has not arisen in the human heart, (and what has never occurred to the human mind.)

Note Section in parenthesis is from the NHL translation of the last phrase.

Epiphany 4

First Reading *Song of Solomon 1:1–4, Tanakh*

Oh, give me of the kisses of your mouth,
For your love is more delightful than wine.
Your ointments yield a sweet fragrance,
Your name is like finest oil —
Therefore do maidens love you.
Draw me after you, let us run!
The king has brought me to his chambers.
Let us delight and rejoice in your love,
Savoring it more than wine —
Like new wine they love you!

Second Reading *Song of Solomon 2:1–6*

I am a rose of Sharon,
A lily of the valleys.
Like a lily among thorns,
So is my darling among the maidens.
Like an apple tree among trees of the forest,

So is my beloved among the youths.
I delight to sit in his shade;
And his fruit is sweet to my mouth.
He brought me to the banquet room
And his banner of love was over me,
"Sustain me with raisin cakes,
Refresh me with apples,
For I am faint with love."
His left hand was under my head,
His right arm embraced me.

Psalm *Ode 3*

I am putting on Your love O Lord,*
    I am clothing myself with You, for You Love me.
How would I know how to love You, Lord,*
    if You did not love me?
And who can tell us about love?*
    Only one who is loved.
I love You my Beloved and my soul loves You.*
    I am where You repose and I will be no stranger.
For You are not petty or jealous,*
    my high merciful Lord.
I have gone to unite with You,*
    for the lover has found his Beloved,
and because I love the Son,*
    I shall become Your child.
Whoever joins the immortal becomes immortal.*
    Whoever delights in the Living One is living.
This is the Spirit of the Lord.*
    It does not lie. It teaches us his ways.
Be wise. Be understanding,*
    and let your eyes be open. Hallelujah!

Gospel *Luke 8:1–3, SV and Gospel of Philip 59:7–11, 63:32–64:5, NHL*

Jesus travelled through towns and villages, preaching and announcing the good news of God's imperial rule. The twelve were with him, and also some women whom he cured of evil spirits and diseases: Mary, the one from Magdala, from whom seven demons had taken their leave, and Joanna, the wife of Chuza, Herod's steward, and Susanna, and many others, who provided for them out of their resources. . . .

There were three who always walked with the Lord: Mary his mother and her sister and Magdalene, the one who was called his companion. His sister and his mother and his companion were each a Mary . . .

And the companion of the Savior is Mary Magdalene. But Christ loved her more than all the disciples and used to kiss her often on her mouth. The rest of the disciples were offended by it and expressed disapproval. They said to him, "Why do you love her more than all of us?" The Savior answered and said to them, "Why do I not love you like her?"

Epiphany 5

First Reading *Daniel 10:1–14, Tanakh*

In the third year of King Cyrus, an oracle was revealed to Daniel, who was called Belteshazzar. That oracle was true, but it was a great task to understand the prophecy; understanding came to him through the vision.

At that time, I, Daniel, kept three full weeks of mourning. I ate no tasty food, nor did any meat or wine enter my mouth. I did not anoint myself until the three weeks were over. It was on the twenty-fourth day of the first month, when I was on the bank of the great river, the Tigris, that I looked and saw a man dressed in linen, his loins girt in fine gold. His body was like beryl, his face had the appearance of lightning, his eyes were flaming torches, his arms and legs had the color of burnished bronze, and the sound of his speech was like the noise of a multitude.

I, Daniel, alone saw the vision; the men who were with me did not see the vision, yet they were seized with a great terror and fled into hiding. So I was left alone to see this great vision. I was drained of strength, my vigor was destroyed, and I could not summon up strength. I heard him speaking; and when I heard him speaking, overcome by a deep sleep, I lay prostrate on the ground. Then a hand touched me, and shook me onto my hands and knees. He said to me, "O Daniel, greatly beloved man, understand the words that I say to you and stand up, for I have been sent to you." After he said this to me, I stood up, trembling. He then said to me "Have no fear, Daniel, for from the first day that you set your mind to get understanding, practicing abstinence before your God, your prayer was heard, and I have come because of your prayer . . . So I have come to make you understand what is to befall your people in the days to come, for there is yet a vision for those days."

Second Reading *Gospel of Philip 73:2–8, 75:22–24, 56:26–32, 57:19–22, 70:8–9 NHL*

Those who say they will die first and then rise are in error. If they do not first receive the resurrection while they live, when they die they will receive nothing. So also when speaking about Baptism they say, "Baptism is a great thing," because if they receive it they will live.

It is necessary that we put on the living *new human being*. Therefore when he is about to go down into the water, he unclothes himself, in order that he may put on the living *new human being* . . .

Some are afraid lest they rise naked. Because of this they wish to rise in the flesh, and they do not know it is those who wear the flesh who are naked. It is those who unclothe themselves who are not naked . . .

In this world those who put on garments are better than the garments. In the kingdom of heaven the garments are better than those who have put them on. . . . One will clothe himself in this light sacramentally in the union . . .

Note italics for inclusive language.

Psalm *Ode 30*

Drink deeply from the living fountain of the Lord. It is opening for You.*

Come, all who are thirsty and drink, and rest by the fountain of the Lord.

How beautiful and pure. It rests the soul, water sweeter than honey.*

The honeycombs of bees are nothing in comparison.

Epiphany

This water flows from the lips of the Lord.*
  It's Name is from the Lord's heart.
It is invisible and has no borders.*
  It is unknown until it comes into our midst.
Those who drink it are blessed*
  and they rest. Hallelujah!

Gospel *Secret Gospel of Mark 1, 2 SV*

And they come into Bethany, and this woman was there whose brother had died. She knelt down in front of Jesus and says to him, "Son of David, have mercy on me." But the disciples rebuked her. And Jesus got angry and went with her into the garden where the tomb was. Just then a loud voice was heard from inside the tomb. Then Jesus went up and rolled the stone away from the entrance to the tomb. He went right in where the young man was, stuck out his hand, dragged him by the hand, and raised him up. The young man looked at Jesus, loved him, and began to beg him to be with him. Then they left the tomb and went into the young man's house. (Incidentally, he was rich.) Six days later Jesus gave him an order; and when evening had come, the young man went to him, dressed only in a linen cloth. He spent that night with him, because Jesus taught him the mystery of God's domain. From there Jesus got up and returned to the other side of the Jordan.

The sister of the young man whom Jesus loved was there, along with his mother and Salome, but Jesus refused to see them.

Commentary Why was this portion of the Gospel of Mark deleted? Now known as "Secret Mark" it actually belongs between Mark 10:34 and 10:35.

Once properly restored, the sequence goes like this:

Mark 10:17–22 about the rich young man who, hearing the message that would require him to sell all his possessions, goes away.

Mark 10:23–34 Jesus teaching about how difficult it is for the rich to find life

Secret Mark 1 The rich young man returns and experiences his spiritual death and resurrection. Thus the rich young man finally gets the message and Jesus initiates him into new life. Essentially, this is a baptism story. In the early church the candidate disrobed, was baptized, and then clothed in linen cloth.

Restoring Secret Mark to the place where it belongs may also shed light on the puzzling story in Mark 14:51–52 and provide the identity of the young man in the Gethsemane story who comes dressed in only a linen cloth and when Jesus is arrested runs away naked leaving his linen cloth behind.

Note further that linen is the material used in wrapping the dead for burial and is significant in the death and resurrection stories of Jesus. See Mark 15:46, Matt 27:59, Luke 23:53 and 24:12, John 19:40, 20:5–7.

Discovery of Secret Mark helps solve several puzzles.

The Daniel passage and the story of the man dressed in linen has its meaning for Daniel and also points to Jesus and to the young man and every person who enters into new life through spiritual death and resurrection.

Epiphany 6

First Reading *Revelation 22:12–17, NRSV*

"See, I am coming soon; my reward is with me, to repay according to everyone's work. I am the Alpha and the Omega, the first and the last, the beginning and the end."

Blessed are those who wash their robes, so that they will have the right to the tree of life and may enter the city by the gates. Outside are the dogs and sorcerers and fornicators and murderers and idolaters, and everyone who loves and practices falsehood.

"It is I, Jesus, who sent my angel to you with this testimony for the churches. I am the root and the descendant of David, the bright morning star."

The Spirit and the bride say, "Come."

And let everyone who hears say, "Come."

Let anyone who wishes take the water of life as a gift.

Second Reading *Gospel of Philip 63:12–21, NHL*

An ass which turns a millstone did a hundred miles walking. When it was loosed it found that it was still at the same place.

There are men who make many journeys, but make no progress toward a destination. When evening came upon them they saw neither city nor village, neither human artifact nor natural phenomenon, power nor angel. In vain have the wretches labored.

Psalm *Ode 1*

Lord, You are on my head like a crown*
   and I shall never be without You.
Your crown of truth was woven for me*
   and caused Your branches to blossom in me.
Your crown is not dry and sterile.*
   You live and blossom on my head.
Your fruits are full and complete*
   and filled with Your salvation.

Gospel *Oxyrhynchus 840, SV*

And taking the disciples along, Jesus led them into the inner sanctuary itself, and began walking about in the temple precinct.

This Pharisee, a leading priest, Levi by name, also entered, ran into them, and said to the Savior, "Who gave you permission to wander around in this inner sanctuary and lay eyes on these sacred vessels, when you have not performed your ritual bath, and your disciples have not even washed their feet? Yet in a defiled state you have invaded this sacred place, which is ritually clean. No one walks about in here, or dares lay eyes on these sacred vessels, unless they have bathed themselves and changed clothes.

And the Savior stood up immediately, with his disciples, and replied, "Since you are here in the temple, I take it you are clean."

He replies to the Savior, "I am clean. I bathed in the pool of David, you know, by descending into it by one set of steps and coming up out of it by another. I also changed to white and ritually clean clothes. Only then did I come here and lay eyes on these sacred vessels."

In response the Savior said to him: "Damn the blind who won't see. You bathe in these stagnant waters where dogs and pigs wallow day and night. And you wash and scrub the outer layers of skin, just like prostitutes and dance-hall girls, who wash and scrub and perfume and paint themselves to entice men, while inwardly they are crawling with scorpions and filled with all sorts of corruption. But my disciples and I — you say we are unbathed — have bathed in lively, life-giving water that comes down from (above) . . .

Note Compare Jesus teaching about inner washing in Thomas 89, Matt 23:25–26, Luke 11:39–41.

Commentary by Robert Funk The temple had *a leading priest* on duty charged with making sure that those who entered were ritually clean. The priest's further identity as *a Pharisee* connects him with other opponents of Jesus in the gospel tradition who dispute with him over questions of ritual.

The *sacred vessels* are the precious items used for libations in the temple service and kept in small rooms opening off of the Court of the Men of Israel. The *ritual bath* was required to achieve a state of levitical purity. See John 13:10: "People who have bathed need only wash their feet."

Priests on duty in the temple are known to have *changed their clothes* after bathing. This fragment is our only evidence that putting on new clothes was required of laymen too. This may well indicate that the author is not well informed about temple regulations.

As is characteristic through the gospel tradition, Jesus answers a challenge with a challenge of his own.

The priest details the steps of his cleansing process. A large double pool found nearby the temple may have been used for this purpose (see "the pool of Bethesda" in John 5). The term *pool of David* is otherwise unattested.

Stagnant waters (as in artificial pools) need replenishment, unlike flowing of "living" streams. Jesus' reference to *dogs and pigs* is not meant literally, as though these animals were actually wallowing in the priests' ritual bathing pools! Instead Jesus is pointing to thoroughly unclean sorts of people as in Matt 7:6; see further 2 Peter 2:22; Revelation 22:15.

Jesus dismisses *washing and scrubbing* as mere external adornment, often covering up the evil inside. The sentiment is similar to that found in Mark 7:1–23, Q 11:39–40, and Thomas 89.

Picturing moral corruption with *scorpions crawling inside* is reminiscent of invective addressed by Jesus elsewhere against the

Pharisees (Matt 23:25). More commonly in biblical tradition, the presence or threat of scorpions suggests danger or unusually severe punishment (Deut 8:15; 1 Kgs 12:11, 15; Ezek 2:6; Luke 10:19; Rev 9:3, 5, 10).

Jesus contrasts ritual bathing with Christian baptism, called *lively, life-giving water* from heaven.

Robert Funk in *The Complete Gospels*, Robert Miller, ed., p. 420–421

Continuing Commentary Would Jesus actually have referred to "prostitutes and dance-hall girls,who wash and scrub and perfume and paint themselves to entice men while inwardly they are crawling with scorpions and filled with all sorts of corruption"? These judgments seem quite different from his acceptance of the woman taken in adultery in John 7:53–8:11, so do they actually originate with him? Or might these words be placed on Jesus lips by someone else?

Dating of the text may be helpful here. Robert Funk, in his introduction to Oxyrhynchus 840 says, "An educated guess for the date of composition is sometime before 200 C.E., a more precise dating may be impossible unless the fragment could be identified with another known text."

In regard to what we might learn from the story, we could ask further questions. In whom might crawling scorpions and all sorts of corruption be residing? Might they be living within the women who service the men or within the men themselves? Jesus is clear in his teaching about projections, "Why do you notice the sliver in your friend's eye, but overlook the timber in your own eye? How can you say to your friend, 'Let me get the sliver out of your eye,' when there is that timber in your own? You phony, first take the timber out of your own eye and then you'll see well enough to remove the sliver within your friend's eye." Matthew 7:3–5, SV

This story from Oxyrhynchus 840 is included in this lectionary for two reasons: first, because of the intention of full disclosure of all the Gospel material available and secondly to raise again the persistent questions of origin: which parts of the tradition may have originated with Jesus? Which sayings may have been added later by others? In either case what value might it have? If this text sparks lively discussion, then it is serving its purpose.

Epiphany 7

First Reading *Sirach 38:1–15, NRSV*

Honor physicians for their services, for the Lord created them;
for their gift of healing comes from the Most High . . .
The skill of physicians makes them distinguished,
and in the presence of the great they are admired.
The Lord created medicines out of the earth,
and the sensible will not despise them.
Was not water made sweet with a tree in order that its power
    might be known?
And the Lord gave skill to human beings to be glorified in mar-
    vellous works.
By them the physician heals and takes away pain;
the pharmacist makes a mixture from them.
God's works will never be finished;
and from God health spreads over all the earth.
My child, when you are ill, do not delay,
but pray to the Lord and who will heal you.
Give up your faults and direct your hands rightly,
and cleanse your heart from all sin . . .
Then give the physicians *their* place, for the Lord created them;
do not let *physicians* leave you, for you need *them*
There may come a time when recovery lies in the hands of
    physicians,
for they too pray to the Lord to grant them success in diagnosis
and in healing, for the sake of preserving life.
Whoever sins against *their* Maker,
let such a one come under the care of a physician!

Note italics for inclusive language.

Second Reading *Gospel of Philip 77:35–78:11, NHL*

Spiritual love is wine and fragrance. All those who anoint
themselves with it take pleasure in it. While those who are
anointed are present, those nearby also profit from the fragrance. If those anointed with ointment withdraw from them
and leave, then those not anointed, who merely stand nearby,
still remain in their bad odor.

The Samaritan gave nothing but wine and oil to the wounded *person*. It is nothing other than the ointment. It healed the wounds, for "love covers a multitude of sins." (1 Peter 4:8)

Psalm *Ode 32*

To the blessed ones joy lives in the heart,*
    Light from You lives in them.
The Word comes from the Truth,*
    You come from Your Self.
You are strong from holy power from the skies*
    You are unshaken forever and ever. Hallelujah!

Gospel *Egerton Gospel 1–3, SV*

Just then a leper comes up to him and says, "Teacher, Jesus, in wandering around with lepers and eating with them in the inn, I became a leper myself. If you want to, I'll be made clean." The master said to him, "Okay — you're clean!" And at once his leprosy vanished from him. Jesus says to him, "Go and have the priests examine your skin. Then offer for your cleansing what Moses commanded — and no more sinning . . .

The legal experts come to him and interrogate him as a way of putting him to the test. They ask, "Teacher, Jesus, we know that you are from God, since the things you do put you above all the prophets. Tell us, then, is it permissible to pay to rulers what is due them? Should we pay them or not?" Jesus knew what they were up to, and became indignant. Then he said to them, "Why do you pay me lip service as a teacher, but not do what I say? How accurately Isaiah prophesied about you when he said, "This people honors me with their lips, but their heart stays far away from me; their worship is empty, because they insist on teachings that are human commandments."

Epiphany 8

First Reading *Genesis 35:22b–26, Tanakh*

Now the sons of Jacob (Israel) were twelve in number. The sons of Leah: Reuben — Jacob's first born — Simeon, Levi, Judah, Issachar, and Zebulun. The sons of Rachel: Joseph and

Benjamin. The sons of Bilhah, Rachel's maid: Dan and Naphtali. And the sons of Zilpah, Leah's maid: Gad and Asher. These are the sons of Jacob who were born to him in Paddan-aram.

Second Reading *Gospel of Philip 61:12–20, 63:25–30, NHL*

God is a dyer. As the good dyes, which are called "true," dissolve with the things dyed in them, so it is with those whom God has dyed. Since his dyes are immortal, they are immortal by means of his colors. Now God dips what he dips in water . . .

The Lord went into the dye works of Levi. He took seventy-two different colors and threw them into the vat. He took them out all white. And he said, "Even so the Truly Human Being comes as a dyer."

Note NHL reads "Even so has the Son of Man come as a dyer."

Psalm *Baruch 3:29–32, NRSV*

Who has gone up into heaven and taken Wisdom,*
  and brought her down from the clouds?
Who has gone over the seas, and found her,*
  and will buy her for pure gold?
No one knows the way to her,*
  or is concerned about the path to her.
But the one who knows all things knows her,*
  He found her by his understanding.
The one who prepared the earth for all time*
  filled it with four-footed creatures;
the one who sends forth the light, and it goes;*
  He called it, and it obeyed him, trembling;
the stars shone in their watches, and were glad,*
  He called them, and they said, "Here we are!"
They shone with gladness for him who made them.*
  This is our God; no other can be compared to him.
He found the whole way to knowledge,*
  and gave her to his servant Jacob and to Israel, whom he
    loved.

Epiphany

Afterward Wisdom appeared on earth*
and lived with humankind.

Gospel *Gospel of the Ebionites 2, SV*

There was this man named Jesus, who was about thirty years
old, who chose us. And when he came to Capernaum, he
entered the house of Simon, who was nicknamed Peter. He then
began to speak as follows:

"As I was walking along by the lake of Tiberias, I chose John
and James, son of Zebedee, and Simon and Andrew and
Thaddeus and Simon the Zealot and Judas the Iscariot. Then I
summoned you, Matthew, while you were sitting at the toll
booth, and you followed me. Therefore, I want you to be twelve
apostles, to symbolize Israel."

Note At present, there are no extant copies of The Gospel of
the Ebionites. We know of its existence because it is quoted in the
writings of early church father Epiphanius of Salamis (ca.
315–403).

Commentary In biology, ontogeny recapitulates phylogeny: the
life of the individual of a species recapitulates the history of the
entire species. In similar fashion, the story of Jesus shows him reca-
pitulating the entire history of his people, Israel. Case in point is in
naming twelve apostles symbolizing the twelve tribes of Israel.

There were twelve springs of water (Exod 15:27), twelve pillars
according to the twelve tribes of Israel (Exod 24:4), twelve stones
corresponding to the names of the sons of Israel (Exod 28:21).
And so Jesus appoints twelve who shall also be springs, pillars,
and reliable stones.

Last Sunday after Epiphany

First Reading *Gospel of Philip 53:24–54:18, and 56:3–15 and
59:12–17, NHL*

Names given to the worldly are very deceptive, for they
divert our thoughts from what is correct to what is incorrect.
Thus one who hears the word, "God" does not perceive what
is correct, but perceives what is incorrect. So also with "the
father" and "the son" and "the holy spirit" and "life" and

"light" and "resurrection" and "the church" and all the rest —
people do not perceive what is correct but they perceive what is
incorrect, unless they have come to know what is correct . . .

One single name is not uttered in the world, the name which
the father gave to the son; it is the name above all things: the
name of the father. For the son would not become father unless
he wore the name of the father.

Those who have this name know it, but they do not speak it.
But those who do not have it do not know it.

But truth brought names into existence in the world for our
sakes because it is not possible to learn it without these names.

Truth is one single thing; it is also many things and for our
sakes to teach about this one thing in love through many things
. . .

"Jesus" is a hidden name. "Christ" is a revealed name. For
this reason "Jesus" does not exist in any other language, but
his name is always "Jesus," as he is called.

"Christ" is also his name: in Syriac it is "Messiah," in Greek
it is "Christ." Certainly all the others have it according to their
own language. "The Nazarene" is he who reveals what is hidden. Christ has everything in himself, whether man or angel or
mystery, and the father . . .

"The father" and "the son" are single names, "the holy
spirit" is a double name. For they are everywhere: they are
above, they are below; they are in the concealed, they are in the
revealed. The holy spirit is in the revealed: it is below. It is in
the concealed: it is above.

Second Reading *Gospel of Philip 57:28–58:10, NHL*

Jesus took them all by stealth, for he did not appear as he
was, but in the manner in which they would be able to see him.
He appeared to them all. He appeared to the great as great. He
appeared to the small as small. He appeared to the angels as an
angel, and to men as a man. Because of this his word hid itself
from everyone. Some indeed saw him, thinking that they were
seeing themselves, but when he appeared to his disciples in glory
on the mount he was not small. He became great, but he made
the disciples great, that they might be able to see him in his
greatness.

Epiphany

Psalm *Ode 4*

No one, O my God, may take Your holy place, *
 nor alter it, for no one has such power.
You designed Your sanctuary before You drew the world. *
 What is older will not be undone by the younger.
You give Your heart, O Lord, to Your believers *
 You will not fail or be fruitless.
One hour of Your faith is more precious *
 than all days and years.
Who puts on Your grace and is rejected? *
 Your seal is known: Creatures know it.
Hosts possess it. Archangels are robed in it. *
 You give Your fellowship.
Not You, but we, were in need. *
 Sprinkle Your dew upon us.
Open Your bountiful springs. *
 Pour forth Your milk and honey.
You regret nothing You have promised. *
 You know the end, You give freely,
You withdraw, and You give again. *
 You knew all, God, and from the beginning set it in order.
And You, O Lord, make all things. Hallelujah!

Gospel *Gospel of Thomas 13 and 61, SV*

Jesus said to his disciples, "Compare me to someone and tell me what I am like."

Simon Peter said to him, "You are like a just angel."

Matthew said to him, "You are like a wise philosopher."

Thomas said to him, "Master, my mouth is utterly unable to say what you are like."

Jesus said, "I am not your teacher. Because you have drunk, you have become intoxicated from the bubbling spring that I have tended."

And he took him, and withdrew, and spoke three things to him. When Thomas came back to his friends, they asked him, "What did Jesus say to you?"

Thomas said to them, "If I tell you one of the sayings he spoke to me, you will pick up rocks and stone me, and fire will come from the rocks and devour you . . .

Jesus said, "Two will recline on a couch; one will die, one will live."

Salome said, "Who are you, mister? You have climbed onto my couch and eaten from my table as if you are from someone."

Jesus said to her, "I am the one who comes from what is whole. I was granted from the things of my Father."

"I am your disciple."

"For this reason I say, if one is whole, one will be filled with light, but if one is divided, one will be filled with darkness."

Season of Lent

Ash Wednesday

First Reading *Isaiah 58:1–8, Tanakh*

Cry with full throat, without restraint;
Raise your voice like a ram's horn!
Declare to My people their transgression,
To the House of Jacob their sin.
To be sure, they seek Me daily,
Eager to learn My ways.
Like a nation that does what is right,
That has not abandoned the laws of its God,
They ask Me for the right way,
They are eager for the nearness of God:
"Why, when we fasted, did You not see?
When we starved our bodies, did You pay no heed?"
Because on your fast day
You see to your business
And oppress all your laborers!
Because you fast in strife and contention,
And you strike with a wicked fist!
Your fasting today is not such
As to make your voice heard on high.
Is such the fast I desire,
A day for men to starve their bodies?
Is it bowing the head like a bulrush

And lying in sackcloth and ashes?
Do you call that a fast,
A day when the Lord is favorable?
No, this is the fast I desire:
To unlock fetters of wickedness,
And untie the cords of the yoke
To let the oppressed go free;
To break off every yoke.
It is to share your bread with the hungry,
And to take the wretched poor into your home;
When you see the naked, to clothe him,
And not to ignore your own kin.
Then shall your light burst through like the dawn
And your healing spring up quickly;"

Second Reading *Job 42:1–6, Tanakh*

Job said in reply to the LORD:
"I know that You can do everything,
That nothing you propose is impossible for You.
Who is this who obscures counsel without knowledge?
Indeed, I spoke with understanding
Of things beyond me, which I did not know.
Hear now, and I will speak;
I will ask and You will inform me.
I had heard you with my ears,
But now I see you with my eyes;
Therefore I recant and relent,
Being but dust and ashes."

Psalm 102 *Psalm 102:1–12, BCP 1979*

Lord, hear my prayer, and let my cry come before you; *
   hide not your face from me in the day of my trouble.
Incline your ear to me;*
   when I call, make haste to answer me,
For my days drift away like smoke,*
   and my bones are hot as burning coals.
My heart is smitten like grass and withered,*
   so that I forget to eat my bread.

Because of the voice of my groaning*
  I am but skin and bones.
I have become like a vulture in the wilderness,*
  like an owl among the ruins.
I lie awake and groan;*
  I am like a sparrow, lonely on a house-top.
My enemies revile me all day long,*
  and those who scoff at me have taken an oath against me.
For I have eaten ashes for bread*
  and mingled my drink with weeping.
Because of your indignation and wrath*
  you have lifted me up and thrown me away.
My days pass away like a shadow,*
  and I wither like the grass.
But you, O Lord, endure for ever,*
  and your Name from age to age.

Gospel *Gospel of Thomas 6–7, 14, 27, 104, SV*

  His disciples asked him, "Do you want us to fast? How should we pray? Should we give to charity? What diet should we observe?"

  Jesus says, "Don't lie, and don't do what you hate, because all things are disclosed before heaven. After all, there is nothing hidden that won't be revealed, and there is nothing covered up that will remain undisclosed."

  Jesus says, "Blessed is the lion that the human will eat, so that the lion becomes human. And foul is the human that the lion will eat, and the lion still will become human." . . .

  Jesus said to them, "If you fast, you will bring sin upon yourselves, and if you pray, you will be condemned, and if you give to charity, you will harm your spirits. When you go into any region and walk in the countryside, when people take you in, eat what they serve you and heal the sick among them. After all, what goes into your mouth won't defile you; what comes out of your mouth will." . . . "If you do not fast from the world, you will not find the Father's domain. If you do not observe the Sabbath day as a Sabbath day, you will not see the Father." . . .

Lent

They said to Jesus, "Come let us pray today, and let us fast." Jesus said, "What sin have I committed, or how have I been undone? Rather, when the groom leaves the bridal suite, then let people fast and pray."

Note In place of Blessed, the SV reads, "Lucky . . ."

First Sunday of Lent

First Reading *Ecclesiastes 3:1–8, NJB*

There is a season for everything, a time for every occupation
　　under heaven:
A time for giving birth, a time for dying;
a time for planting, a time for uprooting what has been planted.
A time for killing, a time for healing,
a time for knocking down, a time for building.
A time for tears, a time for laughter;
a time for mourning, a time for dancing.
A time for throwing stones away, a time for gathering them;
a time for embracing, a time to refrain from embracing.
A time for searching, a time for losing;
a time for keeping, a time for discarding.
A time for tearing, a time for sewing;
a time for keeping silent, a time for speaking.
A time for loving, a time for hating;
a time for war, a time for peace.

Second Reading *Gospel of Philip 67:27–35, 70:13–17, NHL*

The Lord did everything in a Mystery: a Baptism and a Chrism and a Eucharist and a Redemption and a Bridal Chamber.

The Lord said, "I came to make the things below like the things above, and the things outside like those inside. I came to unite them in that place." He revealed himself in this place through types and images . . .

Christ came to repair the separation that was from the beginning and again unite the two, and to give life to those who died as a result of the separation and unite them. But the woman and the man are united in the bridal chamber. Indeed those who have been united in the Bridal Chamber will no longer be separated.

Psalm *Ode 41:1–7*

Let all the Lord's babes praise You, Lord.*
Let us receive the Truth of Trust in You.
You will acknowledge Your children.*
Let us sing of Your love
We live in You, Lord, by Your grace*
We receive Life by Your Anointed One.
A great Day is shining upon us*
Wonderful are You who shows us Your Glory.
Let all of us agree in Your Name O Lord.*
Let us honor You in Your goodness.
Let our faces shine in Your light*
Let our hearts meditate in Your love by night and by day.
Let us exult in the exultation of You, Lord.

Gospel *Gospel of Thomas 21–23, SV*

Mary said to Jesus, "What are your disciples like?"

He said, "They are like little children living in a field that is not theirs. When the owners of the field come, they will say, 'Give us back our field.' They take off their clothes in front of them in order to give it back to them, and they return their field to them. For this reason I say, if the owners of a house knew that a thief is coming, they will be on guard before the thief arrives, and will not let the thief break into their house (their domain) and steal their possessions. As for you, then, be on guard against the world. Prepare yourselves with great strength, so the robbers can't find a way to get to you, for the trouble you expect will come. Let there be a person among you who understands. When the crop ripened, he came quickly carrying a sickle and harvested it. Anyone here with two good ears had better listen!"

Jesus saw some babies nursing. He said to his disciples, "These nursing babies are like those who enter the Father's domain."

They said to him, "Then shall we enter the Father's domain as babies?"

Jesus said to them, "When you make the two into one, and when you make the inner like the outer and the outer like the inner, and the upper like the lower, and when you make the male and female into a single one, so that the male will not be male nor the female be female, when you make eyes in place of an eye, a hand in place of a hand, a foot in place of a foot, an image in place of an image, then you will enter the Father's domain."

Jesus says, "I shall choose you, one from a thousand and two from ten thousand, and they will stand as a single one."

Second Sunday of Lent

First Reading *Proverbs 1:20–31, NRSV*

Wisdom cries aloud in the streets,
Raises her voice in the squares.
At the head of the busy streets she calls;
At the entrance of the gates, in the city, she speaks out:
"How long will you simple ones love simplicity,
You scoffers be eager to scoff,
You dullards hate knowledge?
You are indifferent to my rebuke;
I will not speak my mind to you,
And let you know my thoughts.
Since you refused me when I called,
And paid no heed when I extended my hand,
You spurned all my advice,
And would not hear my rebuke,
I will laugh at your calamity,
And mock when terror comes upon you,
When terror comes like a disaster,
And calamity arrives like a whirlwind,
When trouble and distress come upon you.
When they shall call me but I will not answer;
They shall seek me but not find me.
Because they hated knowledge,

And did not choose fear of the Lord;
They refused my advice,
and disdained all my rebukes,
They shall eat the fruit of their ways,
And have their fill of their own counsels."

Second Reading *Job 28:1–12, NJB*

Silver has its mines
    and gold a place for refining.
Iron is extracted from the earth,
    the smelted rocks yield copper.
The miner makes an end of darkness
    when he pierces to the uttermost depths the black and light-
      less rock.
Mines the lamp folk dig in places where there is no foothold,
    and hang suspended far from humankind.
That earth from which bread comes
    is ravaged underground by fire.
Down there, the rocks are set with sapphires,
    full of spangles of gold.
Down there is a path unknown by birds of prey,
    unseen by the eye of any vulture;
a path not trodden by the lordly beasts,
    where no lion ever walked.
The miner attacks its flinty sides,
    upturning mountains by their roots,
driving tunnels through the rocks,
    on the watch for anything precious.
The miner explores the sources of rivers,
    and brings to daylight secrets that were hidden.
But tell me, where does Wisdom come from?
    Where is understanding to be found?

Psalm *Ode 13*

Look, the Lord is our mirror.*
    Open your eyes and see your eyes in him.
Learn the way of your face and praise the Spirit of the Lord.*
    Wipe the make-up from your face and love the Holiness of
      the Lord.

Lent

Dress yourself in the Lord.*

Dressed in the Lord you will be spotless at all times.

Gospel *Gospel of Thomas 24–26, 28–30, SV*

His disciples said, "Show us the place where you are, for we must seek it." (Jesus) said to them, "Anyone here with two ears had better listen! There is light within a person of light, and it shines on the whole world. If it does not shine, it is dark."

Jesus says, "Love your friends like your own soul, protect them like the pupil of your eye."

Jesus says, "You see the sliver in your friend's eye, but you don't see the timber in your own eye. When you take the timber out of your own eye, then you will see well enough to remove the sliver from your friend's eye . . ."

Jesus says, "I took my stand in the midst of the world, and in flesh I appeared to them. I found them all drunk, and I did not find any of them thirsty. My soul aches for the children of humanity, because they are blind in their hearts and do not see, for they came into the world empty, and they also seek to depart from the world empty. But meanwhile they are drunk. When they shake off their wine, then they will change their ways."

Jesus says, "If the flesh came into being because of spirit, that is a wonder. But if spirit came into being because of the body, it is a wonder of wonders. Indeed, I am amazed at how this great wealth comes to make its home in this poverty."

Jesus says, "Where there are three, they are without God, and where there is only one, I am with that one."

Note Gospel of Thomas 30 is from the Greek, SV. The rest are from the Coptic.

Third Sunday of Lent

First Reading *Genesis 2:18–25, Tanakh*

The LORD God said, "It is not good for man to be alone; I will make a fitting helper *as his partner.*" And the LORD God formed out of the earth all the wild beasts and all the birds of the sky, and brought them to the man to see what he would call them; and whatever the man called each living creature, that would be its name. And the man gave names to all the cattle and to the birds of the sky and to all the wild beasts; but for Adam no fitting helper was found. So the LORD God cast a deep sleep upon the man; and, while he slept, He took one of his ribs and closed up the flesh at that spot. And the LORD God fashioned the rib that He had taken from the man into a woman; and He brought her to the man. Then the man said,

> "This one at last
> Is bone of my bones
> And flesh of my flesh.
> This one shall be called Woman,
> For from man was she taken."

Hence a man leaves his father and mother and clings to his wife, so that they become one flesh.

The two of them were naked, the man and his wife, yet they felt no shame.

Second Reading *Job 28:12–20, The Jerusalem Bible*

> But tell me, where does Wisdom come from?
> Where is understanding to be found?
> The road to it is still unknown to human beings,
> not to be found in the land of the living.
> "It is not in me," says the Abyss;
> "Nor here," replies the Sea.
> It cannot be bought with solid gold,
> not paid for with any weight of silver.
> nor be priced by the standard of the gold of Ophir,
> or of precious onyx or sapphire.
> No gold, no glass can match it in value,
> nor for a fine gold vase can it be bartered.
> Nor is there need to mention coral, nor crystal;
> beside wisdom, pearls are not worth the fishing.
> Topaz from Cush is worthless in comparison,
> and gold, even refined, is valueless.
> But tell me, where does Wisdom come from?
> Where is understanding to be found?

Psalm *Ode 7:2–6*

> You are my joy, Lord, and I move toward You. *
>   Your Way is excellent. You are my Helper, Lord,

Lent

You let me know You generously in simplicity. *
    Your kindness humbles Your magnitude.
You become like me so I can receive You. *
    You think like me so I can become You.
I did not tremble when I saw You *
    For You are gracious to me.
You take on my nature so I can learn from You, *
    You take on my form so I will not turn away.

Gospel *Gospel of Thomas 32–38, SV*

Jesus says, "A city built on a high hill and fortified cannot fall, nor can it be hidden."

Jesus says, "What you will hear in your ear, in the other ear proclaim from your rooftops. After all, no one lights a lamp and puts it under a basket, nor does one put it in a hidden place. Rather, one puts it on a lampstand so that all who come and go will see its light."

Jesus says, "If a blind person leads a blind person, both of them will fall into a hole."

Jesus says, "One can't enter a strong man's house and take it by force without tying his hands. Then one can loot his house."

Jesus says, "Don't fret, from morning to evening and from evening to morning, about your food — what you are going to eat, or about your clothing, what you are going to wear. You're much better than the lilies, which don't card and never spin. As for you, when you have no garment, what are you going to put on? Who could add to your life span? That same one will give you your garment."

His disciples said, "When will you be revealed to us, and when will we see you?"

Jesus said, "When you strip without being ashamed, and you take your clothes and put them under your feet like little children and trample them, then you will see the son of the living one and you will not be afraid."

Jesus says, "Often you have desired to hear these sayings that I am speaking to you, and you have no one else from whom to hear them. There will be days when you will seek me and you will not find me."

Note Gospel of Thomas 36 is from the Greek. Saying 37 is Greek and Coptic conflated. All others are from the Coptic.

Commentary Thomas 33, reads, "hear in your ear, in the other ear proclaim . . ." Marvin Meyer helps us here, "This difficult phrase may well represent an instance of dittography — that is, a scribe's inadvertent duplication of words already transcribed. Otherwise, it may indicate the ear of another, or perhaps one's own *inner* ear." *The Complete Gospels*, p. 311

Fourth Sunday of Lent

First Reading *from Hypostasis of the Archons and On the Origin of the World, NHL*

Then the Female Spiritual Principle came in the Serpent, the Instructor; and she taught them, saying,"What did he say to you? Was it, "From every tree in the Garden shall you eat; yet do not eat from the Tree of recognizing evil? Do not eat from the Tree of Knowledge?"

The earthy Woman said, "He not only said, 'Don't eat from them' but 'Don't touch them, lest you die.'" The Serpent, the Instructor, said to her, "Don't be afraid, You certainly shall not die; for it was out of jealousy that he said this to you. Rather your eyes shall open, your mind will become sober, and you will come to be like gods, recognizing the distinctions which exist between evil and good." And the Female Instructing Principle was taken from the Snake, and she left it behind, merely a thing of the earth.

Now Eve had confidence in the words of the Instructor. She gazed at the two trees and saw that they were beautiful and appetizing, and liked them; she took some of the fruit and ate it; and she gave some also to her husband, and he too ate it.

Then their intellect became open. For when they had eaten, the light of knowledge had shone upon them. When they clothed themselves with shame, they knew they were naked with regard to knowledge. They recognized that they were naked of the Spiritual Element, and took fig leaves and bound them upon

Lent

their loins. When they sobered up, they saw they were naked
and they became enamored of one another. They understood
very much.

Note This passage is conflated and adapted from Hypostasis
of the Archons and On the Origin of the World from *The Nag
Hammadi Library*, 1977, p. 155 and 174

Second Reading *Job 28:20–28, The Jerusalem Bible*

But tell me, where does Wisdom come from?
Where is understanding to be found?
Wisdom is outside the knowledge of every living thing,
hidden from the birds of the sky.
Perdition and Death can only say, "We have heard reports of
    it."
God alone has traced its path and found out where it lives.
(For God sees to the ends of the earth,
and observes all that lies under heaven.)
When he willed to give weight to the wind
and measured out the waters with a gauge,
when he made the laws and the rules for the rain
and mapped a route for the thunderclaps to follow,
then he had it in sight, and cast its worth,
assessed it, fathomed it.
And he said to man, "Wisdom? it is fear of the Lord.
Understanding? — avoidance of evil."

Psalm *Ode 7:7–13*

The Father of Knowledge is the Word of Knowledge*
    You who create wisdom are wiser than Your works.
You who created me when I was not*
    Knew what to do when I came into being.
In Your abundance You are gracious to me*
    and allow me to ask for and receive Your sacrifice
You are incorruptible, the perfection of the worlds and their
        Father.*
    You allow Yourself to be seen in Your works
that You may be recognized as their creator,*

that all may not suppose that they are self-made.

Your way is knowledge. You broaden it and make it perfect.*

　Over it are the traces of Your light from the beginning to the
　　end.

You are resting in Your Son, You are pleased with Your Son,*

　You take possession of all things because of Your salvation.

You the Highest One are known in Your Holy Ones and in
　　songs of your Coming.*

　Those who sing go forth to meet You with joy and a harp of
　　many tunes.

Gospel *Gospel of Thomas 39–46, SV*

Jesus says, "The Pharisees and the scholars have taken the keys of knowledge and hidden them. They themselves have not entered, nor have they allowed to enter those who wish to. You, however, be wise as serpents and as innocent as doves."

Jesus says, "A grapevine has been planted apart from the Father. Since it is not strong, it will be pulled up by its root and will perish."

Jesus says, "Those who have something in hand will be given more, and those who have nothing will be deprived of even the little they have."

Jesus says, "Become passers-by."

His disciples said to him, "Who are you to say these things to us?"

(Jesus said to them), "You don't understand who I am from what I say to you. Rather, you have become like the Judeans, for they love the tree but hate its fruit, or they love the fruit but hate the tree."

Jesus says, "Whoever blasphemes against the Father will be forgiven, and whoever blasphemes against the son will be forgiven, but whoever blasphemes against the holy spirit will not be forgiven, either on earth or in heaven."

Jesus says, "Grapes are not harvested from thorn trees, nor are figs gathered from thistles, for they yield no fruit. Good persons produce good from what they've stored up; bad persons produce evil from the wickedness they've stored up in their hearts, and say evil things. For from the overflow of the heart they produce evil."

Jesus says, "From Adam to John the Baptist, among those born of women, no one is so much greater than John the Baptist that his eyes should not be averted. But I have said that whoever among you becomes a child will recognize the Father's kingdom and will become greater than John."

Note Re: kingdom, SV reads imperial rule.

Commentary Regarding Thomas 43, Marvin Meyer helps us here, "The critical treatment of "the Judeans" here is typical of early Christian writing, which reflects the point of view of a small, sectarian group securing its identity over against the majority culture. Since there is no reason to think that Thomas Christians were themselves not Jewish (see Thomas 27), one should refrain from interpreting the saying in an anti-Semitic vein." *The Complete Gospels* p. 312

Fifth Sunday of Lent

First Reading *Isaiah 2:2–4, Tanakh*

In the days to come,
The Mount of the LORD's House
Shall stand firm above the mountains
And tower above the hills;
And all the nations
Shall gaze on it with joy.
And the many peoples shall go and say:
"Come,
Let us go up to the Mount of the LORD,
To the House of the God of Jacob;
That he may instruct us in His ways,
And that we may walk in His paths."
For instruction shall come forth from Zion,
The word of the LORD from Jerusalem.
Thus He will judge among the nations
And arbitrate for the many peoples,
And they shall beat their swords into plowshares
And their spears into pruning hooks;
Nation shall not take up
Sword against nation;
They shall never again know war.

Second Reading *Gospel of Philip 82:30–84:13, NHL*

Most things of the world as long as their inner parts are hidden, stand upright and live. If they are revealed they die, as is illustrated by the visible *human being*: for as long as the intestines of *a person* are hidden, the person is alive; when the intestines are exposed and come out, the person will die. So also with the tree: while its root is hidden it sprouts and grows. If its root is exposed, the tree dries up. So it is with every birth that is in the world, not only with the revealed but with the hidden. For so long as the root of wickedness is hidden, it is strong. But when it is recognized, it is dissolved. When it is revealed it perishes. That is why the word says, "Already the ax is laid at the root of the trees" (Matthew 3:10). It will not merely cut — what is cut sprouts again — but the ax penetrates deeply until it brings up the root. Jesus pulled out the root of the whole place, while others did it only partially. As for ourselves, let each one of us dig after the root of evil which is within one, and let one pluck it out of one's heart from the root. It will be plucked out if we recognize it. But if we are ignorant of it, it takes root in us and produces its fruit in our heart. It masters us. We are its slaves. It takes us captive, to make us do what we do not want; and what we do want we do not do. It is powerful because we have not recognized it. While it exists it is active. Ignorance is the mother of all evil. Ignorance will result in death, because those that come from ignorance neither were nor are nor shall be. But those who are in the truth will be perfect when all the truth is revealed. For truth is like ignorance: while it is hidden it rests in itself, but when it is revealed and is recognized, it is praised inasmuch as it is stronger than ignorance and error. It gives freedom. The word said, "If you know the truth, the truth will make you free." (John 8:32) Ignorance is a slave. Knowledge is freedom. If we know the truth, we shall find the fruits of the truth within us. If we are joined to it, it will bring our fulfillment.

Psalm *Ode 7:14–18*

Seers go before You and You are seen.*
　　Seers praise You for Your Love. You are near and You see.
Hatred leaves the earth, jealousy drowns, ignorance is
　　　destroyed*

for the knowledge of the Lord has come.
Let singers sing of Your grace, Lord most high, let them sing.*
Let their hearts be like day, their harmonies like Your excel-
lent beauty.
Let there be nothing without life, knowledge, or speech,*
For You, Lord, give mouth to Your creation
You open the voice of our mouth to praise You.*
Praise Your Power and reveal Your Grace! Hallelujah!

Gospel *Thomas 47–53, SV*

Jesus says, "It is impossible for *a person* to mount two horses
or to stretch two bows. And it is impossible for a servant to
serve two masters; otherwise, he will honor the one and treat
the other contemptuously. *No one* drinks old wine and immediately desires to drink new wine. And new wine is not put into
old wineskins, lest they burst; nor is old wine put into new
wineskins, lest it spoil it. An old patch is not sewn into a new
garment, because a tear would result."

Jesus says, "If two make peace with each other in a single
house, they will say to the mountain, 'Move from here!' and it
will move."

Jesus says, "Blessed are the solitary and elect, for you will
find the kingdom. For you are from it, and to it you will
return."

Jesus says, "If they say to you, 'Where have you come from?'
say to them, 'We have come from the light, from the place where
the light came into being by itself, established itself, and
appeared in their image.' If they say to you, 'Is it you?' say 'We
are its children, and we are the chosen of the living Father.' If
they ask you, 'What is the evidence of your Father in you?' say
to them, 'It is motion and rest.'"

His disciples said to him, "When will the rest for the dead
take place and when will the new world come?"

He said to them, "What you are looking forward to has
already come, but you do not recognize it."

His disciples said to him, "Twenty-four prophets have spoken in Israel and they all spoke of you."

He said to them, "You have disregarded the living one who
is in your presence, and have spoken of the dead."

His disciples said to him, "Is circumcision useful or not?"

He said to them, "If it were useful, their father would produce children already circumcised from their mother. Rather, the true circumcision in spirit has become profitable in every respect."

Note Gospel of Thomas 47 and 49 are NHL where person and one are rendered man. All other sayings above are SV.

Holy Week

During Holy Week, the Gospels continue with teachings ascribed to Jesus until Good Friday when we hear the Passion narrative from the Gospel of Peter. Supporting readings are primarily from Job, the symbolic suffering servant who serves as a prototype for Jesus. Both Job and Jesus creatively confront the problem of injustice, suffering, and evil. For an insightful commentary on the meaning of their sufferings and their confrontations with God, consult Carl G. Jung, *Answer to Job*.

Please note the pattern in the pairs of readings from Job: the second is normally a response to the first. Following the dialogue between God and Satan, Job and each of his three friends have their say.

Passion Sunday

First Reading *Job 1:1–12, NRSV*

There was once a man in the land of Uz whose name was Job. That man was blameless and upright, one who feared God and turned away from evil. There were born to him seven sons and three daughters. He had seven thousand sheep, three thousand camels, five hundred yoke of oxen, five hundred donkeys, and very many servants; so that man was the greatest of all the people of the east.

His sons used to go and hold feasts in one another's houses in turn; and they would send and invite their sisters to eat and drink with them. And when the feast days had run their course, Job would send and sanctify them, and he would rise early in the morning and offer burnt offerings according to the number of them all; for Job said, "It may be that my children have sinned, and cursed God in their hearts." This is what Job always did.

One day the sons of God came to present themselves before the LORD, and Satan also came among them. Then the LORD said to Satan, "Where have you come from?" Satan answered the LORD, "From going to and fro on the earth, and from walking up and down on it." The LORD said to Satan, "Have you considered my servant Job? There is no one like him on the earth, a blameless and upright man who fears God and turns away from evil." Then Satan answered the LORD, "Does Job fear God for nothing? Have you not put a fence around him and his house and all that he has, on every side? You have blessed the work of his hands, and his possessions have increased in the land. But stretch out your hand now, and touch all that he has, and he will curse you to your face." The LORD said to Satan, "Very well, all that he has is in your power; only do not stretch out your hand against him!" So Satan went out from the presence of the LORD.

Second Reading *Job 1:13–22, NRSV*

One day when his sons and daughters were eating and drinking wine in the eldest brother's house, a messenger came to Job and said, "The oxen were plowing and the donkeys were feeding beside them, and the Sabeans fell on them and carried them off, and killed the servants with the edge of the sword; I alone have escaped to tell you."

While he was still speaking, another came and said, "The fire of God fell from heaven and burned up the sheep and the servants, and consumed them; I alone have escaped to tell you."

While he was still speaking, another came and said, "The Chaldeans formed three columns, made a raid on the camels and carried them off, and killed the servants with the edge of the sword; I alone am escaped to tell you."

While he was still speaking, another came and said, "Your sons and daughters were eating and drinking wine in their eldest brother's house, and suddenly a great wind came across the desert, struck the four corners of the house, and it fell on the young people, and they are dead; I alone am escaped to tell you."

Then Job arose, tore his robe, shaved his head, and fell on the ground and worshiped. He said, "Naked I came from my mother's womb, and naked shall I return there; the LORD gave, and the LORD has taken away; blessed be the name of the LORD."

In all this Job did not sin or charge God with wrong-doing.

Psalm *Ode 5*

I thank You, O Lord, because I love You.*
> O highest one, do not abandon me for You are my hope.

Freely I receive Your grace. Freely I live on it.*
> My persecutors will come, but let them not see me.

Let a cloud of darkness fall on their eyes.*
> Let thick gloom darken them.

Let light be gone and I be invisible so they will not seize me.*
> Let their counsel be thick darkness.

Let their cunning turn on their own heads,*
> for their counsel is nothing.

Lord, You are my hope, I will not fear.*
> You are as a garland on my head and I will not be moved.

Should everything shake, I stand firm.*
> If all visible things perish, I will not die.

You, Lord, are with me*
> and I am with You. Hallelujah!

Gospel *Gospel of Thomas 54–60, 62–63, SV*

Jesus says, "Blessed are the poor, for your is the kingdom of heaven."

Jesus says, "Whoever does not hate father and mother cannot be my disciple, and whoever does not hate brothers and sisters, and carry the cross as I do, will not be worthy of me."

Jesus says, "Whoever has come to know the world has discovered a carcass, and whoever has discovered a carcass, of that person the world is not worthy."

Jesus says, "The kingdom of the Father is like a man who had good seed. His enemy came by night and sowed weeds among the good seed. The man did not allow them to pull up

the weeds; he said to them, 'I am afraid that you will go intend-
ing to pull up the weeds and pull the wheat along with them.'
For on the day of the harvest the weeds will be plainly visible,
and they will be pulled up and burned."

Jesus says, "Blessed is the *person* who has suffered and
found life."

Jesus says, "Look to the living one as long as you live, otherwise you might die and then try to see the living one, and you
will be unable to see."

(Jesus) saw a Samaritan carrying a lamb and going to Judea.
He said to his disciples, "Why does that man carry the lamb
around?"

They said to him, "So that he may kill it and eat it."

He said to them, "While it is alive, he will not eat it, but
only when he has killed it and it has become a carcass."

They said, "Otherwise he can't do it."

He said to them, "So also with you, seek for yourselves a
place for rest, or you might become a carcass and be
eaten." . . .

Jesus says, "I disclose my mysteries to those who are worthy
of my mysteries. Do not let your left hand know what your
right hand is doing."

Jesus says, "There was a rich man who had a great deal of
money. He said, 'I shall invest my money so that I may sow,
reap, plant, and fill my storehouses with produce, that I may
lack nothing.' These were the things he was thinking in his
heart, but that very night he died. Anyone here with two ears
had better listen!"

Note Translation is SV except Sayings 54, 57, 58 and 60 which
are NHL. In Saying 58, person is rendered man in NHL.

Monday in Holy Week

First Reading *Job 2:1–6, NRSV*

One day the sons of God came to present themselves before
the LORD, and Satan also same among them to present himself
before the LORD.

The LORD said to Satan, "Where have you come from?"
Satan answered the LORD, "From going to and fro on the

earth, and from walking up and down on it." The LORD said to Satan, "Have you considered my servant Job? There is no one like him on the earth, a blameless and upright man who fears God and turns away from evil. He still persists in his integrity, although you incite me against him, to destroy him for no reason." Then Satan answered the LORD, "Skin for skin! All that people have they will give to save their lives. But stretch out your hand now and touch his bone and his flesh, and he will curse you to your very face." The LORD said to Satan, "Very well, he is in your power; only spare his life."

Second Reading *Job 2:7–13, NRSV*

So Satan went out from the presence of the LORD, and inflicted loathsome sores on Job from the sole of his foot to the crown of his head. Job took a potsherd with which to scrape himself, and sat among the ashes.

Then his wife said to him, "Do you still persist in your integrity? Curse God, and die." But he said to her, "You speak as any foolish woman would speak. Shall we receive the good at the hand of God, and not to receive the bad?" In all this Job did not sin with his lips.

Now when Job's three friends heard of all these troubles that had come upon him, each of them set out from his home — Eliphaz the Temanite, Bildad the Shuhite, and Zophar the Naamathite. They met together to go and console and comfort him. When they saw him from a distance, they did not recognize him, and they raised their voices and wept aloud; they tore their robes and threw dust in the air upon their heads. They sat with him on the ground seven days and seven nights, and no one spoke a word to him, for they saw that his suffering was very great.

Psalm *Ode 20*

I am Your priest O Lord and serve You as priest.*
    I offer You Your thought.
Your thought is not like the world, nor of the flesh,*
    nor of those who serve the flesh.
You Lord, offer Your goodness, Your stainless heart and lips.*
    Your interior world, which is faultless.
Let hearts not oppress hearts,*

Holy Week

nor souls harm souls.
Do not buy a stranger. That stranger is you.*
   Do not trick your neighbor.
Do not take the clothing from him that hides his nakedness,*
   but dress in the grace of the Lord generously.
Walk in Paradise and from the tree of the Lord make a garland
    for your head.*
   Loop it around your hair. Be happy and rest in the rest of
    the Lord.
You will inhabit the kindness and grace of the Lord. *
   Be fat in truth with the praise of holiness.
The glory of the Lord will go before you. *
   Praise and honor the Name of the Lord. Hallelujah!

Gospel *Oxyrhynchus 1224:5–6*

When the scholars and Pharisees and priests observed (Jesus), they were indignant because he reclined at table in the company of sinners. But Jesus overheard them and said, "Those who are well don't need a doctor. And pray for your enemies. For the one who is not against you is on your side. The one who today is at a distance, tomorrow will be near you."

Tuesday in Holy Week

First Reading *Job 3:1, 11–12, 16, 20–26, NRSV*

After this Job opened his mouth and cursed the day of his birth. Job said: . . . "Why did I not die at birth, come forth from the womb and expire?

Why were there knees to receive me, or breasts for me to suck? . . . Or why was I not buried like a stillborn child, like an infant that never sees the light? . . .

Why is light given to one in misery, and life to the bitter in soul, who long for death, but it does not come, and dig for it more than for hidden treasures; who rejoice exceedingly, and are glad when they find the grave?

Why is light given to one who cannot see the way, whom God has fenced in? For my sighing comes before my bread, and my groanings are poured out like water. Truly the things that I fear comes upon me, and what I dread befalls me. I am not at ease, nor am I quiet; I have no rest; but trouble comes."

Second Reading *Job 4:1–9, 5:17–19, 27, NRSV*

Then Eliphaz the Temanite answered: "If one ventures a word with you, will you be offended? But who can keep from speaking?

See, you have instructed many; you have strengthened the weak hands. Your words have supported those who were stumbling, and you have made firm the feeble knees.

But now it has come to you and you are impatient; it touches you, and you are dismayed. Is not your fear of God your confidence, and the integrity of your ways your hope?

Think now, who that was innocent ever perished? Or where were the upright cut off? As I have seen, those who plow iniquity and sow trouble reap the same. By the breath of God they perish, and by the blast of his anger they are consumed . . .

How happy is the one whom God reproves; therefore do not despise the discipline of the Almighty. For he wounds, but he binds up; he strikes, but his hands heal.

He will deliver you from six troubles; in seven no harm shall touch you . . .

See, we have searched this out; it is true. Hear and know it for yourself."

Psalm *Ode 31*

Sung to Christ
Chasms vanish before You, Lord.*
　　Darkness fades with Your appearing.
Error wanders off and disappears because of You.*
　　Contempt finds no path and is submerged in Your Truth,
　　　　Lord.
You open Your mouth and speak grace and happiness.*
　　You sing a new chant to Your Father's Name.
You raise Your voice to the sky*
　　and in Your hands offer children to Your Father.
In the Way Your Father gives You,*
　　Your face is justified.
Christ responds
Come, you who have suffered and receive joy.*
　　Possess your souls through grace. Accept Eternal Life.
They condemned me when I stood on my feet, guiltless.*
　　They divvied the spoil though nothing was theirs.

I endured, held my peace, was silent,*
  so they could not get to me.
I was a firm rock pounded by waves, braving the blows.*
  I bore their bitterness humbly to redeem and instruct my
    people.
I could not ignore my promise to the patriarchs*
  to whom I promised the salvation of their seed. Hallelujah!

Gospel *Dialogue of the Savior (excerpts), NHL*

The Savior said to his disciples, "Already the time has come, brothers and sisters, that we should leave behind our labor and stand in the rest; for the person who stands in the rest will rest forever . . . I will teach you when the time of dissolution will come . . ."

His disciples said, "Lord who is the one who seeks and who is the one who reveals?" The Lord said, "The one who seeks is the one who reveals . . .. The one who speaks is also the one who hears, and the one who sees is also the one who reveals."

Mariam said, "O Lord, behold, when I am bearing the body, for what reason do I weep, and for what reason do I laugh?" *(The answer is badly obliterated in the text.)*

Judas said, "Tell us, Lord, before the heavens and the earth were, what was it that existed?" The Lord said, "It was darkness and water and a spirit that was upon a water. But I say to you, as for what you seek after and inquire about, behold it is within you . . . The true mind came to be within . . .He who is able, let him deny himself, and repent. And he who knows, let him seek and find and rejoice."

Mariam asked, "Brothers, the things about which you ask . . . where will you keep them?"

Wednesday in Holy Week

First Reading *Job 6:1–4, 8–17, 7:11–21, NRSV*

Then Job answered: "O that my vexation were weighed, and all my calamity laid in the balances! For then it would be heavier than the sand of the sea: therefore my words have been rash. For the arrows of the Almighty are in me; my spirit drinks their poison; the terrors of God are arrayed against me . . .

O that I might have my request, and that God would grant my desire; that it would please God to crush me, that he would let loose his hand and cut me off! This would be my consolation: I would even exult in unrelenting pain; for I have not denied the words of the Holy One.

What is my strength that I should wait? And what is my end, that I should be patient? Is my strength the strength of stones, or is my flesh bronze?

In truth, I have no help in me, and any resource is driven from me.

Those who withhold kindness from a friend forsake the fear of the Almighty. My companions are treacherous like a torrent-bed, like freshets that pass away, that run dark with ice, turbid with melting snow. In time of heat they disappear; when it is hot, they vanish from their place . . .

Therefore, I will not restrain my mouth; I will speak in the anguish of my spirit; I will complain in the bitterness of my soul . . .

When I say, 'My bed will comfort me, my couch will ease my complaint,' then you scare me with dreams and terrify me with visions, so that I would choose strangling and death rather than this body.

I loathe my life; I would not live forever. Let me alone, for my days are a breath. What are human beings, that you make so much of them, that you set your mind on them, visit them every morning, test them every moment?

Will you not look away from me for awhile, let me alone until I swallow my spittle? If I sin, what do I do to you, you watcher of humanity? Why have you made me your target? Why have I become a burden to you? Why do you not pardon my transgression and take away my iniquity? For now I shall lie in the earth; you will seek me, but I shall not be."

Second Reading *Job 8:1–10, 20–22, NRSV*

Then Bildad the Shuhite answered: "How long will you say these things, and the words of your mouth be a great wind? Does God pervert justice? Or does the Almighty pervert the right? If your children sinned against him, he delivered them into the power of their transgression. If you will seek God and

Holy Week

make supplication to the Almighty, if you are pure and upright, surely then he will rouse himself for you and restore to you your rightful place. Though your beginning was small, your latter days will be very great.

For inquire now of bygone generations, and consider what their ancestors have found; for we are but of yesterday, and we know nothing, for our days on earth are but a shadow, Will they not teach you and tell you and utter words out of their understanding? . . .

See, God will not reject a blameless person, nor take the hand of evildoers, He will yet fill your mouth with laughter, and your lips with shouts of joy.

Those who hate you will be clothed with shame, and the tent of the wicked will be no more."

Psalm *Ode 41:8–15*

Christ speaks
All those who see me will be amazed*
  for I am an alien among you.
The Father of Truth remembers me*
  and possesses me from the beginning.
Through his riches he gives me birth.*
  Through the thought of his heart he gives me birth again.
Response
Your Word is our Way.*
  The Savior gives life and does not reject us.
Those who are humble are raised in You.*
  The Son of the Most High appears in Your perfection.
Light finds daybreak in Your Word*
  that was in You before time began.
The Anointed One is known before the foundation of the world.*
  You give Eternal life to souls by the Truth in Your Name.
Sing a new chant to You Lord*
  from those who love You! Hallelujah!

Gospel *Dialogue of the Savior (excerpts), NHL*

Matthew said, "Lord, I wish to see that place of life, that place in which there is no evil, but rather it is the pure light."

The Lord said, "Brother Matthew, you cannot see it, as long as you wear the flesh."

Matthew said, "O Lord, even if I cannot see it, let me know it." The Lord said, "Every one of you who has known himself has seen it; everything that is fitting for him to do, he does it. And he has been doing it in his goodness."

The Lord said, "If one does not understand how the fire came to be, he will burn in it, because he does not know his root. If one does not first understand the water he does not understand anything. For what is the use for him to receive baptism in it? If one does not understand how the body that he wears came to be, he will perish with it. And he who does not know the Son, how will he know the Father? And he who will not know the root of all things, they (all things) are hidden from him. The *person* who will not know the root of wickedness is not a stranger to it. *Those* who will not understand how *they* came will not understand how *they* will go, and are not strangers to this world which will perish and which will be humbled."

Maundy Thursday

First Reading *Job 9:1–2, 14–24, NRSV*

Then Job answered: "Indeed I know that this is so; but how can a mortal be just before God? If one wished to contend with him, one could not answer him once in a thousand . . .

How then can I answer him, choosing my words with him? Though I am innocent, I cannot answer him; I must appeal for mercy to my accuser. If I summoned him and he answered me, I do not believe that he would listen to my voice. For he crushes me with a tempest, and multiplies my wounds without cause; he will not let me get my breath, but fills me with bitterness.

If it is a contest of strength, he is the strong one! If it is a matter of justice, who can summon him?

Though I am innocent, my own mouth would condemn me; though I am blameless, he would prove me perverse. I am blameless; I do not know myself; I loathe my life.

It is all one, therefore I say, he destroys both the blameless and the wicked. When disaster brings sudden death, he mocks at the calamity of the innocent. The earth is given into the hand of the wicked; he covers the eyes of its judges — if it is not he, who then is it?"

Second Reading *Job 11:1–6, 13–18, 13:1–4, 12, 5, NRSV*

Then Zophar the Naamathite answered: "Should a multitude of words go unanswered, and should one full of talk be vindicated? Should your babble put others to silence, and when you mock, shall no one shame you?

For you say, 'My conduct is pure, and I am clean in God's sight.'

But oh, that God would speak, and open his lips to you, and that he would tell you the secrets of wisdom! For wisdom is many-sided. Know then that God exacts of you less than your guilt deserves . . .

If you direct your heart rightly, you will stretch out your hands toward him. If iniquity is in your hand, put it far away, and do not let wickedness reside in your tents.

Surely then you will lift up your face without blemish; you will be secure, and will not fear. You will forget your misery; you will remember it as waters that have passed away. And your life will be brighter than the noonday; its darkness will be like the morning.

And you will have confidence, because there is hope; You will be protected and take your rest in safety . . ."

Then Job answered: "Look, my eye has seen all this, my ear has heard and understood it. What you know, I also know; I am not inferior to you. But I would speak to the Almighty, and I desire to argue my case with God. As for you, you whitewash with lies; all of you are worthless physicians . . . Your maxims are proverbs of ashes, your defenses are defenses of clay . . . If you only keep silent, that would be your wisdom!"

Psalm *The Dance of Christ, Acts of John 94, Seers Version*

Before he was arrested, . . . Jesus assembled us all and said, "Before I am delivered to them, let us sing a hymn to the Father, and so go to meet what lies before us." So he told us to form a

circle, holding one another's hands, and he stood in the middle
and said, "Answer Amen to me." So he began to sing the hymn.

Glory be to You, Father,
Glory be to you, Mother,
Glory be to You, Logos,
Glory be to You, Spirit,
Glory be to You, Holy One,
Glory be to Your Glory,
We praise You, Father,
We praise you, Mother,
We thank You, Light . . .
I will be saved, and I will save,
I will be loosed, and I will loose,
I will be wounded, and I will wound,
I will be born, and I will bear,
I will eat, and I will be eaten,
I will hear, and I will be heard,
I will be thought, being wholly thought,
I will be washed, and I will wash.
Grace dances
I will pipe, and all of you dance
I will mourn, and all of you beat your breasts,
The Eighth sings praises with us,
The Twelfth dances on high,
To the Universe belongs the Dancer,
Whoever does not dance does not know what happens,
I will flee, and I will remain,
I will adorn, and I will be adorned,
I will be united and I will unite,
I have no house and I have houses,
I have no place, and I have places,
I have no temple, and I have temples,
I am a lamp to you who see me,
I am a mirror to you who know me,
I am a door to you who knock on me,
I am a way to you the traveller,
Repeat "Glory be" section above.

Note If you want to use the dance of Christ as done in the early church, simply follow the directions given in the text: a leader stands in the center of a circle and chants each line as others respond by chanting "Amen."

Gospel Thomas *12,15,16,18,19, 31, SV*

The disciples said to Jesus, "We know that you are going to leave us. Who will be our leader?" Jesus said to them, "No matter where you are, you are to go to James the Just, for whose sake heaven and earth came into being."

Jesus says, "When you see one who was not born of woman, fall on your faces and worship. That one is your Father."

Jesus says, "Perhaps people think that I have come to cast peace upon the world. They do now know that I have come to cast conflicts upon the earth: fire, sword, war. For there will be five in a house: there'll be three against two and two against three, father against son and son against father, and they will stand alone."

The disciples said to Jesus, "Tell us, how will our end come?" Jesus said, "Have you found the beginning, then, that you are looking for the end? You see, the end will be where the beginning is. Congratulations to the one who stands at the beginning: that one will know the end and will not taste death."

Jesus says, "Congratulations to the one who came into being before coming into being. If you become my disciples and pay attention to my sayings, these stones will serve you. For there are five trees in Paradise for you; they do not change, summer or winter, and their leaves do not fall. Whoever knows them will not taste death."

Jesus says, "No prophet is welcome on his home turf; doctors don't cure those who know them."

Commentary James the Just is a blood brother of Jesus. After the death of Jesus, James became the leader of the Jerusalem church. Did Jesus know ahead of time that he would soon die? Did he actually appoint his brother James to be his successor? Or might these words be created by the writer of the Gospel of Thomas who knew what did, in fact, occur after the crucifixion?

Good Friday

First Reading *Zechariah 14:1, 4–9, Tanakh*

Lo a day of the LORD is coming . . . On that day, he will set His feet on the Mount of Olives, near Jerusalem on the east; and the Mount of Olives shall split across from east to west, and one part of the Mount shall shift to the north and the other to the south, a huge gorge. And the Valley in the Hills shall be stopped up, for the Valley of the Hills shall reach only to Azal; it shall be stopped up as it was stopped up as a result of the earthquake in the days of King Uzziah of Judah. — And the LORD my God, with all the holy beings, will come to you.

In that day, there shall be neither sunlight nor cold moonlight, but there shall be a continuous day — only the LORD knows when — of neither day nor night, and there shall be light at eventide

In that day, fresh water shall flow from Jerusalem, part of it to the Eastern Sea and part to the Western Sea, throughout the summer and winter.

And the LORD shall be king over all the earth; in that day there shall be one LORD with one name.

Second Reading *Gospel of Philip, 69:14–25, 70:1–4, 85:10–21, NHL*

There were three buildings specifically for sacrifice in Jerusalem. The one facing west was called "the Holy." Another facing south was called the "Holy of the Holy." The third facing east was called "the Holy of the Holies," the place where only the high priest enters. Baptism is "the Holy" building. Redemption is "the Holy of the Holy." "The Holy of the Holies" is the Bridal Chamber . . .

Its veil was rent from top to bottom. For it was fitting for some from below to go upward . . . It was rent from top to bottom. Those above opened to us who are below, in order that we may go into the secret of the truth. This is what is held in high regard, since it is strong! But we shall go in there by means of lowly types and forms of weakness. They are indeed lowly when compared with the perfect glory. There is glory which surpasses glory. There is power which surpasses power.

Holy Week

Therefore the perfect things have opened to us, together with the hidden things of truth. The holies of the holies were revealed, and the bridal chamber invited us in . . .

Psalm *Ode 27 and Ode 28:7–12*

Christ speaks
I extend my hands and hallow You my Lord!*
    I expand my hands in Your sign
My outstretched arms are Your holy cross . . . *
    They scorned me because in me there was no anger.
Because I did good I was hated.*
    They surrounded me like mad dogs who stupidly attack their
        masters.
Their thought is corrupt, their mind is perverted.*
    I carried water in my right hand. With sweetness I endured
        the bitter.
They sought my death. They failed.*
    They cast lots against me. They failed.

Gospel *Gospel of Peter 1–6, SV*

. . . but of the Judeans no one washed his hands, neither Herod nor any one of his judges. Since they were unwilling to wash, Pilate stood up. Then Herod the King orders the Lord to be taken away, saying to them, "Do what I commanded you to do to him."

Joseph stood there, the friend of Pilate and the Lord, and when he realized that they were about to crucify him, he went to Pilate and asked for the body of the Lord for burial. And Pilate sent to Herod and asked for his body. And Herod replied, "Brother Pilate, even if no one had asked for him, we would have buried him, since the sabbath is drawing near. For it is written in the Law, 'The sun must not set upon one who has been executed.'" And he turned him over to the people on the day before the Unleavened bread, their feast.

They took the Lord and kept pushing him along as they ran; and they would say, "Let's drag the son of God along, since we have him in our power." And they threw a purple robe around him and sat him upon the judgment seat and said, "Judge justly, king of Israel." And one of them brought a crown of thorns and set it on the head of the Lord. And others standing about would spit in his eyes, and others slapped his face, while others poked him with a rod. Some kept flogging him as they said, "Let's pay proper respect to the son of God."

And they brought two criminals and crucified the Lord between them. But he himself remained silent, as if in no pain. And when they set up the cross, they put an inscription on it, "This is the king of Israel." And they piled his clothing in front of him; then they divided it among themselves, and gambled for it. But one of those criminals reproached them and said, "We're suffering for the evil that we've done, but this fellow, who has become a savior of humanity, what wrong has he done to you?" And they got angry at him and ordered that his legs not be broken so he would die in agony.

It was midday and darkness covered the whole of Judea. They were confused and anxious for fear the sun had set since he was still alive. For it is written that, "The sun must not set upon one who has been executed." And one of them said, "Give him vinegar mixed without something bitter to drink." And they mixed it and gave it to him to drink. And they fulfilled all things and brought to completion the sins on their head. Now many went about with lamps, and, thinking that it was night, they laid down. And the Lord cried out, saying, "My power, my power, you have abandoned me." When he said this, he was taken up. And at that moment, the veil of the Jerusalem temple was torn in two.

And when they pulled the nails from the Lord's hands and set him on the ground. And the whole earth shook and there was great fear. Then the sun came out and it was found to be the ninth hour. Now the Judeans rejoiced and gave his body to Joseph so that he might bury it, since Joseph had observed how much good he had done. Joseph took the Lord, washed his body and wound a linen shroud around him, and brought him to his own tomb, called "Joseph's Garden."

Commentary When the body of the Lord is placed on the ground, the whole earth shakes. Might an earthquake have occurred at that moment? It is perfectly possible, because

Jerusalem lies along a geological fault line. This is a place where quite literally the earth on one side of the fault is moving north as the other appears to be moving south. Periodic earthquakes and earth movements do occur here. More important, however, is the symbolic meaning described in Zechariah and earlier in Isaiah during the time of King Uzziah. The quaking of the earth is a sign that the Day of the Lord has dawned, a new age is being born.

Holy Saturday
First Reading *Zechariah 12:9–12a, Tanakh*

In that day . . . I will fill the House of David and the inhabitants of Jerusalem with a spirit of pity and compassion; and they shall lament to Me about those who are slain, wailing over them as over a favorite son and showing bitter grief as over a first-born. In that day, the wailing in Jerusalem shall be as great as the wailing of Hadad-rimmon in the plain of Megiddon. The land shall wail, each family by itself.

Second Reading *Wisdom of Solomon 2:1–5, NRSV*

Short and sorrowful is our life, and there is no remedy when a life comes to its end, and no one has been known to return from Hades. For we were born by mere chance, and hereafter we shall be as though we had never been, for the breath in our nostrils is smoke, and reason is a spark kindled by the beating of our hearts; when it is extinguished, the body will return to ashes, and the spirit will dissolve like empty air. Our name will be forgotten in time, and no one will remember our works; our life will pass away like the traces of a cloud, and be scattered like mist that is chased by the rays of the sun and overcome by its heat. For our allotted time is the passing of a shadow, and there is no return for our death, because it is sealed up and no one turns back.

Psalm *Ode 42*

Christ speaks
I extend my hands and come near You, my Lord,*
> Stretching my hands as spread on a tree is my sign, my Way to You.

I became useless to those who did not know me;*
    I hid from those who did not take hold of me.
My persecutors died. I am with those who love me.*
    Those who trust in me seek me because I am living.
I rise up and am with them and speak through their mouths.*
    They reject those who persecute them. I lock them in the
       yoke of love.
Like the arm of the groom over the bride,*
    so is my love over those who trust in me.
I was not rejected, although I was considered to be.*
    I did not perish, although they thought it of me.
Hell saw me and was shattered;*
    Death ejects me along with many others.
I have been gall and bitterness to death.*
    I went down with it to the utmost depth.
Death released my feet and head*
    because it could not endure my face.
I made a congregation of living among the dead.*
    I spoke to them with living lips so my word would not be
       empty.
The dead ran to me, crying, "Son of God, pity us,*
    be kind, bring us out of the bonds of darkness.
Open for us the door through which we may go forth to You.*
    We perceive that our death has not touched You.
May we also be saved with You because You are our Savior."
    I heard their voice and stored their faith in my heart
I set my Name upon their heads*
    for they are free and they are mine. Hallelujah!

Gospel *Gospel of Peter 7–8, SV*

    Then the Judeans and the elders and the priests perceived what evil they had done to themselves, and began to beat their breasts and cry out, "Our sins have brought woes upon us! The judgment and the end of Jerusalem are at hand!" But I began weeping with my friends. And quivering with fear in our hearts, we hid ourselves. After all, we were being sought by them as criminals and as ones wishing to burn down the temple. As a result of all these things, we fasted and sat mourning and weeping night and day until the sabbath.

When the scholars and the Pharisees and the priests had gathered together, and when they heard that all the people were moaning and beating their breasts, and saying "If his death has produced these overwhelming signs, he must have been entirely innocent!", they became frightened and went to Pilate and begged him, "Give us soldiers so that we may guard his tomb for three days, in case his disciples come and steal his body and the people assume he has risen from the dead and so us harm." So Pilate gave them the centurion Petronius with soldiers to guard the tomb. And elders and scholars went with them to the tomb. And all who were there with the centurion and the soldiers helped roll a large stone against the entrance to the tomb. And they put seven seals on it. Then they pitched a tent there and kept watch.

Easter Season

Easter Day

First Reading *Job 14:1–2, 7–14a, Tanakh*

A mortal, born of woman is short-lived and sated with trouble,
blossoms like a flower and withers,
vanishes like a shadow and does not endure . . .
There is hope for a tree;
If it is cut down, it will renew itself;
Its shoots will not cease.
If its roots are old in the earth,
And its stump dies in the ground,
At the scent of water it will bud
And produce branches like a sapling.
But mortals languish and die;
Humans expire; where *are they?*
The eaters of the sea fail,
And the river dries up and is parched.
So mortals lie down never to rise;
they will awake only when the heavens are no more,
Only then be aroused from sleep.
O that you would hide me in Sheol,
conceal me until Your anger passes,
Set me a fixed time to attend to me.
If *a person* dies, can *that person* live again?

Second Reading *Gospel of Peter 9–11, SV*

Early at first light on the sabbath, a crowd came from Jerusalem and the surrounding countryside to see the sealed tomb. But during the night before the Lord's day dawned, while the soldiers were on guard, two by two during each watch, a loud noise came from the sky, and they saw the skies open up and two men come down from there in a burst of light and approach the tomb. The stone that had been pushed against the entrance began to roll by itself and moved away to one side; then the tomb opened up and both young men went inside.

Now when the soldiers saw this, they roused the centurion from his sleep, along with the elders. (Remember, they were also there keeping watch.) While they were explaining what they had seen, again they see three men leaving the tomb, two supporting the third, and a cross was following them. The heads of the two reached up to the sky, while the head of the third, whom they led by the hand, reached beyond the skies. And they heard a voice from the skies that said, "Have you preached to those who sleep?" And an answer was heard from the cross: "Yes!"

These men then consulted with one another about going and reporting these things to Pilate. While they were still thinking about it, again the skies appeared to open and some sort of human being came down and entered the tomb. When those in the centurion's company saw this, they rushed out into the night to Pilate, having left the tomb they were supposed to be guarding. And as they were recounting everything they had seen, they became deeply disturbed and cried, "Truly, he was a son of God!" Pilate responded by saying, "I am clean of the blood of the son of God; this was all your doing." Then they all crowded around Pilate and began to beg and urge him to order the centurion and his soldiers to tell no one what they saw. "You see," they said, "it is better for us to be guilty of the greatest sin before God than to fall into the hands of the Judean people and be stoned." Pilate then ordered the centurion and the soldiers to say nothing.

Psalm *Ode 17:1–5*

Christ is praying
I was crowned by You, God, by a crown You made me alive,*

You, my Lord, justify me and become my certain salvation.
I am freed from myself and uncondemned.*
  The chain falls from my wrists.
I take on the face and ways of a new person,*
  I walk in You and am redeemed.
The thought of truth drives me*
  I walk in it and do not wander off.
Those who see me are amazed,*
  supposing me to be a stranger.

Gospel *Gospel of Peter 12–13, SV*

Early on the Lord's day, Mary of Magdala, a disciple of the Lord, was fearful on account of the Judeans and, since they were enflamed with rage, she did not perform at the tomb of the Lord what women are accustomed to do for their loved ones who die. Nevertheless, she took her friends with her and went to the tomb where he had been laid. And they were afraid that the Judeans might see them and were saying, "Although on the day he was crucified we could not weep and beat our breasts, we should now perform these rites at his tomb. But who will roll away the stone for us, the one placed at the entrance of the tomb, so that we may enter and sit beside him and do what ought to be done?" (remember, it was a huge stone.) "We fear that someone might see us. And if we are unable to roll the stone away we should, at least, place at the entrance the memorial we brought him, and we should weep and beat our breasts until we go home."

And they went and found the tomb open. They went up to it, stooped down, and saw a young man sitting there in the middle of the tomb; he was handsome and wore a splendid robe. He said to them, "Why have you come? Who are you looking for? Surely not the one who was crucified? He is risen and gone. If you don't believe it, stoop down and take a look at the place where he lay, for he is not there. You see, he is risen and has gone back to the place he was sent from." Then the women fled in fear.

Commentary Only the Gospel of Peter provides a resurrection story in which the body of Jesus leaves the tomb. All other Gospels begin with the tomb being empty. Taken literally, the story might

Easter

seem preposterous. Taken symbolically, it contains rich meaning. For example, who might the two men be who come for Jesus? Might they be the same two, Moses and Elijah, who appear in the Transfiguration story? (Mark 9:2–13, Luke 9:28–36, Matthew 17:1–13)

Note also that in Luke's version of the resurrection story, when the women come to the tomb, they are greeted by "two men in dazzling clothes" (Luke 24:4). Luke's Ascension story give us the third time when the "two men in white robes" are present (Acts 1:10)

Something else unique to the Gospel of Peter is that resurrection and ascension are simultaneous, rather than separate.

As Arthur J. Dewey points out, "The original stage of Peter may well be the earliest passion story in the gospel tradition and, as such, may contain the seeds of subsequent passion narratives."

Second Sunday of Easter

First Reading *Exodus 12:16–19, Tanakh*

You shall celebrate a sacred occasion on the first day, and a sacred occasion on the seventh day; no work at all shall be done on them; only what every person is to eat, that alone may be prepared for you. You shall observe the Feast of Unleavened Bread, for on this very day I brought your ranks out of the land of Egypt; you shall observe this day throughout the ages as an institution for all time. In the first month, from the fourteenth day of the month at evening, you shall eat unleavened bread until the twenty-first day of the month at evening. No leaven shall be found in your houses for seven days. For whoever eats what is leavened, that person shall be cut off from the community of Israel, whether he is a stranger or a citizen of the country.

Second Reading *Gospel of Peter 14, SV*

Now it was the last day of Unleavened Bread, and many began to return to their homes since the feast was over. But we, the twelve disciples of the Lord, continued to weep and mourn, and each one, still grieving on account of what had happened, left for his own home. But I, Simon Peter, and Andrew, my

brother, took our fishing nets and went away to the sea. And
with us was Levi, the son of Alphaeus, whom the Lord . . .

Psalm *Ode 17:6–9*

You know me and bring me up*
　You are the summit of perfection
You glorify me by kindness*
　You lift my thought to truth.
You show me Your Way.*
　I open closed doors, shatter bars of iron. My shackles melt.
Nothing appears closed*
　because I am the Door to everything.
I free slaves, leaving no one in bonds.*
　I spread my knowledge and love,
I sow my fruits in their hearts and transform them.*
　I bless them. They live.
I gather them and save them.*
　They become the limbs of my body and I am their head.
Response
Glory to You, our Head, our Lord Messiah. Hallelujah!

Gospel *John 21:1–14, SV*

　　Some time after these events, Jesus again appeared to his disciples by the Sea of Tiberias. This is how he did it: When Simon
Peter and Thomas, the one known as "the Twin", were together,
along with Nathaniel from Cana, Galilee, the sons of Zebedee,
and two other disciples, Simon Peter says to them, "I'm going
to go fishing."

　　"We're coming with you," they reply.

　　They went down and got into the boat, but that night they
didn't catch a thing.

　　It was already getting light when Jesus appeared on the
shore, but his disciples didn't recognize that it was Jesus.

　　"Lads, you haven't caught any fish, have you?" Jesus asks
them.

　　"No," they replied.

　　He tells them, "Cast your net on the right side of the boat
and you'll have better luck."

　　They do as he instructs them and now they can't haul it in

for the huge number of fish. The disciple Jesus loved most exclaims to Peter, "It's the Master!"

When Simon heard "It's the Master," he tied his cloak around himself, since he was stripped for work, and threw himself into the water. The rest of them came in the boat, dragging the net full of fish. They were not far from land, only about a hundred yards offshore.

When they got to shore, they see a charcoal fire burning, with fish cooking on it, and some bread. Jesus says to them, "Bring some of the fish you've just caught."

Then Simon Peter went aboard and hauled the net full of large fish ashore — one hundred fifty-three of them. Even though there were so many of them, the net still didn't tear.

Jesus says to them, "Come and eat."

None of the disciples dared to ask, "Who are you?" They knew it was the Master. Jesus comes, takes the bread and gives it to them, and passes the fish around as well.

This was now the third time after he had been raised from the dead that Jesus appeared to his disciples.

Commentary Regarding the phrase, *tied his cloak around himself, since he was stripped for work:* This sentence is usually rendered as "put on his outer garment for he was naked" or similarly; so understood it is highly anomalous in view of Peter's jumping into the water that follows. Peter's action means literally "girded himself" and the word for "naked" need mean only "not fully clad." As translated here the difficulty disappears. Peter was stripped to the waist for heavy work in the boat and so girded up the garments tied about his waist, so as to swim and wade ashore. (From *The Complete Gospels* p. 244)

Compare this story with the calling of the disciples and the great catch of fish in Luke 5:4–11. Just as the historical Jesus called the disciples to go fishing for people, so the Resurrected Jesus calls them again to go fishing for people, this time with the symbol of one hundred fifty three fish. At that time, the number of known species of fish was believed to be 153, a major undercount by today's knowledge! Yet the symbol remains: all kinds of fish are included in the net, so are all kinds of people.

Note "Jerome tells us that the Greek zoologists had recorded 153 different kinds of fish; and so by mentioning this number John may have been symbolizing the totality and range of the disciples' catch." Raymond E. Brown, *The Gospel According to John*, Volume 29a, page 1074, in *The Anchor Bible*, Doubleday 1970.

Third Sunday of Easter

First Reading *Genesis 1:1–5, Tanakh*

When God began to create heaven and earth — the earth being unformed and void, with darkness over the surface of the deep and a wind (spirit) from God sweeping over the water — God said, "Let there be light"; and there was light. God saw that the light was good,and God separated the light from the darkness. God called the light Day, and the darkness He called Night. And there was evening and there was morning, a first day.

Second Reading *Gospel of Philip 53:14–23, NHL*

Light and darkness, life and death, right and left, are brothers of one another. They are inseparable. Because of this neither are the good good, nor the evil evil, nor is life life, nor death death. For this reason each will dissolve into its original nature. But those who are exalted above the world are indissoluble, eternal.

Psalm *Ode 8:1–12*

Open your hearts to the exultation of the Lord*
　　And flow your love from your heart to your lips in a holy life.
Carry fruit to the Lord.*
　　Talk and look in his light.
Stand up with your shoulders back,*
　　you who sank low.
You who were silent, speak.*
　　Your mouth has been opened.
You were despised. Now feel uplifted.*
　　Your goodness is high.
The right hand of the Lord is with you.*
　　The Lord will help you.
Christ begins speaking
Hear the Word of truth*

Drink knowledge I offer from the Most High.
Your flesh cannot know what I say to you,*
    nor your garments what I show you.
Keep my Mystery. It keeps you.*
    Keep my faith. It keeps you.
Know my knowledge, you who know me in truth.*
    Love me tenderly, you who love.
I do not turn my face from my own.*
    I know them.

Gospel *Gospel of Mary 2–3, SV*

(Six manuscript pages of the Gospel of Mary are missing. The scene is an encounter with the resurrected Jesus. Someone is asking a question.)

" . . . Will matter then be utterly destroyed or not?"

The Savior replied, "Every nature, every modeled form, every creature, exists in and with each other. They will dissolve again into their own proper root. For the nature of matter is dissolved into what belongs to its nature. Anyone with two ears capable of hearing should listen!"

Then Peter said to him, "You have been expounding every topic to us; tell us one further thing. What is the sin of the world?"

The Savior replied, "There is no such thing as sin; rather, you yourselves are what produces sin when you act according to the nature of adultery, which is called 'sin.' For this reason, the Good came among you approaching what belongs to every nature. It will set it within its root."

Then he continued. He said, "This is why you get sick and die, for you love what deceives you. Anyone with a mind should use it to think!

"Matter gave birth to a passion which has no true image because it derives from what is contrary to nature. Then a disturbing confusion occurred in the whole body. This is why I told you, 'Be content of heart.' And do not conform to the body, but form yourselves in the presence of that other image of nature. Anyone with two ears capable of hearing should listen!"

Fourth Sunday of Easter

First Reading *Ezekiel 1:28b–3:3, RSV*

I saw the appearance of the likeness of the glory of the LORD and I fell upon my face, and I heard the Voice of one speaking. And he said to me, "Son of Man, stand upon your feet, and I will speak with you." And when he spoke to me, the Spirit entered into me and set me upon my feet; and I heard him speaking to me. And he said to me, "Son of Man, I send you to the people of Israel, to a nation of rebels, who have rebelled against me; they and their fathers have transgressed against me to this very day. The people are impudent and stubborn: I send you to them; and you shall say to them, 'Thus says the Lord GOD,' And whether they hear or refuse to hear (for they are a rebellious house) they will know that there has been a prophet among them.

And you, Son of Man, be not afraid of them, nor be afraid of their words, though briers and thorns are with you and you sit upon scorpions; be not afraid of their words, nor be dismayed at their looks, for they are a rebellious house. And you shall speak my words to them whether they hear or refuse to hear, for they are a rebellious house.

"But you, Son of Man, hear what I say to you; be not rebellious like that rebellious house; open your mouth, and eat what I give you." And when I looked, behold, a hand was stretched out to me, and, lo, a written scroll was in it; and he spread it out before me; and it had writing on the front and on the back, and there were written on it words of lamentation and woe.

And he said to me, "Son of man, eat what is offered to you; eat this scroll that I give you and fill your stomach with it." Then I ate it; and it was in my mouth as sweet as honey.

Second Reading *Gospel of Philip 79:18–33, NHL*

Farming in the world requires the cooperation of four essential elements. A harvest is gathered into the barn only as a result of the natural action of water, earth, wind and light. God's farming likewise has four elements — faith, hope, love, and knowledge. Faith is our earth, that in which we take root.

And hope is the water through which we are nourished. Love is the wind through which we grow. Knowledge is the light through which we ripen. Grace exists in four ways: it is earthborn; it is heavenly; it comes from the highest heaven; and it resides in truth.

Psalm *Ode 8:13–22*

> *The Lord sings*
> Before they were, I knew them*
>   and set my seal on their faces.
> I fashioned their limbs and prepared my breasts for them*
>   for them to drink my holy milk and live on it.
> I took pleasure in them*
>   and am not ashamed of them.
> Through my workmanship they are*
>   and are the strength of my thought.
> Who can stand against my handiwork?*
>   Who is not subject to my handiwork?
> I willed and fashioned my mind and heart,*
>   they are mine, and with my own hand I created them.
> My goodness goes before them*
>   and they will not lack my name. I am with them.
> *The Odist responds and speaks to the people*
> Pray and grow, survive in the love of the Lord.*
>   You are loved in the loved one.
> You survive in Christ who lives.*
>   You are saved in Christ who was saved.
> In all ages you will be found incorruptible*
>   through the name of your Father. Hallelujah!

Gospel *Gospel of Mary 4–5, SV*

When the Blessed One had said this, he greeted them all. "Peace be with you!" he said. "Acquire my peace within yourselves!

"Be on your guard so that no one deceives you by saying, 'Look over here!' or 'Look over there!' For the seed of the true humanity exists within you. Follow it! Those who search for it will find it.

Go then, preach the good news of the domain. Do not lay

down any rule beyond what I ordained for you, nor promulgate law like the lawgiver, or else it will dominate you."

After he said these things, he left them.

But they were distressed and wept greatly. "How are we going to go out to the rest of the world to preach the good news about the domain of the seed of the true humanity?" they said. "If they didn't spare him, how will they spare us?"

Then Mary stood up. She greeted them all and addressed her brothers. "Do not weep and be distressed nor let your hearts be irresolute. For his grace will be with you all and will shelter you. Rather we should praise his greatness, for he has joined us together and made us true human beings."

When Mary said these things, she turned their minds toward the Good, and they began to ask about the words of the Savior.

Commentary *seed of true humanity:* This term is usually translated, "Son of Man." "It is rendered differently here because it has a different connotation in the Gospel of Mary: it refers to the archetypal Image of humanity within each person." Karen L. King, *The Complete Gospels*, p. 362

In the book of Ezekiel, the Voice calls Ezekiel to stand up and then calls forth the Son of Man (seed of True Humanity) within Ezekiel. In the Gospel of Mary, the Voice of the Resurrected Jesus also calls forth the seed of true humanity from within Mary Magdalene and the disciples. In the Gospel of Philip, the seed of our true humanity within us grows through the four elements of faith, hope, love, and knowledge. Compare this with Paul's shorter list of "faith, hope, and love" which lacks the fourth essential element: direct knowledge of the Source of Life.

Fifth Sunday of Easter

First Reading *Acts of Peter and the Twelve Apostles 2:11–4:15, NHL 3rd edition*

We went down to the sea at an opportune moment, which came to us from the Lord. We found a ship moored at the shore ready to embark, and we spoke with the sailors of the ship about our coming aboard with them. They showed great kindliness to us as was ordained by the Lord. And after we had embarked, we sailed a day and a night. After that a wind came up behind the ship and brought us to a small city in the midst of the sea.

And I, Peter, inquired about the name of this city from residents who were standing on the dock. A man among them answered, saying, "The name of this city is Habitation, that is, Foundation . . . endurance. And the leader among them holding the palm branch at the edge of the dock. And after we had gone ashore with the baggage, I went into the city to seek advice about lodging.

A man came out wearing a cloth bound around his waist, and a gold belt girded it. Also a napkin was tied over his chest, extending over his shoulders and covering his head and his hands.

I was staring at the man because he was beautiful in his form and stature. There were four parts of his body that I saw: the soles of his feet and a part of his chest and the palms of his hands and his visage. These things I was able to see. A book cover like those of my books was in his left hand. A staff of styrax wood was in his right hand. His voice was resounding as he slowly spoke, crying out in the city, "Pearls! Pearls!"

I, indeed, thought he was a man of that city. I said to him, "My brother and my friend!" He answered me, then, saying, "Rightly did you say, 'My brother and my friend.' What is it you seek from me?" I said to him, "I ask you about lodging for me and the brothers also, because we are strangers here." He said to me, "For this reason have I myself just said, 'My brother and my friend,' because I also am a fellow stranger like you."

And having said these things, he cried out, "Pearls! Pearls!" The rich men of that city heard his voice. They came out of their hidden storerooms. And some were looking out from the storerooms of their houses. Others looked out from their upper windows. And they did not see that they could gain anything from him, because there was no pack on his back, nor bundle inside his cloth and napkin. And because of their disdain they did not even acknowledge him. He, for his part, did not reveal himself to them. They returned to their storerooms, saying, "This man is mocking us."

And the poor of that city heard his voice, and they came to

the man who sells pearls. They said, "Please take the trouble to show us the pearl so that we may, then, see it with our own eyes. For we are the poor. And we do not have the price to pay for it. But allow us to say to our friends that we saw a pearl with our own eyes."

He answered, saying to them, "If it is possible, you yourselves come to my city, so that I may not only show it to you, but give it to you for nothing."

Commentary Just as Jesus the Nazarene had taught about the "pearl of great value" (Matt 13:46) so the Resurrected Jesus continues offering pearls to those who are ready and willing to ask and receive the gift. Those who hold tightly to what they have are closing themselves off and shutting the doors to the greatest value.

Second Reading *Treatise on Resurrection 48:4–49:8, NHL*

What, then, is the resurrection? It is always the disclosure of those who have risen. For if you remember reading in the Gospel that Elijah appeared and Moses with him, do not think the resurrection is an illusion. It is no illusion, but it is truth. Indeed, it is more fitting to say that the world is an illusion, rather than the resurrection which has come into being through our Lord and Savior, Jesus Christ.

But what am I telling you now? Those who are living shall die. How do they live in an illusion? The rich have become poor, and the kings have been overthrown. Everything is prone to change. The world is an illusion! — lest, indeed, I rail at things to excess!

But the Resurrection does not have this aforesaid character; for it is the truth which stands firm. It is the revelation of what is, and the transformation of things, and a transition into newness.

For imperishability descends upon the perishable; the light flows down upon the darkness, swallowing it up; and the Pleroma fills up the deficiency. These are the symbols and the images of the resurrection. This is what makes the good.

Psalm *Ode 9*

Christ is speaking
Open your ears and I will speak to you.*
    Give me your soul that I may give you mine.

Here is the Word of the Lord and his desires,*
 his holy thought about the Messiah.
In the will of the Lord is your life.*
 His purpose is your eternal life.
Be rich in God the Father and receive the purpose of the high
  one.*
 In his grace be strong and redeemed.
I tell you and the holy ones peace*
 and if you hear, you will not fall into war.
Whoever knows him will not perish.*
 Whoever receives him will not be confused.
His eternal crown is truth.*
 Those who wear it on their heads are blessed.
It is made of precious stones*
 and wars were fought over the crown.
Goodness took it*
 and gave it to you.
Put on the crown in a covenant with the Lord.*
All who have conquered will be inscribed in the book of the
  Lord.
Their book is victory, and she is yours.*
Victory sees you before her and wills you saved. Hallelujah!

Gospel *Gospel of Mary 6–7, SV*

 Peter said to Mary, "Sister, we know that the Savior loved you more than any other woman. Tell us the words of the Savior that you know, but which we haven't heard."

 Mary responded, "I will report to you as much as I remember that you don't know. And she began to speak these words to them.

 She said, "I saw the Lord in a vision and I said to him, 'Lord, I saw you today in a vision.'

 "He said to me, 'Congratulations to you for not wavering at seeing me. For where the mind is, there is the treasure.'

 "I said to him, 'Lord, how does a person who sees a vision see it — with the soul or with the spirit?'

 "The Savior answered, 'The visionary does not see with the soul or with the spirit, but with the mind which exists between

these two — that is what sees the vision and that is what . . .'"
(Four manuscript pages are missing here.)

Commentary "Soul, spirit, and mind are the three components of human consciousness. The soul is directed toward what is lower, the spirit toward what is higher. The mind, mediating between the two, allows the soul in the world to perceive a vision of the higher spiritual Reality.

"Four pages are missing from the Coptic manuscript of the Gospel of Mary at this point. There are no parallel Greek fragments so we can only speculate about the contents." Karen L. King, *The Complete Gospels* p. 363

Sixth Sunday of Easter

First Reading *Acts of Peter and the Twelve Apostles 8:15–9:19, NHL 3rd edition*

Lithargoel had the appearance of a physician, since an unguent box was under his arm, and a young disciple was following him, carrying a pouch full of medicine. We did not recognize him . . .

He said to Peter, "Peter!" And Peter was frightened, for how did he know that his name was Peter? Peter responded to the Savior, "How do you know me, for you called my name?" Lithargoel answered, "I want to ask you who gave you the name Peter to you?" He said to him, "It was Jesus Christ, the son of the living God. He gave this name to me." He answered, "It is I. Recognize me, Peter." He loosened his garment, which clothed him — the one into which he had changed himself because of us — revealing to us in truth that it was he.

We prostrated ourselves on the ground and worshipped him. We comprised eleven disciples. He stretched forth his hand and caused us to stand. We spoke with him humbly. Our heads were bowed down in unworthiness as we said, "What you wish, we will do. But give us power to do what you wish at all times."

Commentary The merchant tells Peter that his name is Lithargoel, which is interpreted in the text as a lightweight stone that gleams like the eye of a gazelle, in other words a pearl. So the merchant not only offers pearls, but is the pearl.

Lithargoel, who is the Resurrected Jesus, now is not only a pearl merchant but also a physician. Thus the healing ministry of the historic Jesus continues through the Resurrected Jesus.

Second Reading *Gospel of Philip 67:9–27, NHL*

Truth did not come into the world naked, but it came in types and images. One will not receive truth in any other way. There is a rebirth and an image of rebirth. It is certainly necessary to be born again through the image. Which one? Resurrection. The image must rise again through the image. The bridal chamber and the image must enter through the image into the truth: this is the restoration.

Not only must those who produce the name of the father and the son and the holy spirit do so, but those who have produced them for you. If one does not acquire them, the name "Christian" will be taken from him. But one receives them in the aromatic unction of the power of the cross. This power the angels called "the right and the left." For this person is no longer a Christian but a Christ.

Psalm *Ode 10*

O Lord You change my mouth by Your Word*
    and open my heart by Your light.
You make Your deathless life inhabit me*
    and let me speak the fruit of Your peace
to convert souls who want to come to You*
    and lead captives into freedom.
Christ responds,
I took courage, became strong, and captured the world,*
    yet captivity was mine for the glory of the High One, God
      my Father.
The Gentiles who were scattered abroad were gathered
    together*
    and I was not polluted by my love for them.
They praised me in high holy places.*

Traces of light entered their heart as they became my people forever. Hallelujah!

Gospel *Gospel of Mary 9, SV*

(After four missing pages, the manuscript continues in the middle of Mary's account of the ascent of the soul out of its bondage.)

"And Desire said, 'I did not see you go down, yet now I see you go up. So why do you lie since you belong to me?'

"The soul answered, 'I saw you, You did not see me nor did you know me. You mistook the garment I wore for my true self. And you did not recognize me.'

"After it had said these things, the soul left rejoicing greatly.

"Again, it came to the third Power, which is called 'Ignorance.' It examined the soul closely, saying, 'Where are you going? You are bound by fornication. Indeed you are bound! Do not pass judgment!'

"And the soul said, 'Why do you judge me, since I have not passed judgment? I am bound, but I have not bound! Do not pass judgment!' They did not recognize me, but I have recognized that the universe is to be dissolved, both the things of earth and those of heaven.'

"When the soul had overcome the third Power, it went upward and it saw the fourth Power. It had seven forms. The first form is Darkness; the second, Desire; the third, Ignorance; the fourth, Zeal for Death; the Fifth the Domain of the Flesh; the sixth the Foolish Wisdom of the Flesh, the seventh is the Wisdom of the Wrathful Person. These are the seven Powers of Wrath.

"They interrogated the soul, 'Where are you coming from, human-killer, and where are you going, space-conqueror?'

"The soul replied, 'What binds me has been slain, and what surrounds me has been destroyed, and my desire has been brought to an end, and my ignorance has died. In a world, I was set loose from a world and a type, from a type which is above, and from the chain of forgetfulness that exists in time. From now on, for the rest of the course of the due measure of the time of the age, I will rest in silence.'"

When Mary said these things, she fell silent, since it was up to this point that the Savior had spoken to her.

Commentary For an excellent commentary on this passage, please see the footnotes in *The Complete Gospels*, p. 364–65.

Seventh Sunday of Easter

First Reading *Acts of Peter and the Twelve Apostles 9:20–11:26, NHL 3rd edition*

The Lord gave them the unguent box and the pouch that was in the hand of the young disciple. He commanded them like this, saying, "Go into the city from which you came, which is called Habitation. Continue in endurance as you teach all who believed in my name, because I have endured in hardships of the faith. I will give you your reward. To the poor of the city give what they need in order to live until I give them what is better, which I told you that I will give you for nothing."

Peter answered and said to him, "Lord, you have taught us to forsake the world and everything in it. We have renounced them for your sake. What we are concerned about now is the food for a single day. Where will we be able to find the needs that you ask us to provide for the poor?"

The Lord answered and said, "O Peter, it was necessary that you understand the parable that I told you! Do you not understand that my name, which you teach, surpasses all riches, and the wisdom of God surpasses gold, and silver and precious stones?"

The Lord gave them the pouch of medicine and said, "Heal all the sick of the city who believe in my name." Peter was afraid to reply to him for the second time. He signaled to the one who was beside him, who was John: "You talk this time." John answered and said, "Lord before you we are afraid to say many words. But it is you who asks us to practice this skill. We have not been taught to be physicians. How then will we know how to heal bodies as you have told us?"

He answered, "Rightly have you spoken, John, for I know that the physicians of this world heal what belongs to the world. The physicians of souls, however, heal the heart. Heal the bodies first, therefore, so that through the real powers of healing for their bodies, without medicine of the world, they may believe in you, that you have power to heal the illnesses of the heart also.

Commentary The ministry of the historic Jesus included healing. Now that healing ministry is passed on to Peter and all the members of his Risen Body.

You have power to heal the illnesses of the heart.

Second Reading *Gospel of Philip 63:32–64:5, 59:2–6, NHL*

And the companion of the Savior is Mary Magdalene. But Christ loved her more than all the disciples and used to kiss her often on her mouth. The rest of the disciples were offended by it and expressed disapproval. They said to him, "Why do you love her more than all of us?" The Savior answered and said to them, "Why do I not love you like her?" . . .

For it is by a kiss that the perfect conceive and give birth. For this reason we also kiss one another. We receive conception from the grace which is in each other.

Psalm *Ode 11:9–19*

You renew me, Lord, by clothing me and holding me in Your
     light.*
   From above You give me uncorrupt ease
I am like land deep and happy in its orchards,*
   You, Lord, are sun on the face of the land.
My eyes are clear, dew is on my face.*
   My nostrils enjoy Your aroma, Lord.
You take me to Paradise where I know joy,*
   where I worship Your glory.
Blessed are they planted in Your land, in Paradise,*
   who grow in the growth of Your trees and change from
     gloom into light.
Your servants are lovely. They do good,*
   they turn from evil toward Your pleasantness.
The pungent odor of the trees is changed in Your land.*
   Everyone is like Your remnant.

Blessed are the workers of Your living water.*

You are everywhere, always before Your servants.

There is much space in Paradise but no wasteland. Everything is filled with fruit.*

Praise be to You, O God, the eternal delight of Paradise. Hallelujah!

Gospel *Gospel of Mary 10, SV*

Andrew said, "Brothers, what is your opinion of what was just said? I for one don't believe that the Savior said these things, because these opinions seem so different from his thought."

After reflecting on these matters, Peter said, "Has the Savior spoken secretly to a woman and not openly so that we would all hear? Surely he did not wish to indicate that she is more worthy than we are?"

Then Mary wept and said to Peter, "Peter, my brother, what are you imagining about this? Do you think that I've made all this up secretly by myself or that I am telling lies about the Savior?"

Levi said to Peter, "Peter, you have a constant inclination to anger and you are always ready to give way to it. And even now you are doing exactly that by questioning the woman as if you're her adversary. If the Savior considered her to be worthy, who are we to disregard her? For he knew her completely and loved her devotedly.

"Instead, we should be ashamed and, once we clothe ourselves with perfect humanity, we should do what we are commanded. We should announce the good news as the Savior ordered, and not be laying down any rules or making laws."

After he said these things, Levi left and began to announce the good news.

Season of Pentecost

The Day of Pentecost

First Reading *Ezekiel 37:1–14, Tanakh*

The hand of the Lord came upon me. He took me out by the spirit of the LORD and set me down in the valley. It was full of bones. He led me all around them; there were very many of them spread over the valley, and they were very dry. He said to me, "O *Son of Man*, can these bones live again?" I replied, "O Lord GOD, only you know." And He said to me, "Prophesy over these bones and say to them: O dry bones, hear the word of the LORD! Thus says the Lord GOD to these bones: I will cause breath to enter you and you shall live again. I will lay sinews upon you, and cover you with flesh, and form skin over you. And I will put breath into you, and you shall live again. And you shall know that I am the LORD!"

I prophesied as I had been commanded. And while I was prophesying, suddenly there was a sound of rattling, and the bones came together, bone to matching bone. I looked, and there were sinews on them, and flesh had grown, and skin had formed over them; but there was no breath in them.

Then He said to me, "Prophesy to the breath, prophesy, O *Son of Man*! Say to the breath: Thus said the Lord GOD: Come, O breath, from the four winds, and breathe into these slain, that they may live again." I prophesied as He commanded me. The breath entered them, and they came to life and stood up on their feet, a vast multitude.

And he said to me, "O *Son of Man*, these bones are the whole House of Israel. They say, 'Our bones are dried up, our hope is gone; we are doomed.' Prophesy, therefore, and say to them: Thus said the Lord GOD: I am going to open your graves and lift you out of the graves, O My people, and bring you to the land of Israel. You shall know, O My people, that I am the LORD, when I have opened your graves and lifted you out of your graves. I will put My breath into you and you shall live again, and I will set you upon your own soil. Then you shall know that I the LORD have spoken and have acted" — declares the LORD.

Second Reading *Acts 2:1–15, NRSV*

When the day of Pentecost had come, they were all together in one place. And suddenly from heaven there came a sound like the rush of a violent wind, and it filled the entire house where they were sitting. Divided tongues, as of fire, appeared among them, and a tongue rested on each of them. All of them were filled with the Holy Spirit and began to speak in other languages, as the Spirit gave them ability.

Now there were devout Jews from every nation under heaven living in Jerusalem. And at this sound the crowd gathered and was bewildered, because each one heard them speaking in the language of each. Amazed and astonished, they asked, "Are not all these who speak Galileans? And how is it that we hear, each of us, in our own native language? Parthians, Medes, Elamites, and residents of Mesopotamia, Judea, Cappodocia, Pontus and Asia, Phrygia and Pamphilia, Egypt and the parts of Libya belonging to Cyrene, and visitors from Rome, both Jews and proselytes, Cretans and Arabs — in our own languages we hear them speaking about God's deeds of power." All were amazed and perplexed, saying to one another, "What does this mean?" But others sneered and said, "They are filled with new wine."

But Peter, standing with the eleven, raised his voice and addressed them, "Men of Judea and all who live in Jerusalem, let this be known to you, and listen to what I say. Indeed, these are not drunk, as you suppose, for it is only nine o'clock in the morning. No, this is what was spoken through the prophet Joel:

'In the last days it will be, God declares,
that I will pour out my Spirit upon all flesh,
and your sons and your daughters shall prophesy,
and your young men shall see visions,
and your old men shall dream dreams.
Even upon my slaves, both men and women,
In those days I will pour out my Spirit;
and they shall prophesy.
And I will show portents in the heaven above
and signs on the earth below, blood, and fire, and smoky mist.
The sun shall be turned to darkness,
and the moon to blood,
Before the coming of the Lord's great and glorious day.
Then everyone who calls on the name of the Lord shall be saved.'"

Psalm *Ode 6*

As the hand moves over the harp and the strings speak,*
  so Your Spirit speaks in my members and I speak by Your love.
You transform what is foreign and bitter.*
  You are from the beginning and will be to the end.
Nothing will be Your adversary*
  Nothing will resist You.
You, Lord, multiply Your knowledge*
  You are zealous to make us know what You give us through Your grace.
You give us praise for Your Name*
  and our spirits praise Your Holy Spirit.
A stream goes forth and becomes a long and broad river.*
  It flooded and broke and carried away the Temple.
Ordinary people could not stop it,*
  nor could those whose art is to halt the waters.
It spread over the face of the whole earth, filling everything,*
  and the thirsty of the earth drink and their thirst is relived and quenched.
The drink comes from You, the Highest One.*

Blessed are the ministers of that drink who are entrusted
  with Your water.
They assuage dry lips.*
  They raise up those who have fainted.
Souls that are about to depart they draw back from death.*
  Limbs that become crooked they make straight.
They give strength to our feebleness and light to our eyes*
  Everyone knows them in You, Lord, and by Your water they
  live forever.

Gospel *The Sophia of Jesus Christ 90:14–92:5, NHL*

After Jesus Christ rose from the dead, his twelve disciples
and seven women continued to be his followers and went to
Galilee onto the mountain called "Divination and Joy." When
they gathered together and were perplexed about the underlying reality of the universe and the plan and the holy providence
and the power of the authorities and about everything that the
Savior is doing with them in the secret of the holy plan, the
Savior appeared, not in his previous form, but in the invisible
spirit. And his likeness resembled a great angel of light. But his
resemblance I must not describe. No mortal flesh could endure
it, but only pure and perfect flesh, like that which he taught us
about on the mountain called "Of Olives" in Galilee.

And he said, "Peace be to you! My peace I give to you!" And
they all marveled and were afraid.

The Savior laughed and said to them: "What are you thinking about? Why are you perplexed? What are you searching
for?"

Philip said, "For the underlying reality and the plan."

Commentary The traditional reading for the Day of Pentecost
is the story from second chapter of the Acts of the Apostles in
which the setting is the City of Jerusalem. Yet most of Jesus' life
and ministry were set in the villages of Galilee. In this story from
the Sophia of Jesus Christ, the setting is once again a mountain in
Galilee where the twelve disciples and seven women are gathered
for a peak experience.

Having witnessed the death of Jesus and feeling shattered and
scattered like the bones in Ezekiel's vision, the followers of Jesus

are now together in one place, and through their encounter with him become living members of his risen body, ready to receive and proclaim insightful teachings. Notice that the Risen One comes to them in peace and with laughter.

Introduction to the Sundays after Pentecost

During the Pentecost season, the gospels are from the two earliest written Gospels: Thomas followed by the Q Gospel, that common source of sayings embedded in Luke and Matthew. The second reading will normally be a precursor that supports the Gospel.

The first reading comes from two documents: the Secret Book of James and then the Didache.

Scholar Ron Cameron tells us that in Secret James an unknown author appropriates and speaks through the person of James, the brother of Jesus. The written form of the book comes from the beginning of the second century, but its content is much earlier and includes oral tradition with "dialogue and discourse that are essentially a collection of sayings in relatively primitive form."[1]

The Didache is a document with a longer and a shorter title. The longer title is The Teaching of the Twelve Apostles. The shorter title is simple The Didache which is Greek for "The Teaching."

The Didache evolved from oral and written sources 60–80 CE reaching its final form sometime in the first part of the second century. The Teaching springs from the record of Jesus in the synoptic Gospels. It continues with guidance regarding baptism, fasting, eucharist, ministry of bishops and deacons in local churches, and how to show hospitality to itinerant teachers.

Scholars debate the place of origin. Edgar Goodspeed says, "probably in the region of Antioch"[2] Kurt Niederwimmer says, "I do not think, however, that the major city of Antioch should be considered its location.[3] Cyril C. Richardson says "That the Didache comes from Alexandria is suggested by several factors."[4] There may be no clear consensus, but the content provides valuable insight into early church faith and life with implications for present day communities of faith.

The Seers Version is a conflation of the work of Cyril C. Richardson, Edgar J. Goodspeed, and Linda M. Maloney.

The pattern for the readings in the Sundays after Pentecost is to begin with a course reading describing encounters with the Risen Christ first from the Secret Book of James and then from the Didache.

Notes 1. Ron Cameron in *The Complete Gospels*, p. 232 2. Edgar J. Goodspeed, *The Apostolic Fathers*, New York, Harper, 1950, p. 9 3. Kurt Niederwimmer in *The Didache*, A Commentary, by Minneapolis, Fortress Press, 1998. 4. Cyril C. Richardson, *Early Christian Fathers*, Philadelphia, Westminster 1953, p. 163

Pentecost 2

First Reading *The Secret Book of James 2, SV*

Now the twelve disciples used to sit together at the same time, remembering what the Savior had said to each one of them, whether secretly or openly, and setting it down in books. I was writing what went in my book — suddenly the Savior appeared, after he had departed from us, and while we were watching for him. And so, five hundred days after he rose from the dead, we said to him, "You went away and left us!"

"No," Jesus said, "but I shall go to the place from which I have come. If you wish to come with me, come on!"

They all replied, "If you bid us, we'll come."

He said, "I swear to you, no one will ever enter heaven's domain at my bidding, but rather because you yourselves are full. Let me have James and Peter, so that I may fill them."

Second Reading *Deuteronomy 20:5–9, Tanakh*

Then the officials shall address the troops as follows: "Is there anyone who has built a new house but has not dedicated it? Let him go back to his home, lest he die in battle and another dedicate it. Is there anyone who has planted a vineyard but has never harvested it? Let him go back to his home, lest he die in battle and another harvest it. Is there anyone who has paid the bride-price for a wife, but has not yet married her? Let him go back to his home, lest he die in battle and another marry her."

The officials shall go on addressing the troops and say, "Is there anyone afraid and disheartened? Let him to back to his home, lest the courage of his comrades flag like his." When the officials have finished addressing the troops, army commanders shall assume command of the troops.

Psalm *Ode 16*

As the work of the farmer is the plough*
    and the work of the helmsman the steering of the ship,
so my work is the song praising You, Lord!*
    My art and occupation are in praise of You
Your love feeds my heart and Your sweet fruits touch my lips*
    You are my love, O Lord, and so I will sing to You.
Celebrating You makes me strong and filled with faith.*
    Your Spirit in my mouth sings of Your glory and beauty,
the work of Your hands and the craft of Your fingers,*
    Your horizonless mercy, the power of Your Word.
Your Word investigates the invisible and reveals Your thought.*
    Our eyes see Your labor. Our ears hear Your mind.
You spread out the earth and place the waters in the sea.*
    You measure the firmament and set the stars.
You create and You rest.*
    Created things follow a pattern. They do not know the rest.
Throngs follow Your Word. The gold coin of light is the sun*
    the gold coin of darkness is the night
You make the sun to clarify the day but evening blurs the face
    of the earth.*
    Their alternation speaks of Your Beauty!
Nothing exists without You, O Lord. You were before anything
    was.*
    Our worlds are made by Your Word, Your thought and Your
    heart*
Glory and honor to Your Name! Hallelujah!

Gospel *Thomas 64, SV*

Jesus says: "Someone was receiving guests. When he had prepared the dinner, he sent his slave to invite the guests. The slave went to the first and said, 'My master invites you.' The first replied, 'Some merchants owe me money; they are coming to me tonight. I have to go and give them instructions. Please excuse me from dinner.'

The slave went to another and said, 'My master has invited you.' The second said to the slave, 'I have bought a house, and I have been called away for a day. I shall have no time.'

The slave went to another and said, 'My master invites you.' The third said to the slave, 'My friend is to be married, and I am to arrange the banquet. I shall not be able to come. Please excuse me from dinner.'

The slave went to a another and said, 'My master invites you.' The fourth said to the slave, 'I have bought an estate, and I am going to collect the rent. I shall not be able to come. Please excuse me.'

The slave returned and said to his master, 'Those whom you invited to dinner have asked to be excused.' The master said to his slave, 'Go out on the streets and bring back whomever you find to have dinner.'"

Commentary Jesus the Jew is addressing his primarily Jewish followers who would have been familiar with the Hebrew Scriptures. He may have had in mind Wisdom's dinner (Prov 9:1–6) in which she invites people to feast on insight. When Jesus offers his story of invitations to dinner, the excuses are similar to those who are excused from serving in the military! (Deuteronomy above) What sort of dinner is Jesus talking about? Might tasting of it nourish a person for something as intense as going into battle? Might it also include Wisdom's invitation to insight?

If you compare this dinner story with its counterparts in Luke 14:16–24 and Matt 22:1–10, you can see how they have retold and expanded it. Thomas provides the version most likely to have been told by Jesus.

Pentecost 3

First Reading *The Secret Book of James 3, SV*

And when he called these two (James and Peter), he took them aside, and commanded the rest to carry on with what they had been doing.

The Savior said, "You have received mercy . . . So don't you want to be filled? And is your heart drunk? So don't you want to be sober? You ought, then, to be ashamed! And now, waking or sleeping, remember that you have seen the *Son of Man, (The Truly Human Being)*, and with him you have spoken, and to him you have listened. *Woe* to those who have seen the *Son of Man* (The Truly Human Being). *Blessed are* those who have not seen that man, and who have not associated with him, and who have not listened to a thing from him. Yours is life! Know, therefore, that he treated you when you were sick, so that you might reign. *Woe* to those who have been relieved of their sickness, for they will relapse again into sickness. *Blessed are* those who have not been sick, and have experienced relief before they became sick. *Yours is the Kingdom of God.* Therefore, I say to you, become full and leave no place within you empty, or else the one who is coming will be able to mock you."

Then Peter responded, "Look three times you have told us, 'Become full,' but we are full."

The Lord replied, "This is why I told you, 'Become full,' so that you might not be lacking; those who are lacking will not be saved. For fulness is good, and lacking, bad. Therefore, inasmuch as it's good for you to lack but bad for you to be filled, whoever is full tends to be lacking. One who lacks is not filled in the same way that another who lacks is filled; but whoever is full receives his just deserts. Therefore, it's fitting to lack while it's possible to fill yourselves, and to be filled while it's possible to lack, so that you may be able to fill yourselves the more. Therefore, become full of the spirit but lacking in reason. For reason is of the soul; indeed, it is the soul."

Note The text above is the Scholars Version, except those phrases in italics where Francis Williams' translation in the Nag Hammadi Library is used.

NHL *Son of Man* is translated in SV *Son of Adam*
NHL *Blessed are* is translated in SV *Congratulations to*
NHL *Woe to you* is translated in SV *Damn you*
NHL *Kingdom of God* is translated in SV *God's domain*

Second Reading *Teachings of Silvanus 106:22–107:4, 109:11–25, NHL*

For the Tree of Life is Christ . . . For he is Wisdom; he is also the Word. He is the Life, the Power, and the Door. He is the Light, the Messenger, the Good Shepherd. Entrust yourself to this one who became all for your sake.

Knock on yourself as upon a door, and walk upon yourself as on a straight road. For if you walk on the road, it is impossible for you to go astray. And if you knock with this one (Wisdom), you knock on hidden treasuries.

For since Christ is Wisdom, he makes the foolish man wise . . .

Let Christ alone enter your world, and let Christ bring to naught all powers which have come upon you. Let him enter the temple which is within you so that he may cast out all the merchants. Let him dwell in the temple which is within you, and may you become for him a priest and a Levite, entering in purity.

Blessed are you, O soul, if you find this one in your temple.

Blessed are you still more if you perform his service.

Psalm *Wisdom of Solomon 7:24–30, NRSV*

For wisdom is more mobile than any motion;*
> because of her pureness she pervades and penetrates all things.

For she is a breath of the power of God,*
> and a pure emanation of the glory of the Almighty;

therefore nothing defiled gains entrance into her.*
> For she is a reflection of eternal light,

a spotless mirror of the working of God,*
> and an image of his goodness

Although she is but one, she can do all things;*
> in every generation she passes into holy souls

and makes them friends of God, and prophets;*
> for God loves nothing so much as the person who lives with wisdom.

She is more beautiful than the sun,*
> and excels every constellation of the stars.

Compared with the light she is found to be superior,*

for it is succeeded by the night, but against wisdom evil does not prevail.

Gospel *Thomas 65–71 SV, except 68 which is NHL*

Jesus said, "A person owned a vineyard and rented it to some farmers, so they could work it and he could collect crops from them. He sent his slave so the farmers would give him the vineyard's crop. They grabbed him, beat him, and almost killed him, and the slave returned and told his master. His master said, "Perhaps he didn't know them. He sent another slave, and the farmers beat that one as well. Then the laster sent his son and said, "Perhaps they'll show my son some respect." Because the farmers knew that he was the heir to the vineyard, they grabbed him and killed him. Anyone here with two good ears had better listen!"

Jesus says, "Show me the stone that the builders rejected: that is the keystone."

Jesus says, "Those who know all, but are lacking in themselves, are utterly lacking."

Jesus says, "Blessed are you when you are hated and persecuted. Wherever you have been persecuted, they will find no place."

Jesus says, "Blessed are they who have been persecuted within themselves. It is they who have truly come to know the father. Blessed are the hungry, for the belly of him who desires will be filled."

Jesus says, "If you bring forth what is within you, what you have will save you. If you do not have that within you, what you do not have within you, will kill you."

Jesus says, "I will destroy this house, and no one will be able to build it."

Commentary The SV in Thomas 66 is *keystone*. In other translations the word is translated *cornerstone*. Which makes the better sense?

In Thomas 71, the word *house*: A similar statement is found in Mark 14:58, 15:29, Matthew 26:61, 27:40; John. 2:19 where the word is *temple*. Ron Cameron says, "It is noteworthy that Thomas' "temple" saying makes no direct reference to the temple.

Of course, *house* could refer obliquely to the temple. It could also invite a number of other referents: the ruling (Herodian) house; a family household; or metaphorically, the body as the house of the soul." *The Complete Gospels*, p. 316.

Pentecost 4

First Reading *The Secret Book of James 4, SV*

And I responded, "Lord, we can obey you if you wish, for we have forsaken our fathers and our mothers and our villages and have followed you. Give us the means, then, not to be tempted by the evil devil."

The Lord replied, "If you do the Father's will, what credit is that to you — unless he gives you, as part of his gift, your being tempted by Satan? But if you are oppressed by Satan, and are persecuted, and you do his will, I say that he will love you, and will make you equal with me, and will regard you as having become beloved through his providence according to your own choice. So won't you cease being lovers of the flesh and afraid of suffering? Or don't you realize that you have not yet been abused and have not yet been accused unjustly, nor have you yet been locked up in prison, nor have you yet been condemned unlawfully, nor have you yet been buried in the sand, as I myself was, by the evil one? Do you dare to spare the flesh, you for whom the spirit acts as an encircling wall? If you think about the world, about how long it existed before you and how long it will exist after you, you will discover that your life is but a single day, and your suffering but a singly hour. Accordingly, since what is good will not enter the world, you should scorn death and be concerned about life. Remember my cross and my death, and you will live!"

Second Reading *Teachings of Sylvanus 86:17–24, 88:16–21, 89:17–23, NHL*

May God dwell in your camp, may his Spirit protect your gates, and may the mind of divinity protect the walls. Let holy reason become a torch in your mind, burning the wood which is the whole of sin . . .

Live in Christ, and you will acquire a treasure in heaven. Do not become a sausage made of many things which are useless,

and do not become a guide on behalf of your blind ignorance . . .

Cast your anxiety upon God alone. Do not become desirous
of gold and silver which are profitless, but clothe yourself with
wisdom like a robe, put knowledge upon you like a crown, and
be seated upon a throne of perception.

Psalm *Ode 35*

The dew of the Lord rinses me with Silence*
    and a cloud of peace rises over my head, guarding me.
It becomes my salvation.*
    Everybody quivers in horror.
They issue smoke and judgment,*
    but I am silent, near You, my Lord.
You are more than shadow, more than foundation.*
    You carry me like a child by its mother.
You give me Your milk, Your dew,*
    and I grow in Your bounty and rest in Your perfection.
I spread my hands out as my soul points to the Most High.*
    I slip upward toward You who makes me whole. Hallelujah!

Gospel *Thomas 72–79 SV, except 76 and 79, NHL*

A person said to (Jesus), "Tell my brothers to divide my
father's possessions with me."

He said to the person, "Mister, who made me a divider?"

He turned to his disciples and said to them, "I'm not a
divider, am I?"

Jesus says, "The crop is huge but the workers are few, so beg
the harvest boss to dispatch workers to the fields."

He says, "There are many around the drinking trough, but
there is nothing in the well."

Jesus says, "There are many standing at the door, but it is
the solitary who will enter the bridal chamber."

Jesus says, "The kingdom of the father is like a merchant
who had a consignment of merchandise and who discovered a
pearl. That merchant was shrewd. He sold the merchandise and
bought the pearl alone for himself. You too, seek his unfailing
and enduring treasure where no moth comes near to devour
and no worm destroys."

Jesus says, "I am the light that is over all things. I am all:

from me all came forth, and to me all attained. Split a piece of wood; I am there. Lift up the stone, and you will find me there."

Jesus says, "Why have you come out to the countryside? To see a reed shaken by the wind? And to see a person dressed in soft clothes, like your rulers and your powerful ones? They are dressed in soft clothes, and they cannot understand truth."

A woman from the crowd said to him, "Blessed are the womb which bore you and the breasts which nourished you."

He said to her, "Blessed are those who have heard the word of the father and have truly kept it. For there will be days when you will say, 'Blessed are the womb which has not conceived and the breasts which have not given milk.'"

Note *Kingdom of the Father* in SV reads *God's domain.*

Pentecost 5

First Reading *The Secret Book of James 5, SV*

And I answered him, "Lord, don't proclaim the cross and death to us, for they are far from you."

The Lord replied, "I swear to you, none will be saved unless they believe in my cross; for the kingdom of God belongs to those who have believed in my cross. Become seekers of death, therefore, like the dead who are seeking life, for what they seek is manifest to them. So what can be of concern to them? When you inquire into the subject of death, it will teach you about election. I swear to you, none will be saved who are afraid of death; for the kingdom of God belongs to those who are dead. Become better than I; be like the son of the holy spirit."

Second Reading *Teachings of Sylvanus 90:29–91:1–33, NHL*

From now on, then, my son, return to your divine nature. Cast from you these evil deceiving friends! Accept Christ, this true friend, as a good teacher. Cast from you death, which has become a father to you. For death did not exist, nor will it exist at the end.

But since you cast from yourself God, the holy Father, the true Life, the Spring of Life, therefore you have obtained death as a father and have acquired ignorance as a mother. They have robbed you of true knowledge.

But return, my son, to your first father, God, and Wisdom your mother, from whom you came into being from the very first in order that you might fight against all of your enemies, the powers of the Adversary.

Listen, my son, to my advice. Do not be arrogant in opposition to every good opinion, but take for yourself the side of the divinity of reason. Keep the holy commandments of Jesus Christ, and you will reign over every place on earth and will be honored by the angels and archangels. Then you will acquire them as friends and fellow servants, and you will acquire places in heaven.

Psalm *Sirach 51:18–27, NRSV*

For I resolved to live according to wisdom and I was zealous
    for the good,*
  and I shall never be disappointed.
My soul grappled with Wisdom,*
  and in my conduct I was strict.
I spread out my hands to the heavens,*
  and lamented my ignorance of her.
I directed my soul to her,*
  and in purity I found her.
With her I gained understanding from the first;*
  therefore I will never be forsaken.
My heart was stirred to seek her;*
  therefore I have gained a prize possession.
The Lord gave me my tongue as a reward,*
  and I will praise him with it.
Draw near to me, you who are uneducated,*
  and lodge in the house of instruction.
Why do you say you are lacking in these things,*
  and why do you endure such great thirst?
I opened my mouth and said,*
  Acquire wisdom for yourselves without money.
Put your neck under her yoke, and let your souls receive
    instruction;*
  it is to be found close by.
See with your own eyes that I have labored but little*
  and found for myself much serenity.

Gospel *Thomas 80–88 SV, except 86 NHL*

Jesus says, "Whoever has come to know the world has discovered the body, and whoever has discovered the body, of that one the world is not worthy."

Jesus says, "The one who has become wealthy should reign, and the one who has power should renounce it."

Jesus says, "Whoever is near me is near the fire, and whoever is far from me is far from the Father's domain.

Jesus says, "Images are visible to people, but the light within them is hidden in the image of the Father's light. He will be disclosed, but his image is hidden by his light."

Jesus says, "When you see your likeness, you are happy. But when you see your images that came into being before you and that neither die nor become visible, how much you will have to bear!"

Jesus says, "Adam came from great power and wealth, but he was not worthy of you. For had he been worthy, he would not have tasted death."

Jesus says, "The foxes have their holes and the birds have their nests, but the Son of Man has no place to lay his head and rest."

Jesus says, "How miserable is the body that depends on a body, and how miserable is the soul that depends on these two."

Jesus says, "The messengers (Angels) and the prophets will come to you and give you what belongs to you. You, in turn, give them what you have, and say to yourselves, 'When will they come and take what belongs to them?'"

Note Angels is from NHL translation.

Pentecost 6

First Reading *The Secret Book of James 6:1–18, SV*

Then I asked him, "Lord, how will we be able to prophesy to those who ask us to prophesy to them? For there are many who inquire of us, and who look to us to hear an oracle from us."

The Lord replied, "Don't you realize that the head of prophecy was severed with John?"

But I said, "Lord, it's not possible to remove the head of prophecy, is it?"

The Lord said to me, "When you comprehend what 'head' means, and that prophecy issues from the head, understand what 'Its head was removed' means. I first spoke with you parabolically, and you did not understand. Now I am speaking with you openly, and you do not perceive. Nevertheless, for me you were a parable among parables, and the disclosure of openness.

"Be eager to be saved without being urged. Instead, become zealous on your own and, if possible, surpass even me. For that is how the Father will love you.

"Become haters of hypocrisy and evil intent. For intent is what produces hypocrisy, and hypocrisy is far from the truth.

"Don't let the kingdom of heaven wither away. For it is like a date palm shoot whose fruit fell down around it. It put forth buds, and when they blossomed, its productivity was caused to dry up. So it also is with the fruit that came from this singular root: when it was picked, fruit was gathered by many. Truly this was good. Isn't it possible to produce new growth now? Can't you discover how?

"Since I was glorified in this way before now, why do you detain me when I am eager to go? For after my labors you have constrained me to stay with you eighteen more days for the sake of parables. It was enough for some people to pay attention to the teaching and understand 'the shepherds.' and 'the seed,' and 'the building,' and 'the lamps of the virgins,' and 'the wage of the workers,' and 'the silver coins,' and 'the woman.'

"Become eager for instruction. For the first prerequisite for instruction is faith, the second is love, the third is works; now from these comes life. For instruction is like a grain of wheat. When they sowed it they had faith in it; and when it sprouted they loved it, because they envisioned many grains in place of one; and when they worked they were sustained, because they prepared it for food, then kept the rest in reserve to be sown. So it is possible for you, too, to receive for yourselves the kingdom of heaven unless you receive it through knowledge, you will not be able to discover it."

Second Reading *Teachings of Sylvanus 96:19–20, 32–97:3, 98:21–28, 99:13–20, 100:24–29, NHL*

Accept Christ who is able to set you free . . . The divine Teacher is with you always. Christ is a helper, and meets you because of the good which is in you . . .

Live with Christ, and he will save you. For Christ is the true light and the sun of life. For just as the sun is manifest and makes light for the eyes of the flesh, so Christ illuminates every mind and heart . . .

Christ has a single being, and gives light to every place. This is also the way in which Christ speaks of our mind as if it were a lamp which burns and lights up the place. Being in a part of the soul, it gives light to all the parts . . .

You cannot know God through anyone except Christ who has the image of the Father *and Mother*, for this image reveals the true likeness in correspondence to that which is revealed.

Psalm *Sirach 6:23–31, NRSV*

Listen, my child, and accept my judgment;*
  do not reject my counsel.
Put your feet into her fetters,*
  and your neck into her collar.
Bend your shoulders and carry her,*
  and do not fret under her bonds.
Come to her with all your soul,*
  and keep her ways with all your might.
Search out and seek, and she will become known to you;*
  and when you get hold of her, do not let her go.
For at last you will find the rest she gives,*
  and she will be changed into joy for you.
Then her fetters will become for you a strong defense,*
  and her collar a glorious robe.
Her yoke is a golden ornament,*
  and her bonds a purple cord.
You will wear her like a glorious robe,*
  and put her on like a splendid crown.

Gospel *Thomas 89–95, SV*

Jesus says, "Why do you wash the outside of the cup? Don't you understand that the one who made the inside is also the one who made the outside?"

Jesus says, "Come to me, for my yoke is comfortable and my lordship is gentle, and you will find rest for yourselves."

They said to him, "Tell us who you are so we may believe in you."

He said to them, "You examine the face of heaven and earth, but you have not come to know the one who is in your presence, and you do not know how to examine the present moment."

Jesus says, "Seek and you will find. In the past, however, I did not tell you the things about which you asked me then. Now I am willing to tell them, but you are not seeking them."

Jesus says, "Don't give what is sacred to dogs, for they might throw them upon the manure pile. Don't throw pearls to pigs, or they might . . . "

Jesus says, "One who seeks will find, and for one who knocks it will be opened."

Jesus says, "If you have money, don't lend it at interest. Rather, give it to someone from whom you won't get it back."

Pentecost 7

First Reading *The Secret Book of James 6:19–40, SV*

Therefore, I say to you, be sober; don't go astray. Moreover, I have often said to you all together — and also to you alone, James, have I said — be saved. I have commanded you to follow me, and I have taught you how to respond in the presence of the rulers. Observe that I have descended, and have spoken, and have expended myself, and have won my crown, so as to save you. For I descended to dwell with you so that you might also dwell with me. And when I found your houses to be without roofs, I dwelt instead in houses that could receive me at the time of my descent.

"Therefore, rely on me, my brothers; understand what the great light is. The Father does not need me. For a father does not need a son, but it is the son who needs the father. To him do I go, for the Father of the Son is not in need of you.

"Pay attention to instruction, understand knowledge, love life. And no one will persecute you, nor will any one oppress you, other than you yourselves.

"You wretches! You unfortunates! You pretenders to the truth! You falsifiers of knowledge! You sinners against the spirit! Do you even now dare to listen, when you should have spoken from the beginning? Do you even now dare to sleep, when you should have been awake from the beginning, so that heaven's domain (the kingdom of heaven) might receive you? I swear to you, it is easier for a holy one to descend into defilement, and for an enlightened person to descend into darkness, than for you to reign — or even not to!

"I have remembered your tears and your grief and your sorrow; they are far from us. Now, then, you who are outside the Father's inheritance, weep where it's called for, and grieve, and proclaim what is good: how the Son is ascending, as he should. I swear to you, were I sent to those who would listen to me, and were I to have spoken with them, I would never have come down to earth. From now on, then, be ashamed for them.

"See I shall leave you and go away; I don't wish to stay with you any longer — just as you have not wished it either. Now, then, follow me eagerly. Therefore, I say to you, for your sake I descended. You are the beloved; it is you who will become the cause of life for many. Invoke the Father, pray to God frequently, and he will give to you. Congratulations to whoever has envisioned you along with him when he is proclaimed among the angels and glorified among the saints. Yours is life! Rejoice and exult as children of God. Keep his will, so that you may be saved. Accept reproof from me and save yourselves. I am pleading for you with the Father, and he will forgive you much."

Second Reading *Teachings of Sylvanus 100:32–101:21, NHL*

Consider these things about God: he is in every place; on the other hand, he is in no place. With respect to power, to be sure, he is in every place; but with respect to divinity, he is in no place. So then it is possible to know God a little. With respect to his power, he fills every place, but in the exaltation of his divinity, nothing contains him. Everything is in God, but God is not in anything.

Now what is it to know God? God is all which is in the truth. But as it is impossible to look at Christ as at the sun. God sees everyone; no one looks at him. But Christ without being jealous receives and he gives. He is the light of the Father, as he gives light without being jealous. In this manner he gives light to every place.

Psalm *Ode 12*

You fill me with words of truth*
    that I may proclaim them.
Like the flow of waters truth flows from my mouth,*
    and my lips reveal its fruits.
You give me the gold of knowledge*
    for Your mouth, O Lord, is the true Word and the door of
        light.
You are the Highest One who gives Word to Your worlds*
    which interpret Your own beauty, recite Your praise,
confess Your thought, proclaim Your mind,*
    and teach Your works.
For the subtleness of Your Word is inexpressible.*
    Your expression is swift and to the point.
Your path is limitless. You never fail but remain standing.*
    Your descent and Your Way are incomprehensible.
As Your work is, so is Your expectation.*
    You are the Light and the dawning of thought.
Through You worlds converse and the Silent acquire speech.*
    From You comes love and concord and candor.
Those who are penetrated by Your Word*
    know You who make it and come into harmony.
Your mouth, O Highest One, speaks*
    and You become clear by Your Word.
The dwelling place of Your Word is humanity*
    and Your Truth is love.
Blessed are they who have understood everything *
    and have known You, O Lord, in Your Truth. Hallelujah!

Gospel *Thomas 96–100 NHL, except 99, SV*

Jesus says, "The Kingdom of the Father is like a certain woman. She took a little leaven, concealed it in some dough, and made it into large loaves. Let him who has ears hear."

Jesus says, "The Kingdom of the Father is like a certain woman who was carrying a jar full of meal. While she was walking on the road, still some distance from home, the handle of the jar broke and the meal emptied out behind her on the road. She did not realize it; she had noticed no accident. When she reached her house, she set the jar down and found it empty."

Jesus says, "The Kingdom of the Father is like a certain man who wanted to kill a powerful man. In his own house he drew his sword and stuck it into the wall in order to find out whether his hand could carry through. Then he slew the powerful man."

The disciples said to him, "Your brothers and your mother are standing outside."

He said to them, "Those here who do the will of my Father wants are my brothers and my mother. It is they who will enter the kingdom of my Father."

They showed Jesus a gold coin and said to him, "Caesar's men demand taxes from us."

He said to them, "Give Caesar what belongs to Caesar, give God what belongs to God, and give me what is mine."

Pentecost 8

First Reading *The Secret Book of James 7, SV and NHL conflated*

And when we heard these things, we became elated, for we had despaired over what we recounted earlier. But when he saw us rejoicing, he said, "Woe to you who lack an advocate! Woe to you, who stand in need of grace! Blessed will they be who have spoken out and obtained grace for themselves. Compare yourselves to foreigners; how are they regarded by your city? Why are you disturbed when you cast yourselves away of your own accord and separate yourselves from your city? Why abandon your home on your own, making it available for those who wish to live in it? You outcasts and runaways! Damn you, for you will be caught! Or perhaps you think that the Father is a lover of humanity? Or that he is persuaded by prayers? Or that he grants favors to one on behalf of another? Or that he bears with one who seeks? For he knows about desire, as well as what the flesh needs: does it not long for the soul? For without the soul the body does not sin, just as the soul is not saved without the spirit. But if the soul is saved when it is without evil, and the spirit is also saved, then the body becomes free from sin. For the spirit is what animates the soul, but the body is what kills it — in other words, it is the soul which kills itself. I swear to you, he will never forgive the sin of the soul, nor the guilt of the flesh; for none of those who have worn the flesh will be saved. Do you think, then, that many have found the kingdom of heaven? Blessed is he who has seen himself as the fourth one in heaven."

Second Reading *Teachings of Sylvanus 103:11–30, 104:18–19, 106:14–15, NHL*

Do not tire of knocking on the door of reason and do not cease walking in the way of Christ. Walk in it so that you may receive rest from your labors. If you walk in another way, there is no profit in it. For those who walk in the broad way will go down at their end to the perdition of the mire. For the Underworld is open wide for the soul, and the place of perdition is broad.

Accept Christ, the narrow way. For he is oppressed and bears affliction for your sin.

O soul, persistent one, in what ignorance you exist! For who is your guide in the darkness? How many likenesses did Christ take on because of you? . . .

The basic choice, which is humility of heart, is the gift of Christ . . .

Light the light within you. Do not extinguish it.

Psalm *Ode 23*

The holy are happy.*
    Who but they alone will wear joy?
The elect wear grace.*
    Who will be arrayed in grace but those who from the beginning have believed?

Walk in the knowledge of the Lord,*
  and you will know the grace of the Lord of generosity, exultation, and the perfection of knowledge.
The Lord's thought was a letter.*
  The will of the Lord descended from the skies, shot like an arrow, violently released from its bow.
Many hands rushed to the letter, to catch it, take it, and read it,*
  yet it slipped from their fingers and they were terrified of it and its seal.
They couldn't loosen the seal,*
  for the power of the seal was greater than they.
Others saw the letter and chased it, wondering where it would land*
  and who might read it, who might hear it.
But a wheel caught the letter and rolled over it and it stuck there,*
  and it was a sign of the kingdom and of providence.
Everything moving near the wheel, the wheel cut down,*
  and it destroyed a multitude of enemies and it bridged rivers and crossed over and uprooted forests, leaving a huge ditch.
As if a body were on the wheel, a head turned down to the feet.*
  The wheel turned on the feet and on whatever struck it.
The letter commanded over all districts, and there appeared a head.*
  It became a child of truth from the Father on high, who possessed all,
and the thought of many became nothing,*
  and the apostates and seducers became headstrong yet fled and tormentors were blotted out.
The letter became a great tablet,*
  a volume written by the finger of God.
On it was the Name of the Father and the Son,*
  and the Holy Spirit, and their word of rule forever. Hallelujah!

Gospel *Thomas 101–107 SV, except 101, NHL*

Jesus says, "Whoever does not hate his father and his mother as I do cannot become a disciple to me. And whoever does not love his father and his mother as I do cannot become a disciple to me. For my mother gave me falsehood, but my true Mother gave me life."

Jesus says, "Damn the Pharisees! They are like a dog sleeping in the cattle manger: the dog neither eats nor lets the cattle eat."

Jesus says, "Congratulations to those who know where the rebels are going to attack. They can get going, collect their imperial resources, and be prepared before the rebels arrive."

They said to Jesus, "Come, let us pray today and let us fast."

Jesus said, "What is the sin that I have committed, or wherein have I been defeated? But when the bridegroom leaves the bridal chamber, then let them fast and pray."

Jesus says, "Whoever knows the father and the mother will be called the child of a whore."

Jesus says, "When you make the two into one, you will become the sons of man (Truly Human Beings), and when you say, 'Mountain, move from here!' it will move."

Jesus says, "The kingdom is like a shepherd who had a hundred sheep. One of them, the largest, went astray. He left the ninety-nine and looked for that one until he found it. When he had gone to such trouble, he said to the sheep, 'I care for you more than the ninety nine."

Commentary How in the world is one to understand being "called a child of a whore"? Consider Robert Winterhalter's interpretation: "In John 8:41, Jesus' adversaries made the snide remark: "We were not born of fornication." Jesus replied, "If God were your Father, you would love me, for I proceeded and came forth from God . . . But you have not known him; I know him. (John 8:42, 55)

Saying 105 records the irony of Jesus' retort more clearly. His critics had the audacity to denounce Mary as a fornicator, or even a whore. Yet Jesus knew his Father-Mother God, and his opponents did not. They were the spiritual bastards who did not know their true Parent. Their fixation on human ancestry had blinded them to the fact that they, too, were sons (and daughters) of God."

Robert Winterhalter, *The Fifth Gospel*, Harper and Row, New York, 1988

Pentecost 9

First Reading *The Secret Book of James 8, SV and NHL conflated*

When we heard these things, we became distressed. But when the Lord saw that we were distressed, he said, "This is why I say this to you that you may know yourselves. For the kingdom of heaven is like an ear of grain which sprouted in a field. And when it ripened, it scattered its fruit and, in turn, filled the field with ears for another year. You also: be eager to reap an ear of life for yourselves that you may be filled with the kingdom!

"As long as I am with you, pay attention to me and obey me; but when I take leave of you, remember me. Remember me because I was with you, though you did now know me. Blessed will be those who have known me. Damn those who have heard and have not believed. Blessed will be those who have not seen, yet have believed!

"Once again I appeal to you. For I am made known to you building a house of great value to you, since you take shelter in it; likewise, it can support your neighbor's house when theirs is in danger of collapsing.

"I swear to you, woe to those for whose sakes I was sent down to this place; blessed will they be who ascend to the Father! Again I admonish you. You who exist, be like those who do not exist, so that you may dwell with those who do not exist.

"Do not make the kingdom of heaven a desert within you. Don't be arrogant about the light that enlightens you. Rather, behave toward yourselves in the way that I have toward you: I placed myself under a curse for you, so that you may be saved."

Second Reading *Teachings of Sylvanus 110:14–111:5, 116:27–117:9, NHL*

Know who Christ is, and acquire him as a friend, for this is the friend who is faithful. He is also God and Teacher. This one, being God, became man for your sake. It is the one who broke the iron bars of the Underworld and the bronze bolts. It is this one who attacked and cast down every haughty tyrant. It is he who loosened from himself the chains of which he had taken hold. He brought up the poor from the Abyss and the mourners from the Underworld. It is he who humbled the haughty powers; he who put to shame the haughtiness through humility; he who has cast down the strong and the boaster through weakness; he who in his contempt scorned that which is considered an honor so that humility for God's sake might be highly exalted; and he has put on humanity . . .

For no one who wants to will be able to know God as he actually is, nor Christ, nor the Spirit, nor the chorus of angels, nor even the archangels, and the thrones of the spirits, and the exalted lordships, and the Great Mind. If you do not know yourself, you will not be able to know all of these.

Open the door for yourself that you may know what is. Knock on yourself that the Word may open for you.

Psalm *Sirach 48:4–14, NRSV*

How glorious you were, Elijah, in your wondrous deeds!*
　　Whose glory is equal to yours?
You raised a corpse from death and from Hades,*
　　by the word of the Most High.
You sent kings down to destruction,*
　　and famous men, from their sick-beds.
You heard rebuke at Sinai*
　　and judgments of vengeance at Horeb.
You anointed kings to inflict retribution,*
　　and prophets to succeed you.
You were taken up by a whirlwind of fire,*
　　in a chariot with horses of fire . . .
Happy are those who saw you*
　　and were adorned with your love!
When Elijah was enveloped in the whirlwind,*
　　Elisha was filled with his spirit.
He performed twice as many signs,*
　　and marvels with every utterance of his mouth.
Never in his lifetime did he tremble before any ruler,*
　　nor could anyone intimidate him at all.
Nothing was too hard for him,*
　　and when he was dead his body prophesied.
In his life he did wonders,*
　　and in death his deeds were marvelous.

Gospel *Thomas 108–113, NHL except 111, SV*

Jesus says, "Whoever drinks from my mouth will become like me: I, too, will become that person, and to that person the hidden things will be revealed."

Jesus says, "The kingdom is like a man who had a hidden treasure in his field without knowing it. And after he died, he left it to his son. The son did not know about the treasure. he inherited the field and sold it. And the one who bought it went plowing and found the treasure. He began to lend money at interest to whomever he wished."

Jesus says, "The one who has found the world, and has become wealthy, should renounce the world."

Jesus says, "The heavens and the earth will roll up in your presence, and whoever is living from the living one will not see death." Does not Jesus say, "Those who have found themselves, of them the world is not worthy"?

Jesus says, "Woe to the flesh that depends on the soul; woe to the soul that depends on the flesh."

His disciples said to him, "When will the Kingdom come?"

Jesus said, "It will not come by waiting for it. It will not be a matter of saying, 'here it is' or 'there it is'. Rather, the kingdom of the Father is spread out upon the earth, and *people* do not see it."

Notes Saying 108 is SV conflated with Bentley Layton translation. Saying 113 *people* NHL reads "men."

Pentecost 10

First Reading *The Secret Book of James 9, SV and NHL conflated*

To this Peter responded, "Sometimes you urge us on toward the kingdom of heaven, yet at other times you turn us away, Lord. Sometimes you make appeals, draw us toward faith, and promise us life, yet at other times you drive us away from the kingdom of heaven."

The Lord replied to us, "I have offered you faith many times; moreover, I have made myself known to you, James, and you have not understood me. On the other hand, now I see you rejoicing again and again. And when you are elated at the promise of life, are you yet despairing and distressed when you are taught about the kingdom of heaven? But you, through faith and knowledge, have received life. Accordingly, disregard rejection when you hear it, but when you hear about the promise, rejoice all the more. I swear to you, whoever receives life and believes in the kingdom will never leave it, not even if the Father wishes to banish him!

"This is all I shall tell you at this time. Now I shall ascend to the place from which I have come. But you, when I was eager to go, have rebuffed me; and instead of accompanying me, you have chased me away. Still, pay attention to the glory that awaits me and, having opened your hearts, listen to the hymns that await me up in the heavens. For today I must take my place at the right hand of my Father.

"I have spoken my last word to you; I shall part from you. For a chariot of spirit has carried me up, and from now on I shall strip myself so that I may clothe myself. So pay attention: blessed are those who have proclaimed the Son before he descended, so that, having come, I might ascend again. Thrice blessed are those who were proclaimed by the Son before they existed, so that you may have a share with them."

Second Reading *Isaiah 61:1–3, Tanakh*

The Spirit of the LORD God is upon me,
Because the LORD has anointed me;
He has sent me as a herald of joy to the humble.
To bind up the wounded of heart,
To proclaim the release to the captives,
Liberation to the imprisoned;
To proclaim a year of the LORD'S favor
And a day of vindication by our God;
To comfort all who mourn —
To provide for the mourners in Zion —
To give them a turban instead of ashes,
The festive ointment instead of a drooping spirit.
They shall be terebinths of victory,
Planted by the LORD for His glory.

Psalm *Ode 32*

> To the blessed ones joy lives in the heart,*
>> Light from You lives in them.
> The Word comes from the Truth,*
>> You come from Your Self.
> You are strong from holy power from the skies*
>> You are unshaken forever and ever. Hallelujah!

Gospel *The Beatitudes, Q9 — Powelson & Reigert*

Around this time, Jesus went out into the hill seeking solitude and spent the entire night in prayer. At daybreak, he came down with his disciples.

A great crowd of people from all parts of Judea, Jerusalem and the coastal region of Tyre and Sidon had come to hear him and be cured of their diseases.

Fixing his eyes on his disciples he began to speak:

Blessed are you poor	Blessed are the poor in spirit,
for yours is the reign of God	for theirs is the reign of heaven.
But woe to you rich,	
for you have received your	
consolation.	
Blessed are you that hunger now,	Blessed are those who hunger
	and thirst after righteousness,
for you shall be filled.	for they shall be filled.
Woe to you who are full now,	
for you shall go hungry.	
Blessed are you that weep now	Blessed are those who mourn
for you shall laugh.	for they shall be comforted.
Woe to you who laugh now,	
for you shall mourn and weep.	

Blessed are the meek,
for they shall inherit the earth.
Blessed are the merciful,
for mercy will be shown them.
Blessed are the pure in heart,
for they shall see God.
Blessed are the peacemakers,
for they shall be called sons of God.
Blessed are those who are persecuted

Blessed are you when people
hate you,
And when they exclude you and
reproach you,
and cast out your name as evil,
on account of the *Truly
Human Being!**
Rejoice in that day, and leap for joy,
for behold, your reward is great
in heaven;
for so their fathers did to the
prophets.
Woe to you, when all people speak
well of you,
for so their fathers did to the
false prophets.
Luke 6:27–35 Kloppenborg

for righteousness' sake,
for theirs is the reign of heaven.
Blessed are you when they
reproach
you and persecute you
and say every evil against you
falsely
on my account.
Rejoice and be glad,
for your reward is great
in heaven,
for so they persecuted the
prophets who came before you.

**Matthew 5:43–44, 38–42
Kloppenborg**

Commentary The Beatitudes of the Q Gospel are strikingly different in Luke and Matthew. They deserve to be heard at the same time. Suggestion: read the introduction, then the Luke version, followed by a meditative pause, and then the Matthew version.

Please note that in the arrangement above each of the "Woes" in Luke have been inserted after their companion "Beatitude." Also note that Matthew has no "Woes"!

Notice that in Luke all the Beatitudes are in the second person, "Blessed are you . . . " In Matthew most of the Beatitudes are in the third person, "Blessed are those who . . . " The "you" version, being more immediate, suggests that it may be the earlier version and closer to what Jesus may have spoken.

Each Beatitude has been traditionally translated into English as "Blessed . . . "

The Greek word *makarios* contains a rich variety of meanings. Some translators render the word as "Congratulations to . . . " Others choose "Happy are . . . " and still others select, "Fortunate are . . . "

Likewise, some translators render the phrase "Woe to you . . . " as "Damn you . . . "

A study the Beatitudes from both the Luke and Matthew versions along with the several ways of rendering "Blessed" and "Woe" may stimulate fresh thought and meaning. New insights and applications may emerge for all who are willing to take this passage seriously.

Pentecost 11

First Reading *The Secret Book of James 10, SV*

When the Lord said this, he went away. So Peter and I knelt down, gave thanks, and sent our hearts up to heaven. We heard with our ears and saw with our eyes the sound of battles and a trumpet's blast and utter turmoil.

And when we passed beyond that place, we sent our minds up further. We saw with our eyes and heard with our ears hymns and angelic praises and angelic rejoicing. Heavenly majesties were singing hymns, and we ourselves were rejoicing.

After this, we also desired to send our spirits heavenward to the majesty. And when we went up, we were not permitted to see or hear a thing. For the rest of the disciples called to us and asked us, "What did you hear from the Teacher? and, "What did he say to you?" and "Where did he go?"

We answered them, "He has ascended. He has given us a pledge, and promised all of us life, and disclosed to us children who are to come after us, having bid us to love them, since we will be saved for their sake."

And when they heard, they believed the revelation, yet were angry about those who would be born. So, not wishing to give them an occasion to take offense, I sent each one to a different place. And I myself went up to Jerusalem, praying that I might obtain a share with the beloved who will be made manifest.

Second Reading *Proverbs 19:11, 20:22, 24:29, 25:21, NRSV*

Those with good sense are slow to anger,
and it is their glory to overlook an offense . . .
Do not say, "I will repay evil";
wait for the Lord and He will help you . . .

Do not say, "I will do to others as they have done to me;
I will pay them back for what they have done." . . .
If your enemies are hungry, give them bread to eat;
if they are thirsty, give them water to drink;
for you will heap coals of fire on their heads,
and the Lord will reward you.

Psalm *Sirach 22:16–18, NRSV*

A wooden beam firmly bonded into a building*
    is not loosened by an earthquake;
so the mind firmly resolved after due reflection*
    will not be afraid in a crisis
A mind settled on an intelligent thought*
    is like a stucco decoration that makes a wall smooth.
Fences set on a high place*
    will not set firm against the wind;
so a timid mind with a fool's resolve*
    will not stand firm against any fear."

Gospel *Q Gospel 6:20–23, 27–38*

Blessed are you when people hate you, exclude you, abuse you and denounce you on my account.

Celebrate when that day comes and dance for joy — your reward will be great in heaven. Remember that their ancestors treated the prophets this way.

Love your enemies. Do good to those who hate you. Bless those who curse you. Pray for those who treat your badly.

When someone strikes you on the right cheek, offer the other cheek, too. When someone takes your coat from you, let them have your shirt as well.

Give to everyone who asks. And if someone robs you, don't demand your property back.

Treat people as you would like them to treat you.

If you love those who love you, what credit is that to you? Even sinners do the same. If you do good only to those who do good to you, what merit is there in that? Even sinners do that. And if you lend to those from whom you hope to receive, what reward is that? Even sinners lend to sinners.

Instead, love your enemies and do good, expecting nothing

in return. You will have a great reward, and you will be children of your Father in heaven. He makes the sun rise on the bad and the good. He sends rain to fall on both the just and the unjust.

Be compassionate as your Father is compassionate. Do not judge, and you will not be judged. Do not condemn, and you will not be condemned. Forgive, and you will be forgiven.

Give, and there will be gifts for you. A full measure of grain, pressed down, shaken together and running over, will be poured into your lap; because the amount you measure out is the measure you will be given back.

Pentecost 12

First reading *Secret James 11, SV*

Now I, (James), pray that a beginning may take place with you. For this is how I can be saved — since they will be enlightened through me, through my faith and through another's that is better than mine, for I wish for mine to be more lowly. Do your best, therefore, to be like them, and pray that you may obtain a share with them. For, apart from what I have recounted, the Savior did not disclose revelation to us. For their sake do we proclaim a share with those for whom this has been proclaimed, those whom the Lord has made his children.

Second Reading *Secret John 1:4–25, 30–32, 2:1–25, NHL*

It happened one day when John, the brother of James — who are the sons of Zebedee — had come up to the temple, that a Pharisee named Arimanius approached him and said to him, "Where is your master whom you followed?" And he said to him, "He has gone to the place from which he came." The Pharisee said to him, "With deception did this Nazarene deceive you, and he filled your ears with lies, and closed your hearts and turned you from the traditions of your fathers."

When I, John, heard these things I turned away from the temple to a desert place. And I grieved greatly in my heart saying, "How then was the savior appointed, and why was he sent into the world by his Father, and who is his Father who sent him, and of what sort is that aeon to which we shall go? . . . "

Straightway, while I was contemplating these things, behold the heavens opened and the whole creation which is below heaven shone, and the world was shaken. I was afraid, and behold I saw in the light a youth who stood by me. While I looked at him he became like an old man. And he changed his likeness again becoming like a servant. There was not a plurality before me, but there was a likeness with multiple forms in the light, and the likenesses appeared through each other, and the likenesses had three forms.

He said to me, "John, John, why do you doubt, or why are you afraid? You are not unfamiliar with the image are you? — that is, do not be timid! — I am the one who is with you always. I am the Father, I am the Mother, I am the Son. I am the undefiled and incorruptible one.

"Now I have come to teach you what is and what was and what will come to pass, that you may know the things which are not revealed and those which are revealed, and to teach you concerning the unwavering race of the perfect *Human Being*. Now, therefore, lift up your face, that you may receive the things that I shall teach you today, and may tell them to your fellow spirits who are from the unwavering race of the perfect *Human Being*.

Psalm *Ode 15*

As the sun is joy to those who seek daybreak,*
   so You are my joy, O Lord.
You are my sun and Your rays uplift me*
   You chase all darkness from my face.
In You I acquire eyes and see Your sacred day.*
   In You I acquire knowledge and You make me happy.
I leave the way of error and go to You*
   and I am saved.
You give me according to Your bounty.*
   You make me according to Your beauty.
I find purity through Your Name*
   I shed corruption through Your grace.
Death dies before my face;*
   Hell is abolished by my Word.
Eternal Life appears in Your land, O Lord,*

and is known to those with faith.
Eternal life is given without limit*
   to all who trust in You. Hallelujah!

Gospel Q Gospel 6:39–49

Can one blind person lead another? Won't they both fall into a ditch? The student is not superior to the teacher, but if the students are well taught they will become like their teacher.

Why do you notice the speck of sawdust in your brother's eye and not the wooden plank in your own? How can you say to your brother, "Let me take out the sawdust from your eye," when you cannot see the plank in your own?

Hypocrite! Remove the plank from your own eye first; then you will see clearly enough to remove the sawdust from your brother's eye.

No good tree produces rotten fruit and no bad tree produces good fruit. Each tree is known by its own fruit. People do not pick figs from thorn bushes, nor gather grapes from blackberry brambles. Good people draw what is good from the treasure of their hearts. Bad people produce what is bad from the evil within them. A person's words flow from what is treasured in the heart.

Why do you call me, "Lord, Lord" and then not do what I say?

I will show you what the person who comes to me, hears what I have to say and acts accordingly is really like. That person is like someone building a house, who digs deeply and lays the foundation on bedrock. The rain pours down, the floods rise in a torrent, and the winds blow and beat upon the house, but it does not fall. It is built on rock.

But the one who listens and does nothing is like the person who builds a house on sand with no foundation. When the river bursts against it, it collapses immediately and is destroyed.

Note Compare Jesus' teachings with this one: "That great cloud rains on all whether their nature is superior or inferior. The light of the sun and the moon illuminates the whole world, both him who does well and him who does ill, both him who stands high and him who stands low." Sadharmapundarika Sutra 5

Pentecost 13

First Reading *Didache 1*

There are two ways, one of life and one of death, and there is a great difference between the two ways.

The way of life is this: "First you shall love God who has created you; second, your neighbor as yourself."[1] Whatever you do not want to happen to you, do not do to another.[2]

The teaching that comes from these words is this: "Bless those who curse you," and "pray for your enemies." Moreover, fast "for those who persecute you." For "what credit is it to you of you love those who love you? Do not even the nations do that? But "you must love those who hate you,"[3] and then you will make no enemies.

"Abstain from the desires of the flesh."[4] If anyone strikes you on your right cheek, turn your other one to him also, and you will be perfect.[5] If anyone "forces you into one miles of service, go two miles with him."; if someone "takes away your coat, give him your shirt too."[6] If someone "takes away from you what is yours, do not demand it back"[7] You could not get it back anyway!

"Give to everyone who asks of you, and do not demand it back."[8] For the Father wants people to give to everyone from the gifts that have been freely given to them. Blessed is the person who gives according to the commandment, for he is guilt-less. But if he is not in need, he will have to stand trial of why he took and for what purpose. If he is imprisoned, he shall be interrogated about what he has done, and "he shall not go free until he has paid back the last penny."[9] Indeed, there is a further saying that relates to this: "Let your donation sweat in your hands until you know to whom you are giving it."[10]

Notes **1.** Matt 22:37–39; Deut 6:5; Lev 19:18. **2.** Cf. Matt 7:12. **3.** Matt 5:44, 46, 47; Luke 6:27, 28, 32, 33. **4.** 1 Pet 2:11. **5.** Cf. Matt 5:39, 48; Luke 6:29. **6.** Matt 5:40, 41. **7.** Luke 6:30. **8.** Luke 6:30. **9.** Matt 5:26. **10.** "to date it has not been possible to give a secure demonstration of its source."

For a discussion, see *The Didache, A Commentary* by Kurt Niederwinner, Minneapolis, Fortress Press 1998.

Second Reading *Book of Thomas the Contender 138:4–27,
139:13–21, NHL*

The Savior said, "Brother Thomas, while you have time in
the world, listen to me and I will reveal to you the things you
have pondered in your mind.

"Now since it has been said that you are my twin and true
companion, examine yourself that you may understand who
you are, in what way you exist, and how you will come to be.
Since you are called my brother, it is not fitting that you be ignorant of yourself. And I know that you have understood, because
you had already understood that I am the knowledge of the
truth. So while you accompany me, although you are uncom-
prehending, you have in fact already come to know, and you
will be called, 'the one who knows himself.'

"For he who has not known himself has known nothing, but
he who has known himself has at the same time already
achieved knowledge about the Depth of the All. So then, you,
my brother Thomas, have beheld what is hidden to people, that
is, that against which they ignorantly stumble."

Now Thomas said to the Lord, "Therefore I beg you to tell
me what I ask before your Ascension, and when I hear from
you about the hidden things, then I can speak about them. And
it is obvious to me that the truth is difficult to perform before
people . . .

Those who speak about things that are invisible and difficult
to explain are like those who shoot arrows at a target at night.
To be sure they shoot their arrows as anyone would — since
they shoot at a target — but it is not visible. Yet when the light
comes forth and hides the darkness, then the work of each will
appear. And you, our light, enlighten, Lord."

Psalm *Ode 18*

My heart is raised and magnified in the love of You, O Highest
    One,*
That I might celebrate Your Name!
My arms and legs are made powerful*
    that they might not fall from Your power.
You heal my bodily sickness*
    Your will is as firm as Your Kingdom.

O lord, that I may help the weak, let me keep Your Word.*
    For them do not deny me Your perfection.
Let the light not be conquered by darkness.*
    Let truth not flee falsehood.
Appoint me to victory. Your right hand is salvation.*
    Receive and preserve us who greet temptation.
Falsehood and death are not in Your mouth.*
    My God, Your will is perfection.
Vanity You do not know, nor does it know You.*
    Error You do not know, nor does it know You.
Ignorance appears like dust and like scum of the sea.*
    The vain supposed it was great and were its child.
The wise understand and meditate.*
    They are unpolluted in their meditations for they share the
        mind of the Lord.
They laugh at error and speak truth*
    breathed into them from You, the Highest One.
Your Name is greatly beautiful. Hallelujah!

Gospel *Q Gospel 7:1–10*

At the time that Jesus entered Capernaum, a Roman officer there had a favorite servant who was sick and near death. Hearing about Jesus, the centurion sent some Jewish elders to ask him to come and heal his servant. They came to Jesus and pleaded urgently with him. "He deserves your help," they said. "He is a friend of our people; in fact, he is the one who built our synagogue."

Jesus was not very far from the house when the centurion approached him and said,"My servant is lying at home paralyzed and in great pain."

Jesus said to him, "I will come myself and cure him."

The centurion replied, "I don't deserve to have you in my house. But just say the word, and my servant will be healed. After all, I myself am under orders, and I have many soldiers under my command. I say to one, 'Go!' and he goes. I order another to come and he comes. And to my servant, 'Do this!' and he does it."

When Jesus heard this, he was amazed and said to the crowd

following him, "I tell you, nowhere in Israel have I found such faith."

Then Jesus said to the centurion, "Go home now and everything will happen as you believed it would." At that moment, the servant was healed.

Pentecost 14

First Reading *Didache 2*

The second commandment of the Teaching: "You shall not murder. You shall not commit adultery." You shall not corrupt children. You shall not fornicate. "You shall not steal." You shall not practice magic. You shall not go in for sorcery. You shall not murder a child, whether by abortion or by killing it once it is born. "You shall not covet what belongs to your neighbor. You shall not swear falsely, You shall not bear false witness."[1] You shall not slander anyone.

You shall not harbor resentment.

You shall not equivocate, either in what you think or in what you say, for equivocation is "a deadly snare."[2] Your speech shall not be false or empty, but fulfilled in action. You shall not be given to greed, or robbery, or wickedness, or malice, or pride. You shall not plot evil against your neighbor.

You shall not hate anyone. Some people, though, you shall call to task; for others you shall pray. Still others you shall love more than your own life.

Notes **1.** Exod 20:13–17; cf. Matt 19:18; 5:33. **2.** Prov 21:6

Second Reading *Malachi 3:1–3, Tanakh*

Behold, I am sending My messenger to clear the way before Me, and the Lord whom you seek shall come to His Temple suddenly. As for the angel of the covenant that you desire, he is already coming. But who can endure the day of his coming, and who can hold out when he appears? For he is like a smelter's fire and like fuller's lye. He shall act like a smelter and purger of silver; and he shall purify the descendants of Levi and refine them like gold and silver, so that they shall present offerings in righteousness.

Psalm *Ode 21*

> I raise my arms high to the grace of the Lord.*
> For You cast off my bonds.
> My helper lifts me to Your grace and salvation.*
> I discard darkness and clothe myself in light.
> My soul acquires a body*
> free from sorrow, affliction, or pain.
> Your Thought, O Lord, restores me.*
> I feed on Your Eternal fellowship.
> I am raised in the light and go to You, near You,*
> Praising and proclaiming You.
> You make my heart flood into my mouth.*
> You make my heart shine on my lips.
> On my face the exaltation of You increases, Lord*
> My face shines forth Your Praise. Hallelujah!

Gospel *Q Gospel 7:18–19, 22–35*

John the Baptist was in prison when he heard what Jesus was doing. He sent two of his own disciples to ask him, "Are you the one who is to come, or are we to wait for another?"

Jesus answered, "Go back and tell John what you hear and see: the blind see again, the lame walk, lepers are made clean, the deaf hear, the dead are raised to life and the poor are given good news. Blessed is the man who does not lose faith in me."

After John's disciples had departed, Jesus spoke to the crowds about John. "What did you go out to the desert to see? A reed shaken by the wind? No? Then what did you go out to see? A man dressed in fine clothes? Those who wear fine clothes live in luxury in royal palaces. But why did you go out? To see a prophet? Yes, I tell you — and much more than a prophet. He is the one about whom it is written:

'See, I send my messengers before you,
He will prepare the road ahead of you.'

"I tell you, of all the children born of women, no one is greater than John the Baptist; yet the least in the realm of God is greater than him.

Up until the time of John the Baptist, we had the law of Moses and the words of the prophets. Since John arrived, the good news about God's realm has been announced. Now people everywhere are pushing to get in.

How should I describe the people of this generation? What are they like?

They are like children who sit in the marketplace and call to one another:

'We played the flute for you and you didn't dance;

We sang sad songs and you would not weep.'

For John the Baptist came, not eating and drinking, and you say, 'Just look at him, a glutton and a drunkard, a friend of tax collectors and outcasts.'

But Wisdom is being proven right by all her children."

Pentecost 15

First Reading *Didache 3*

My child, flee from all evil and from everything like it. Do not be an angry person, for anger leads to murder. Do not be jealous or contentious or impetuous, for from all this flows murderous acts.

My child, do not be lustful, for lust leads to fornication. Do not use foul language or leer, for all this breeds adultery.

My child, do not be a dealer in omens, since it leads to idolatry; nor should you be an enchanter, or an astrologer, or a magician, and do not be present to see or hear such things, for from all of these breed idolatry.

My child, do not be a liar, since lying leads to theft. Do not be avaricious or vain, for all this breeds thievery.

My child, do not be a grumbler against God, since it leads to blasphemy. Do not be presumptuous or disposed to invent evil, for all this breeds blasphemy.

But be humble since "the humble will inherit the earth."[1] Be patient, merciful, guileless, quiet, and good; and always "have respect for the Teaching"[2] you have heard.

You shall not exalt yourself or let yourself be arrogant. You shall not attach yourself to those who are highly placed but shall associate with those who are just and humble.

Accept as good whatever happens to you, knowing that nothing happens without God.

Notes 1. Ps 37:11 Matt 5:5. 2. Isa 66:2.

Second Reading *I Kings 19:19–21, Tanakh*

Elijah set out from there (a cave on Mount Horeb) and came upon Elisha son of Shaphat as he was plowing. There were twelve yoke of oxen ahead of him, and he was with the twelfth. Elijah came over to him and threw his mantle over him. He left the oxen and ran after Elijah, saying: "Let me kiss my father and mother good-by, and I will follow you." And he answered him, "Go back. I am not stopping you." He turned back from him and took the yoke of oxen and slaughtered them; he boiled their meat with the gear of the oxen and gave it to the people, and they ate. Then he arose and followed Elijah and became his attendant.

Psalm *Ode 39*

Raging rivers are the force of You, Lord!*
      They wash away those who despise You!
They entangle their paths and destroy their crossings.*
      They carry away their bodies and destroy their souls.
Their rapids are faster than lightning,*
      But those who cross them in faith will not be hurt.
Those who walk without blame need not cringe.*
      You are their sign, their Way, for those who cross in Your
      Name.
Dress in the Name of the Most High and know the Lord*
      Cross rivers without worry. Rivers obey you.
You, Lord, bridge rivers with Your Word.*
      You walk and cross them on foot.
Your footsteps are firm upon the waters and do not sink.*
      Your feet are like beams of wood fashioned of Truth.
Waves rise on this side and on the other*
      But Your footsteps, Anointed One, do not wash away.
A Way exists for those who cross after You,*
      for those who follow Your Way of faith and love Your Name.
      Hallelujah!

Gospel *Q Gospel 9:57, 10:2–4*

As they walked along the road, they met a man who said to Jesus, "I will follow you wherever you go." Jesus answered, "Foxes have dens and birds have nests, but the son of man, the *Truly Human Being*, has nowhere to rest his head."

To another he said, "Follow me." But that person replied, "Let me go and bury my father first." Jesus answered, "Let the dead bury their dead. Your duty is to go and spread the news of the realm of God."

Another person said, "I will follow you, but first let me go and say good-bye to my family." Jesus said to him, "No one who puts a hand on the plough and continues to look at what was left behind is suited for the realm of God."

"Although the crop is abundant, there are few workers to harvest it, so ask the owner to send more laborers into the fields. Get going, but remember, I am sending you out like lambs among wolves."

"Don't acquire gold, silver or copper. Carry no purse, no knapsack, no sandals. Don't bring a second tunic or a staff. Don't stop to greet people along the way."

Pentecost 16

First Reading *Didache 4*

My child, "you shall be mindful day and night of the one who speaks to you the word of God"[1] and honor that person as you would the Lord. For where the Lord's nature is proclaimed, there is the Lord.

You shall seek daily the faces of the saints, to enjoy their refreshing conversation. You shall not cause division; instead you shall reconcile fighters.

"Your judgments must be fair."[2] You shall not show partiality in calling people to task for their faults. You must not be of two minds about your decision. [3]

Do not be the sort of person who holds out his hands to receive but draws them back when it comes to giving. If your labor has brought you earnings, pay a ransom for your sins.

You shall not hesitate to give, and when you give you shall not grumble, for you will know who the paymaster is who gives good wages.

You shall not turn away anyone who is in need, but you shall share everything with your brother and sister, and you shall not say that anything belongs only to you, for if you are partners in what is eternal, should you not be so all the more in things that perish?

Do not neglect your responsibility[4] to your son or your daughter, but from their youth you shall teach them to revere God.

You shall not give orders in bitterness to your slave or you maid, those who hope in the same God as you, lest they stop revering the God who is over both you and them. For God does not come to call people according to their personal status but comes upon those whom the Spirit has prepared.

As for you who are slaves, obey your masters with reverence and respect, as if they represented God.

You shall hate all hypocrisy, and everything that is not pleasing to the Lord.

You shall not abandon "the Lord's commandments," but "observe" the ones you have been given, "neither adding nor subtracting anything."[5]

In the assembly[6] you shall confess your sins, and not approach prayer with a bad conscience.

This is the way of life.

Notes 1. Heb 13:7. **2.** Deut 1:16, 17; Prov 31:9. **3.** The meaning of this phrase is uncertain. (Robinson) **4.** Literally, "Do not withhold your hand from . . . " **5.** Deut 4:2; 12:32. **6.** For "assembly" some translations read "church".

Commentary How shall we read the passage about slavery? The context of the Didache is one where both slaves and free people were in the same congregation with the same God. The teaching, while accepting of slavery, is about an equality which leads toward abolition of slavery.

Second Reading *2 Kings 4:29–37, Tanakh*

Elisha said to Gehazi, "Gird up your loins, take my staff in your hand, and go. If you meet anyone, do not greet him; and if anyone greets you, do not answer him. And place my staff on the face of the boy." But the boy's mother said, "As the Lord lives and as you live, I will not leave you!" So he arose and followed her.

Gehazi had gone on before them and had placed the staff on the boy's face; but there was no sound or response. He turned back to meet him and told him, "The boy has not awakened." Elisha came into the house, and there was the boy, laid out dead on his couch. He went in, shut the door behind the two of them, and prayed to the LORD. Then he mounted the bed and placed himself over the child. He put his mouth on his mouth, his eyes of his eyes, and his hands on his hands, as he bent over him. And the body of the child became warm. He stepped down, walked once up and down the room, then mounted and bent over him. Thereupon the boy sneezed seven times, and the boy opened his eyes. Elisha called Gehazi and said, "Call the Shumanite woman," and he called her. When she came to him, he said, "Pick up your son." She came and fell at his feet and bowed low to the ground; then she picked up her son and left.

Psalm *Ode 36*

I find rest in the Spirit of the Lord who raises me up. *
  You place my feet on solid rock in high terrain before Your
    Glory.
I praise You continually*
composing my odes.
Christ speaks
The Spirit brought me forth*
  before the face of the Lord.
I was a Son of Man, living my True Humanity,*
  I was named the light, the child of God.
I was the most glorified of the glorious,*
  greatest of the great.
According to the greatness of the Most High, She made me.*
  According to his freshness, He renewed me.
From his perfection he anointed me*
  and I became equal to those near him.
My mouth was open like a dew cloud,*
  my heart overflowed with goodness,

My Way to him was peace,*
and I was united in the soul of his providence.

Gospel *Q Gospel 10:5–22*

Whenever you enter someone's home, let your first words be, "Peace to this house!" If a person who loves peace lives there, they will accept your blessings. If not, your words will come back to you. Stay in this house, taking what food and drink they offer, for the laborer deserves his reward. Do not keep moving from house to house. When you enter a town and the people welcome you, eat the food they provide. Heal the sick who are there. Say to the people of the town, "The realm of God is at your door."

If you enter a town and they do not welcome you, go out into its streets and say, "We wipe off the very dust of your town that clings to our feet, and leave it with you. Yet be sure of this: the realm of God is very near."

I tell you, on that day Sodom and Gomorrah will be better off than that town.

Beware Chorazin! Take heed, Bethsaida! If Tyre and Sidon had seen the miracles performed in your midst, they would have changed their ways long ago, sitting in sackcloth and ashes. It will not go as hard with Tyre and Sidon at the judgment as with you. As for you, Capernaum, do you think you will be exalted to the heavens? No, you shall go crashing down among the dead!

Anyone who listens to you listens to me. Whoever rejects you rejects me, and those who reject me reject the one who sent me.

At this time, Jesus said, "I thank you, Father, for hiding these things from the wise and the clever and revealing them to the childlike. This is the way you want it. Everything has been put in my hand by my father. No one knows who the son is except the father, and who the father is except the son, and anyone to whom the son chooses to reveal him."

Commentary Compare the instructions of Jesus to his disciples with the instructions for the passover meal. "This is how you shall eat (the passover meal): your loins girded, your sandals on your feet, and your staff in your hand; and you shall eat it hurriedly: it is a passover to the Lord." (Exod 12:11, Tanakh)

Just as the Hebrews set out on their journey toward freedom, so the disciples set out on theirs.

Pentecost 17

First Reading *Didache 5–6*

But the way of death is this: First of all it, is evil and full of cursing; murders, adulteries, lusts, fornications, thefts, idolatries, magic, sorceries, robberies, false witnessings, hypocrisies, duplicity, deceit, pride, malice, stubbornness, greediness, filthy talk, jealousy, arrogance, boastfulness, lack of reverence for God. 1

Persecutors of good people, hating truth, loving lies, ignorant of the wages of uprightness, not "adhering to what is good," 2 nor to just judgment, lying awake not for what is good but for what is evil, from whom gentleness and patience are far away. "They love vanity," 3 "look for profit," 4 do not show mercy to a poor person, do not exert themselves for the oppressed, ignoring their Maker, "murder children," 5 corrupt God's image, turn their backs on the needy, who oppress the person who is distressed, advocates of the rich, unjust judges of the poor, and are thoroughly sinful. My children, may you be saved from all this!

See to it "that no one leads you astray" 6 from this way of the Teaching, since the person who does this teaches apart from God. For if you can near the whole yoke of the Lord, you will be perfect; but if you cannot, then do what you can.

Now about food: bear what you can. But keep strictly away from food offered to idols, for that implies worshiping dead gods.

Notes 1. Cf. Matt 15:19; Mark 7:21–22; Rom 1:29–31, Gal 5:19–21. 2. Rom 12:9. 3. Ps 4:2. 4. Isa 1:23. 5. WisSol 12:6. 6. Matt 24:4.

Second Reading *Ezekiel 36:22–28, Tanakh*

Say to the House of Israel: Thus said the Lord GOD: Not for your sake will I act, O House of Israel, but for My holy name, which you have caused to be profaned among the nations to which you have come. I will sanctify My great name which has been profaned among the nations — among whom you have caused it to be profaned. And the nations shall know that I am the LORD — declares the Lord GOD — when I manifest My holiness before their eyes through you. I will take you from among the nations and gather you from all the countries, and I will bring you back to your own land. I will sprinkle clean water upon you, and you shall be clean: I will cleanse you from all your uncleanness and from all your fetishes. And I will give you a new heart and put a new spirit into you: I will remove the heart of stone from your body and give you a heart of flesh; and I will put My spirit into you. Thus I will cause you to follow My laws and faithfully to observe My rules. Then you shall dwell in the land which I gave to your fathers, and you shall be My people and I will be your God.

Psalm *Sirach 28:2–7, NRSV*

> Forgive your neighbor the wrong he has done,*
> and then your sins will be pardoned when you pray.
> Does anyone harbor anger against another,*
> and expect healing from the Lord?
> If one has no mercy toward another like himself,*
> can he then seek pardon for his own sins?
> If a mere mortal harbors wrath,*
> who will make an atoning sacrifice for his sins?
> Remember the end of your life,*
> and set enmity aside.
> remember corruption and death,*
> and be true to the commandments.
> Remember the commandments,*
> and do not not be angry with your neighbor;
> Remember the covenant of the most high,*
> and overlook faults.

Gospel *Q Gospel 10:23–24, 11:2–13*

> When Jesus was alone with his disciples, he turned to them and said, "Fortunate are the eyes that see what you are seeking. Many prophets and kings wished to see what you now see and

never saw it, longed to hear what you now hear and never heard it."

One day it happened that Jesus was praying in a particular place. When he finished, one of his disciples said, "Lord, teach us how to pray just as John the Baptist taught his disciples." He responded, "Say this when you pray:

'Father, may your name be honored; may your reign begin.
Grant us the food we need for each day.
Forgive our failures, for we forgive everyone who fails us.
And do not put us to the test.'"

"Ask and it'll be given to you. Search and you will find. Knock and the door will be opened for you. For everyone who asks receives, and everyone who searches finds, and for those who knock, the door is opened.

"Who among you would hand his son a stone when he has asked you for bread? Who would hand him a snake when it's fish he's asking for? If you, who are imperfect, know how to give good things to your child, how much more will your heavenly Father give to you when you ask."

Pentecost 18

First Reading *Didache 7–8*

Now about baptism: this is how to baptize. Give instruction in the assembly on this Teaching and then "baptize" in running water, "in the name of the Father and of the Son, and Holy Spirit."[1] If you do not have running water, baptize in some other water. If you cannot baptize in cold water, then use warm. If you have neither, pour water on the head three times "in the name of the Father, Son, and Holy Spirit."[2] Before the baptism let the baptizer and the one who is to be baptized, and others who are able, fast. And you must tell the one who is being baptized to fast for one or two days before.

Your fasts must not be on the same days as the hypocrites.[3] They fast on Mondays and Thursdays; but you should fast on Wednesdays and Fridays.

And do not pray like the hypocrites, but "pray as follows"[4] as the Lord directed in his gospel:

"Our Father in heaven, your name be revered, your king-dom come, your will be done on earth as it is done in heaven. Give us today our bread for the day, and forgive our debtors; and do not subject us to temptation, but save us from the Evil One; for your is the power and the glory forever!"

You should pray in this way three times a day.

Notes 1. Matt 28:19. 2. Matt 28:19. 3. Cf. Matt 6:16. 4. Cf. Matt 6:9–13.

Second Reading *2 Esdras 7:78–87, NRSV*

When the decisive decree has gone out from the Most High that a person shall die, as the spirit leaves the body to return again to him who gave it, first of all it adores the glory of the Most High. If it is one of those who have shown scorn and have not kept the way of the Most High, who have desired his law and hated those who fear God — such spirits shall immediately wander about in torments, always grieving and sad, in seven ways.

The first way, because they have scorned the law of the Most High. The second way, because they cannot now make a good repentance so that they may live. The third way, they shall see the reward laid for those who have trusted the covenants of the Most High. The fourth way, they shall consider the torment laid up for themselves in the last days. The fifth way, they shall see how the habitations of the others are guarded by angels in profound quiet. The sixth way, they shall see how some of them will cross over into torments. The seventh way, which is worse than all the ways that have been mentioned, because they shall utterly waste away in confusion and be consumed with shame, and shall wither with fear at seeing the glory of the Most High in whose presence they sinned while they were alive, and in whose presence they are to be judged in the last times.

Psalm *Ode 40*

As honey drips from the honeycomb of bees*
    And milk flows from the woman who loves her child,
      so goes my hope to You, my God.
As a fountain bursts with water,*

My heart bursts with praise for You, Lord, through my lips.
My tongue is sweet from conversing with You.*
I feel the anointing when I sing Your songs.
My face beams when praising You.*
My spirit is overflowing with Your Love and my soul is shin-
ing.
Whoever is fearful will trust in You*
and come to wholeness in You.
Whoever trusts You has Eternal life*
and cannot be corrupted. Hallelujah!

Gospel *Q Gospel 11:14–32*

They brought a man who was blind and mute and who was possessed by a demon to Jesus. He cured the man so that he could speak and see.

The crowds were astonished. But some of them said, "He is in league with Beelzebul, the chief of the evil spirits."

But Jesus answered them, "If it is by the power of Beelzebul that I cast out demons, by whose power do your own people cast them out? If I rely on the help of the chief of the demons, then Beelzebul's own house is divided against itself. Every kingdom divided against itself will be destroyed, and a house divided in two will collapse. So if Satan's house is divided, how can his kingdom survive?

"But if it is by the finger of God that I cast out demons, then the reign of God has arrived!

"Anyone who is not with me is against me. Whoever does not help me gather scatters.

"When an unclean spirit goes out of a person, it wanders through waterless country looking for a place to rest. Not finding one it says, 'I will go back to the home I came from.' But on arrival, finding it swept and tidied, it then goes off and brings seven other spirit more wicked then itself, and they go in and set up house there, so that the person ends up by being worse than before."

As Jesus was speaking, a woman in the crowd raised her voice and said, "Blessed is the womb that gave birth to you and the breasts that nursed you."

He replied, "Blessed rather are those who hear the word of God and observe it."

With the crowds swarming around him, Jesus addressed the people directly,"You are an imperfect generation! You demand a sign, but none will be given except the sign of Jonah. Just as Jonah was a symbol for the people of Nineveh, so will the Son of Man (Truly Human Being) be for today's generation.

"The Queen of Sheba traveled from the ends of the earth to hear the wisdom of Solomon. Today, something greater than Solomon is here. The people of Nineveh heard the preaching of Jonah and changed their ways. But now, something greater than Jonah is here.

"At the judgment, both the Queen of Sheba and the Ninevites will condemn this generation."

Pentecost 19

First Reading *Didache 9*

Now about the Eucharist: This is how to give thanks. First about the cup,

"We thank you,our Father, for the holy vine of David, your child, which you have revealed through Jesus, your child. Glory to you forever."

And about the Bread, "We thank you, our Father, for the life and knowledge which you have made known to us through Jesus your child. Glory to you forever, Just as this piece of bread was scattered over the hills and then was brought together and made one, so let your Church be brought together from the ends of the earth, into your Kingdom. For the glory and the power are yours through Jesus Christ forever."

You must not let anyone eat or drink of your Eucharist except those baptized in the Lord's name. For in reference to this the Lord said, "Do not give what is sacred to dogs."[1]

Note 1. Matt 6:7, but compare Mark 7:24–30 (Matt 15:21–28) where Jesus, in conversation with the Samaritan woman, apparently has a change in his attitude. Might she be helping Jesus overcome his prejudice?

Second Reading *2 Samuel 12:1–12, Tanakh*

The LORD was displeased with what David had done, and

the LORD sent Nathan to David, he came to him and said, "There were two men in the same city, one rich and one poor. The rich man had very large flocks and herds, but the poor man had only one little ewe lamb that he had bought. He tended it and it grew up together with him and his children: it used to share his morsel of bread, drink from his cup, and nestle in his bosom; it was like a daughter to him. One day, a traveler came to the rich man, but he was loath to take anything from his own flocks or herd to prepare a meal for the guest who had come to him; so he took the poor man's lamb and prepared it for the man who had come to him."

David flew into a rage against the man, and said to Nathan, "As the LORD lives, the man who did this deserves to die! He shall pay for the lamb four times over, because he did such things and showed no pity."

And Nathan said to David, "That man is you! Thus said the LORD, the God of Israel: 'It was I who anointed you king over Israel and it was I who rescued you from the hand of Saul. I gave you your master's house and possession of your master's wives; and I gave you the House of Israel and Judah; and if that were not enough, I would give you twice as much and more. Why then have you flouted the command of the LORD and done what displeases Him? You have put Uriah the Hittite to the sword; you took his wife and made her your wife and had him killed by the sword of the Ammonites. Therefore the sword shall never depart from your House — because you spurned Me by taking the wife of Uriah the Hittite and making her your wife.' Thus said the LORD: 'I will make a calamity rise against you from within your own house; I will take your wives and give them to another man before your very eyes and he shall sleep with your wives under this very sun. You acted in secret, but I will make this happen in the sight of all Israel and in broad daylight.'"

Psalm *Micah 6:6–9, Tanakh*

With what shall I approach the LORD,*
   and do homage to God on high?
Shall I approach Him with burnt offerings,*
   With calves a year old?

Would the LORD be pleased with thousands of rams,*
   With myriads of streams of oil?
Shall I give my first-born for my transgression,*
   The fruit of my body for my sins?
"He has told you, O mortal, what is good
   And what does the LORD require of you;
Only to do justice*
   And to love goodness,
And to walk modestly with your God;*
   Then will your name achieve wisdom."

Gospel *Q Gospel 11:33–51, 12:2–3*

Jesus said, "No one lights a lamp and puts it under a bushel basket. They put it on a stand so that everyone can see the light. Your eye is the lamp of your body. When your eye is clear, your entire body fills with light. But if your eye become clouded, your body is in darkness. Be careful that your light never fades into darkness.

"Beware, you who call yourselves perfect in your obedience to the law. You pay tax on mint, dill and cumin, but you ignore justice, mercy and honesty. You should practice these things first.

"You wash the outside of your cups and plates, but inside you are filled with thoughts of greed and theft. Didn't the one who made the outside make the inside too? Wash the inside of the cup and it will all be clean.

"You who claim to be the most devout are hopeless! You love sitting in the front row of the synagogue and having people bow down to you in public. You are whitewashed tombs — beautiful on the surface, but filled with death and decay.

"Beware to those who load people down with the crushing burden of laws and regulations but do nothing to help them. You have taken away the key of knowledge, but instead of unlocking the door, you have blocked the way for those trying to enter.

"You erect monuments to prophets who were murdered by your ancestors. They did the killing, you built the tombs.

"That's why the Wisdom of God said, 'I will send them prophets and messengers. Some they will kill, others they will persecute. This generation will have to answer for the blood of every prophet shed since the beginning of the world from Abel to Zechariah."

"There is nothing covered up now that will not be exposed. Nothing is secret that will not be revealed. Every secret you've kept will become known. What you have whispered in hidden places will be shouted from the housetops."

Commentary For similar stories of revealing that which was hidden, see 2 Kgs 6:8–12 and 2 Macc 12:38–42.

Pentecost 20

First Reading *Didache 10*

After you have finished your meal, give thanks in this way: "We give you thanks, Holy Father, for your holy name, which you have made to dwell in our hearts, and for knowledge and faith and immortality, which you have made known to us through Jesus your child. Glory to you forever. You, almighty Master, have created all things for your name's sake, you have given human beings food and drink to enjoy, so that they would give you thanks, but to us you have given spiritual food and drink and eternal life through Jesus, your child.

"Above all, we thank you that you are powerful. Glory to you forever. Remember, Lord, your church, to save it from all evil and to make it perfect in your love. Make it holy 'and gather' it 'together from the four winds,' 1 into your kingdom which you have prepared for it. For the power and the glory are yours forever."

"Let Grace come and let this world pass away."

"Hosanna to the God of David!"[2]

"If anyone is holy, let him come. If not, let him repent."

"Our Lord, come!"[3]

"Amen."[4]

Permit the prophets to give thanks as much as they please.[5]

Notes 1. Matt 24:31. 2. Cf. Matt 21:9, 15. 3. Cf. 1 Cor 16:22 and Rev 22:20. 4. These short verses may be called out and echoed by the people. 5. In other words, let them pray freely in the Spirit.

Second Reading *Gospel of Philip 63:21 and 55:6–14 and 57:6–9 and 75:14–24, NHL*

The Eucharist is Jesus . . . Before Jesus came there was no bread in the world, just as Paradise, the place where Adam was, had many trees to nourish the animals but no wheat to sustain *human beings.* They used to feed like the animals, but when Jesus came, *the truly human being,* he brought bread from heaven in order that *humans* might be nourished with the food of *humanity* . . .

Jesus' flesh is the word and Jesus' blood is the holy spirit. Whoever receives these has food and drink and clothing . . .

The cup of prayer contains wine and water, since it is appointed as the type of the blood for which thanks is given. And it is full of the Holy Spirit, and it belongs to the wholly *perfect human being.* When we drink this, we shall receive for ourselves the perfect humanity. The living water is a body. It is necessary that we put on the *living true humanity.* Therefore, when someone is about to go down into the water, that person removes all clothing in order to put on the new and *living humanity.*

Psalm *Wisdom of Solomon 1:1–7, NRSV*

Love righteousness, you rulers of the earth, think of the Lord in
goodness*
and seek the Lord with sincerity of heart;
because he is found by those who do not put him to the test,*
and manifests himself to those who do not distrust him.
For perverse thoughts separate people from God,*
and when his power is tested, it exposes the foolish;
because wisdom will not enter a deceitful soul,*
or dwell in a body enslaved to sin.
For a holy and disciplined spirit will flee from deceit, and will
leave foolish thoughts behind,*
and will be ashamed at the approach of unrighteousness.
For wisdom is a kindly spirit,*
but will not free blasphemers from the guilt of their words;
because God is witness of their inmost feelings,*
and a true observer of their hearts, and a hearer of their
tongues.

Because the spirit of the Lord has filled the world,*
and that which holds all things together knows what is said.

Gospel *Q Gospel 12:4–21*

Jesus said, "Do not fear those who kill the body but cannot kill the soul. Instead, you should respect the one who holds in his hands both your body and your soul. What does a sparrow cost? A few pennies? Yet not a single little bird is forgotten by God. And you? God's care extends to every hair on your head. You are worth more than a flock of sparrows.

"Everyone who acknowledge me in public will be celebrated by the angels. Whoever rejects me before others will be disowned by the angels. Anyone who speaks against the Son of Man (*True Humanity*) will be forgiven, but there is no forgiveness for those who attack the Holy Spirit.

"When you are dragged into court and forced to appear before judges because of your beliefs, don't worry about how to defend yourself or what to say. The words will come to you from the Holy Spirit when you need them."

Someone in the crowd said to him, "Teacher, tell my brother to share the family inheritance with me." Jesus responded, "Friend, who made me a judge?

"There was once a rich man whose lands yielded a good harvest. He thought to himself, 'What shall I do? I don't have enough room to store my crops. I know, I'll tear down my barns and build bigger ones so that I can keep all my grain in them. Then I will say to myself, 'I have enough to last me for years. I can take it easy, eat, drink, and have a good time.'

"But God said to him, 'You fool! This very night you may die. Then who will own this hoard of yours?' So it is with those who pile up possessions but remain poor in the treasures of the spirit."

Commentary Regarding "hairs of the head," see 1 Sam 14:45 and 2 Sam 14:11, 1 Kgs 1:52.

Pentecost 21

First Reading *Didache 11*

Now, you should welcome anyone who comes your way and

teaches you all we have been saying. But if the teacher proves himself a renegade and by teaching otherwise contradicts all this, pay no attention to him. But if he teaches so that justice and knowledge of the Lord increase, welcome and receive him as you would the Lord.

Now about the apostles and prophets: act in line with the Gospel precept.[1] Welcome every apostles on arriving, as if he were the Lord. But he must not stay beyond one day. In case of necessity, however, the next day too. If he stays three days, he is a false prophet. On departing, an apostle must not accept anything except enough food to carry him till he finds his next lodging. If he asks for money, he is a false prophet.

Do not test or examine any prophet who speaks in the Spirit. For "every sin will be forgiven," but this sin "will not be forgiven."[2] However, not everyone making ecstatic utterances is a prophet, but only if he has the ways of the Lord. It is by their conduct that the false prophet and the true prophet can be distinguished. No prophet who orders a meal under the spirit's influence shall eat of it; if he does, he is a false prophet. Again, every prophet who teaches the truth but fails to practice what he preaches is a false prophet. But every reliable and genuine prophet who acts with a view to symbolizing the Mystery of the church,[3] but does not teach others to do what he himself does, shall be judged by you, for his judgment is with God. The ancient prophets acted in the same way.

But whoever says in the spirit, "Give me money", or something else, you shall not listen to him, but if he tells you to give for others who are in need, no one must condemn him.

Notes 1. Matt 10:40–41. 2. Matt 12:31. 3. Cf. 1 Cor 7:36ff and Gospel of Philip.

Second Reading *Tobit 4:5–11, NRSV*

Revere the LORD all your days, my son, and refuse to sin or to transgress his commandments. Live uprightly all the days of your life, and do not walk in the ways of wrongdoing; for those who act in accordance with truth will prosper in all their activities. To all those who practice righteousness give alms from your possessions, and do not let your eye begrudge the gift when you make it. Do not turn your face away from anyone who is poor, and the face of God will not be turned away from you. If you have many possessions, make your gift from them in proportion; if few, do not be afraid to give according to the little you have. So you will be laying up a good treasure for yourself against the day of necessity. For almsgiving delivers from death and keeps you from going into the Darkness. Indeed, almsgiving, for all who practice it, is an excellent offering in the presence of the Most High.

Psalm *Ode 22*

Christ speaks to the Father

You are the One who brings me down from on high*
    and who brings me up from the regions below,
who gathers what is on the earth and hurls them at me,*
    who scatters my enemies and adversaries,
who gives me mastery of binding ropes that I loosen them,*
    who with my hands overthrows the dragon with seven heads
    and places me at his roots to destroy his seed.
You are here and help me*
    and everywhere Your Name circles me.
Your right hand destroys his wicked poison.*
    Your hand smooths the way for those who believe in You
Your hand chooses them from their graves, separating them
      from the dead,*
    taking dead bones and covering them with bodies.
They are motionless. You give them the energy of life.*
    Your Way and Your face are stainless.
To corruption You bring Your world clean and refreshing.*
    The foundation is Your rock on which You build Your king-
      dom where the holy live. Hallelujah!

Gospel *Q Gospel 12:22–40*

Jesus spoke to his disciples: "Don't be anxious about your life. Don't worry about getting enough food or having clothes to wear. Life means more than food and the body is more than clothing. Look at the ravens. They don't plant seeds or gather a harvest. They have neither storehouses nor barns. Yet God feeds them. Aren't you more important than birds? Can any of you, for all your worrying, add a single moment to your life? If worry can't change the smallest thing, then why be anxious about the rest?

"Look at the lilies that grow wild in the fields. They don't weave clothes for themselves. But I tell you, even King Solomon in all his splendor was not dressed as beautifully as these flowers. If that is how God clothes the grasses, which are green today and burned in the sun tomorrow, how much more will God provide for you. How little faith you have!

"Don't be blinded by the pursuit of food, clothing, and possessions. Stop worrying about these things. Only those who lack spirit and soul pursue them. You have a Father who knows what you need. Set your heart on God and these other things will be given to you.

"Don't pile up your treasures here on earth. They will be destroyed by moths and rust and stolen by thieves. Store your riches in heaven where moths and rust are powerless and thieves cannot break in. Wherever your treasure is, your heart will also be.

"If the owner of a house knows when a thief is coming, he will be guard and not let anyone break into the house. You too must be prepared — the son of man will arrive when you least expect him."

Pentecost 22

First Reading *Didache 12*

Everyone "who comes" to you "in the name of the Lord"[1] must be welcomed. Then, when you have taken stock of him, you will know — for you will have insight — what is true and what is false.

If the person who comes is just passing through, help him as much as you can. But he must not stay with you more than two days, or, if necessary, three.

If he wants to settle in with you and has a trade, let him work for his living. But if he has no trade, see to it that no Christian live with you in idleness.

If he refuses to do this, he is trading on Christ. Be on your guard against people like this.

Notes 1. Matt 21:9, Ps 118:26, cf. John 5:43.

Second Reading *Micah 7:1–7, NJB*

I am in trouble! I have become like a harvester in summer-time, like a gleaner at the vintage: not a single cluster to eat, not one of the early figs I so long for.

The devout have vanished from the land: there is not one honest man left. All are lurking for blood, every man hunting down his brother. Their hands are skilled in evil; the official demands . . . , the judge gives judgment for a bribe, the man in power pronounces as he pleases.

Put no trust in a neighbor, have no confidence in a friend; to the woman who shares your bed do not open your mouth. For son insults father, daughter defies mother, daughter-in-law defies mother-in-law; a man's enemies are those of his own household.

The best among them is like a briar, the most honest a hedge of thorn. Today will come their ordeal from the north, now is the time for their confusion.

For my part, I look to Yahweh, my hope is in the God who will save me; my God will hear me.

Psalm *Ode 25*

I am rescued from my chains and flee to You, my God.*
   You are the right hand of my salvation and my helper.
You hold back those who rise against me and they do not
      appear again.*
   Your face is with me. I am saved by Your grace.
But in the eyes of many I am abhorred and excluded.*
   In their eyes I am like lead. I assume strength and help from
      You.
You place a lamp at my right hand and at my left.*
   In me nothing is not bright.
Your Spirit covers me and I take off my garment of skin.*
   Your right hand raises me and removes my sickness.
I grow strong in Your truth, holy in Your goodness.*
   My enemies fear me.
I am of You, Lord, and by Your Name justified by Your gentle-
      ness.*
   Your rest goes on forever. Hallelujah!

Gospel *Q Gospel 12:42–46, 49–59*

Jesus said, "When the owner of an estate wants a manager who can be trusted with all his goods, someone who will make sure the staff is cared for and fed, whom will be put in charge? A trusty and sensible supervisor. Congratulations to that person if he proves faithful and is hard at work when the owner comes home. In that case, the owner will give him a share of the property. But if the manager says to himself, 'The owner is not coming back for a long time,' and begins abusing the workers and feasting and getting drunk, the owner may return unexpectedly. Instead of receiving a reward, the manager will be cut off and will share the fate of the unfaithful.

"Do you suppose that I am here to bring peace? No, I have come to bring the sword of division. My message will divide father and son, mother and daughter, mother-in-law and daughter-in-law.

"Those who prefer their father or mother to me are not deserving. Nor are those who prefer their sons and daughters.

"Unless you carry your own cross and follow me, you are not worthy.

"Those who grasp and clutch at self will lose it. Those who let go of self and follow me will find it.

"When you see clouds in the western sky, you say, 'It's going to rain.' And it does! When the wind blows from the south, you predict scorching weather. And it comes! You know the lay of the land and can read the face of the sky. So why can't you interpret the here and now?

"Why can't you judge for yourself what is right? When you are headed for court with an opponent, try to settle the case on the way and make peace with him. Otherwise he will call you before the judge, who may turn you over to the jailer. Then you may not get out of jail until you've paid your last penny."

Pentecost 23

First Reading *Didache 13*

Every genuine prophet who wants to settle with you "has a right to his support." In the same way, a genuine teacher, just like a "workman, has a right to his support." So you shall take

the first fruits of the produce of the wine press and the threshing floor and of cattle and sheep and give the first fruits to the
prophets, for they are your high priests. If, however, you have
no prophet, give them to the poor. If you make bread, take the
first fruits and give them according to the command. Likewise,
when you open a jar of wine or oil, take the first fruits and give
them to the prophets.

Take the first fruits of money and clothing, and and of all
your possessions, and give as you think best according to the
command.

Note 1. Matt 10:10.

Second Reading *Ezekiel 17:22–23*

Thus says the Lord GOD: "Then I in turn will take and set
in the ground a slip from the lofty top of the cedar; I will pluck
a tender twig from the tip of its crown, and I will plant it on a
tall, towering mountain. I will plant it in Israel's lofty highlands,
and it shall bring forth boughs and produce branches and grow
into a noble cedar. Every bird of every feather shall take shelter
under it, shelter in the shade of its boughs. Then shall all the
trees of the field know that it is I the LORD who have abased
the lofty tree and exalted the lowly tree, who have dried up the
green tree and made the withered bud. I the LORD have spoken and I will act."

Psalm *Ode 26*

I pour praise on You, Lord. I am Yours.*
    I recite Your holy poem. My heart is with You.
Your harp is in my hand,*
    and the odes of Your rest will not be silent.
I cry to You from my whole heart.*
    praise and exult You with my arms raised.
From the east into the west is Your praise!*
    From south far into the north is Your thanksgiving!
From the top of the hills to the greatest peaks is Your
    Perfection!*
    Who can write the odes of the Lord or who can read them?
Who can train the soul for life to save the soul?*

Who can rest high in the firmament so his mouth speaks?
Who can decipher the wonders of the Lord?*
The interpreter perishes and the interpretation remains.
It is enough to know and to rest.*
Singers rest serenely like a flowing river, like an overflowing
spring. Hallelujah!

Gospel *Q Gospel 13:18–35, 14:11*

Jesus said, "What is the realm of God like? How can I describe it to you? It is like a tiny mustard seed that someone tosses into a garden. It grows into a tree and birds nest in its branches.

"To what shall I compare the realm of God? It is like yeast that a woman takes and mixes with three cups of flour until it all rises.

"Enter by the narrow gate. The path that leads to destruction is a wide and easy. Many follow it. But the narrow gate and hard road lead to life. Few discover it.

"I predict that people will come from east and west, and north and south to sit with Abraham *and Sarah*, Isaac *and Rebecca*, and Jacob *and Leah and Rachel* at a great banquet in the realm of heaven. Those who think the realm of God belongs to them will be thrown out into the dark where they will dry tears of bitter regret.

"The last will be first and the first will be last.

"Jerusalem, O Jerusalem, you are a city that kills the prophets and stones those who are sent to you. How often I have wanted to gather your children as a hen gathers her chicks under her wings. But you have not let me. See your house will be abandoned and left in ruins. You will not see me again until you say, 'Blessed is the one who comes in the name of the Lord.'

"Those who praise themselves will be humbled. Those who humble themselves will be praised."

Note Italics indicates names of wives added to the text.

Commentary Jesus retells the Ezekiel story by changing the mighty cedar on a lofty mountain into a mustard seed tossed into a garden. Instead of being high and mighty, this lowly plant is as invasive as an unwanted weed in a garden.

A passage written toward the end of the first century expands on the meaning of the narrow gate: "There is a city built and set on a plain, and it is full of all good things; but the entrance to it is narrow and set in a precipitous place, so that there is fire on the right hand and deep water on the left. There is only one path lying between them, that is, between the fire and the water, so that only one person can walk on the path. If now the city is given to some-one as an inheritance, how will the heir receive the inheritance unless by passing through the appointed danger?" (2 Esdr 7:6–9 NRSV)

Another passage from 2 Esdras parallels Jesus teaching about gathering from east and west, "And now, father, look with pride and see the people coming from the east: to them I will give as leaders Abraham, Isaac, and Jacob, Elijah and Enoch, Zechariah and Hosea, Amos, Joel, Micah, Obadiah, Zephaniah, Nahum, Jonah, Mattathias, Habakkuk, and twelve angels with flowers." (2 Esdr 1:38 – 40 NRSV)

Yet another passage from 2 Esdras also parallels Jesus teaching regarding the hen and her chicks, "Thus says the Lord Almighty: Have I not entreated you as a father entreats his sons or a mother her daughter or a nurse her children, so that you should be my people and I should be your father *and mother*? I gathered you as a hen gathers her chicks under her wings. But now, what shall I do to you?" (2 Esdr 1:28–30 NRSV)

Pentecost 24

First Reading *Didache 14*

On every Lord's Day — his special day — come together and break bread and give thanks, first confessing your sins so that your sacrifice may be pure. Let no one engaged in a dispute with his neighbor meet with you until they are reconciled, so that your sacrifice may not be profaned.

This is the meaning of what was said by the Lord, "Always and everywhere offer me a pure sacrifice; for I am a great king," says the Lord, "and my name is wonderful among the nations."[1]

Note 1. Mal 1:11, 14.

Second Reading *Proverbs 9:1–6, Tanakh*

Wisdom has built her house,
She has hewn her seven pillars.
She has prepared the feast,
Mixed the wine,
And also set the table.
She has sent out her maids to announce
On the heights of the town,
"Let the simple enter here";
To those devoid of sense she says,
"Come, eat my food
And drink the wine that I have mixed;
Give up simpleness and live,
Walk in the way of understanding."

Psalm *Ode 28:1–6*

As the wings of the dove over their nestlings, and the mouths
   of the nestlings toward their mothers' mouths,*
   so also are the wings of the Spirit over my heart.
My heart is happy and leaps for joy,*
   like the infant who leaps for joy in mother's womb.
I believe. I am peaceful. My faith is in You whom I trust.*
   You bless me greatly. My mind is with You.
No sword divides us, No scimitar separates us.*
   I am prepared before destruction comes.
I am in Your arms that do not know death.*
   Eternal Life embraces and kisses me.
Your Spirit is in me.*
   It lives and cannot die. Hallelujah!

Gospel *Q Gospel 14:16–23*

Jesus said, "A man once gave a great banquet and invited
many guests. As the dinner hour approached, he sent a servant
to tell them, 'Come, everything is ready now.' One by one, they
started making excuses. The first guest told the servant, 'I'm
sorry but I just bought a piece of land and have to go see it.'

Another guest said, 'You'll have to excuse me, I'm on my
way to take a look at five pairs of oxen that I've purchased.'

A third guest explained, 'I just got married and I cannot come.'

The servant returned to tell the host about all these excuses.

In a fit of anger, the man shouted, 'Go out right now into the streets and alleys and invite the poor, the crippled, the blind, and the lame.' ·

Soon, the servant reported back, 'I've carried out your orders, but there is still room.'

'Then go farther out to the roads and country lanes,' the man responded, 'and lead people back until my house is filled. But not one of those original guests will share this feast.'"

Commentary For an interesting study of the development of this story read it in the following sequence: Thomas 64, Luke 14:16–24, Matt 22:1–10.

Pentecost 25

First Reading *Didache 15*

Elect for yourselves bishops and deacons who are a credit to the Lord, those who are gentle, generous, faithful, and honest. For their ministry to you is identical with that of prophets and teachers. So do not disregard them, for along with the prophets and teachers they enjoy a place of honor among you.

Correct one another not in anger but in peace as you find it in the gospel. If anyone wrongs a neighbor, let no one speak to that person, and let him not hear a word from you until he repents.

Offer your prayers, give your charity, and do everything just as you find it in the gospel of our Lord.

Second Reading *2 Esdras 13:51–56, NRSV*

I said, "O sovereign Lord, explain this to me: Why did I see the man coming up from the sea?"

He said to me, "Just as no one can explore or know what is in the depths of the sea, so no one on earth can see my Son or those who are with him, except in the time of his day. This is my interpretation of the dream that you saw. And you alone have been enlightened about this, because you have forsaken your own ways and have applied yourself to mine, and have searched out my law; for you have devoted your life to wisdom, and called understanding your mother. Therefore I have shown you these things; for there is a reward laid up with the Most High. For it will be that after three more days I will tell you other things, and explain weighty and wondrous matters to you."

Psalm *Ode 34*

The simple heart finds no hard way.*
> Good thoughts have no barriers.
Deep in the illumined mind is no whirlwind.*
> Surrounded on every side by the beauty of open country, one
> is free of doubt.
Below is like above. Everything is above.*
> Below is nothing, but the ignorant think they see.
Now you know grace. It is for your salvation.*
> Believe and live and be saved. Hallelujah!

Gospel *Q Gospel 17:3–4, 6, 22–35*

Jesus explained to his disciples, "If a companion does something wrong to you, go to the person and point this out. But do it privately. If your friend listens and says, 'I'm sorry,' forgive and your bond will be strengthened."

"But how often must I forgive the same person?" asked one of his disciples, "Seven times?"

Jesus answered, "Not just seven times, but seventy times seven.

"Even if your faith is no bigger than a mustard seed, you can say to this mountain, 'Move!' and it will move. Nothing will be impossible for you."

Jesus was asked, "When will the kingdom of God arrive?"

He replied, "You won't be able to see the kingdom of God when it comes. People won't be able to say, 'it's here' or 'it's over there.' The kingdom of God is among you.

"A time will come when you will long to see the son of man, *the Truly Human Being*, but you'll see nothing. There will be those who will say, 'Look over there' or 'Look right here.' But don't go searching! Stay right where you are. Because the son of man, the *Truly Human One*, will come like lightning flashing from one end of the sky to the other.

"It will be just like it was in the days of Noah. People ate, drank, got married and went on with their lives right up until the day that Noah climbed aboard the ark. Then the flood came and destroyed them. That's how it will be when the son of man, the *Truly Human Being*, is revealed.

"If two people are sleeping, one will be taken, the other left. If two women are grinding grain at the mill, one will be taken, the other will be left."

Pentecost 26

First Reading *Didache 16*

"Watch" over your life: do not let "your lamps" go out, and do not let your loins be weak, but "be ready" for "you do not know the hour when our Lord is coming." Meet together frequently in your search for what is good for your souls, since a "lifetime of faith will be of no advantage"[2] to you unless you prove perfect at the final hour. For in the final days the false prophets and seducers will be multiplied, and the sheep will turn into wolves and love will turn into hate. As lawlessness increases, they will hate and persecute and betray one another. And then the world deceiver will appear in the guise of a son of God. He will work "signs and wonders"[3] and the earth will fall into his hands and he will commit outrages such as have never occurred before.

Then humankind will come into the fiery trial and "many will fall away"[4] and perish, "but those who persevere" in their faith "will be saved"[5] by the Curse himself.[6]

Then "there will be signs"[7] of the Truth: first the sign of stretched out hands in heaven,[8] then the sign of "a loud trumpet call"[9], and thirdly the resurrection of the dead, though not all the dead, but as it has been said, "The Lord will come and all his saints with him. Then the world will see the Lord coming upon the clouds of heaven."[10]

Notes 1. Matt 24:42, 44; Luke 12:35. **2.** Barn 4:9. **3.** Matt 25:25. **4.** Matt 24:10. **5.** Matt 10:22; 24:13. **6.** Who is the Curse? The Didache is following the thinking of Paul in Gal 3:13, "Christ redeemed us from the curse of the law by becoming a curse for us — for it is written 'Cursed is everyone who hangs on a tree'." **7.** Matt 34:30. **8.** As Moses stretched out his hands in the desert to empower the people (Exod 17:11–13) so Jesus stretches out his hands on the cross, and the Resurrected Jesus (Christ) stretches out his hands opening the Way into heaven. (Barn 12:2–4) **9.** Matt 24:31. **10.** Zech 14:5; 1 Thess 3:13; Matt 24:30.

Second Reading *Apocalypse of Paul 18:3–19:20, NHL*

Paul meets a Child along the road and says to him, "By which road shall I go to Jerusalem?" The little child replied, saying, "Say your name so that I may show you the road." The little child knew who Paul was. He wished to make conversation with him through his words in order that he might find an excuse for speaking with him.

The little child spoke, saying, "I know who you are, Paul. You are he who was blessed from his mother's womb. For I have come to you that you may go up to Jerusalem to your fellow apostles. And for this reason you were called. And I am the Spirit who accompanies you . . .

"Let your mind awaken, Paul, and see this mountain upon which you are standing is the mountain of Jericho, so that you may know the hidden things in those that are visible. Now it is to the twelve apostles that you shall go, for they are elect spirits, and they will greet you."

Paul raised his eyes and saw them greeting him.

Commentary The story continues as the Child points out that Paul is already standing on a high mountain and from here he launches into each of the heavens, learning what he needs to know at each level until he reaches the tenth heaven. It is the child and the Spirit who guide Paul into this new awareness.

Clearly, this is a continuing understanding of the function of the child in our spiritual life: "And a little child shall lead them." Isaiah 11:6 "Unless you become as a little child . . . " Luke 18:17 and "The person old in days won't hesitate to ask a child seven

days old about the place of life, and that person will live."
(Thomas 4)

Psalm *Wisdom of Solomon 4:11–18, NRSV*

> Wisdom teaches her children*
> and gives help to those who seek her.
> Whoever loves her loves life,*
> and those who seek her from early morning are filled with
> joy.
> Whoever holds her fast inherits glory,*
> and the Lord blesses the place she enters.
> Those who serve her minister to the Holy One;*
> the Lord loves those who love her.
> Those who obey her will judge the nations,*
> and all who listen to her will live secure.
> If they remain faithful, they will inherit her;*
> their descendants will also obtain her.
> For at first she will walk with them on tortuous paths;*
> she will bring fear and dread upon then,
> and will torment them by her discipline until she trusts them,*
> and she will test them with her ordinances.
> Then she will come straight back to them again and gladden
> them,*
> and will reveal her secrets to them.

Gospel *Q Gospel 19:12–26, 22:28–30*

Jesus said, "A nobleman once went off to a distant land to become king. just before he left, he called together his ten most trusted servants and gave each of them ten silver coins. 'See what you can earn with this money while I am gone,' he instructed them.

"His fellow citizens, however, hated him and sent a delegation saying, 'We don't want this man to rule over us!'

Nevertheless, he received the kingship and returned home. He summoned the servants to find out what each one had done with the money.

The first one said, 'I've turned the ten coins into one hundred!'

'Excellent.' the new king replied. 'Because you've proven trustworthy in this small matter, I'm going to put you in charge of ten towns.'

The second one reported, 'I've earned five times what you gave me.'

'Then you'll be in charge of five towns,' replied the king.

Another servant stepped forward and said, 'Sir, here are your coins. I kept them wrapped in a handkerchief because you're a hard man and I'm afraid of you. You always try to get something for nothing. You reap where you do not sow.'

'Listen to what you're saying!' the king said. 'You're trapped by your own words. You say that I'm a difficult man, that I try to get something for nothing. If that is true, why didn't you do something with the money to make a profit? You've disobeyed me.'

Turning to the others, he said, 'Take the silver coins from him and give them to the fellow who turned ten coins into one hundred.'

'But sir!' they protested. 'He already has a hundred coins.'

'Yes,' the king replied, 'and to the person who has something, more will be given and that person will have abundance. The person who has nothing of real value will lose even what he thinks he has.'"

Jesus said to his followers, "You have stayed close to me through all my trials. You will eat and drink with me in the realm of God."

Season Before Christmas

The date of Easter affects the length of the Pentecost season. When Easter is early, Pentecost is longer. When Easter is later, Pentecost is shorter.

In ancient Celtic custom, the liturgical year begins with All Saints Day, November 1. Immediately after All Saints Day, begins the Season before Christmas. Another common custom is to have the Pentecost season continue until the Advent season, which is composed of four Sundays before Christmas.

Choices in any given year are as follows:

- End the Pentecost Season with the Sunday before All Saints Day and begin the Sundays before Christmas.
- Continue the Pentecost Season until the First Sunday of Advent.
- Continue the Pentecost Season until it finishes.

Clearly, there are gains, losses, and choices on where to place emphasis: Will it be continuing the Pentecost readings in order to complete the Gospel Q teachings ascribed to Jesus? Or to move sooner into the the symbolic material about Jesus birth?

So what is a creative liturgist to do? One might begin by reading all the overlapping material and then make choices according to the leading of the Holy Spirit.

In order to make use of all the Infancy Gospel of James, the gospels are longer. It seems appropriate to have simply one reading rather than two during this season.

Interpreting Nativity Stories

When we look into the Gospel records of Jesus, we find that the earliest written Gospels, Thomas and Q, are collections of sayings attributed to Jesus without any information about his life. Mark, the earliest of the narrative Gospels, surrounds the teachings with other stories of Jesus' life including healings, conflict with authorities, and stories of his trial, crucifixion, death, and resurrection. But in Mark, there is still no mention of the birth of Jesus.

The familiar Nativity stories that many of us have known from childhood come from Matthew and Luke. There are additional Gospels with other versions of the Nativity Story. One of them is a second-century document called the Gospel of James which is featured in this lectionary. When you compare the Gospels of Matthew, Luke, and James, you find some interesting similarities and some significant differences.

All three agree that Mary is a virgin. Luke says Mary is a "virgin engaged to a man whose name was Joseph." (Luke 1:27, NRSV) An angel says to Mary, "The Holy Spirit will come upon you and the power of the Most High will overshadow you . . . " Mary questions this and says, "How can this be since I have no husband?" The angel reassures her and then Mary says, "Let it be . . ." and in that moment she conceives. (Luke 1:35, 38, NRSV)

The Gospel of Matthew spells out Mary's virginity even more clearly by saying that, "Now the birth of Jesus Christ took place in this way. When his mother Mary had been betrothed to Joseph, before they came together she was found to be with child of the Holy Spirit;" (Matt 1:18, RSV)

In the Gospel of James a woman named Salome doubts that Mary is a virgin so she does a very graphic test: Salome "inserted her finger into Mary" (James 20:2 SV) and discovers that Mary is still a virgin after delivering the child.

Many of us feel it difficult if not impossible to accept the virgin birth as a literal fact. Are we expected to stretch our imaginations even further to believe that her virginity was restored after the delivery?

Study the stories a bit more and compare what these three versions say regarding the place of birth: Luke says the Child is born in a stable with a manger for a bed. Matthew places the Holy Family in a house where the Wise Men visit. James uses a cave for the setting. So which is it: a stable, a house, or a cave?

Compare some of the other details: Luke says that an angel comes to Mary in the daytime. Matthew says an angel appears to Joseph in his dreams. These are details that are easy to reconcile simply by saying that Mary heard the message during the day and Joseph at night.

Luke says the angels brought their message to the Shepherds in their fields at night. Matthew says the Wise Men followed a star and came with their gifts for the holy Child. You will find no shepherds in Matthew, no wise men in Luke.

These stories with very different details lived side by side until the thirteenth century when Francis of Assisi conflated the stories and created outdoors, where everyone could see, the first complete and full size nativity scene: Holy Family with a live baby, shepherds, angels, wise men, and plenty of animals. The only missing character is King Herod, who is nowhere in sight.

Look at various creches and nativity scenes on Christmas cards we have today and once in awhile you will see one where the scene is a cave with a stable inside. So if you work at it, you can reconcile most of the details into one somewhat coherent story.

Whether or not one chooses to accept the story as a literal account by arguing that "With God all things are possible," important questions remain. What do these stories really mean? What difference might they make in our lives now?

Consider the possibility that these stories might be absolutely true symbolically. They are myth in the best sense of that word. Sometimes we might assume that "myth" is another way of saying, "not true, false." On the other hand, consider again one of Joseph Campbell's definitions. "Myth is a tale told to tell the truth."[1] Myth is a vehicle that conveys meaning to us. Important truths are carried inside these extraordinary stories.

Virgin Birth stories are found in other religious traditions. There are stories which say that the Buddha was born from his virgin Mother Maya. In China, stories say that Lao Tsu and Confucius were also virgin born. This list of those who are said to be virgin born includes Zoroaster in Persia, Ra in Egypt, Prometheus, Plato, and even Alexander the Great in Greece, Romulus and Remus in

Rome, and Quetzalcoatl in Mexico. There are virgin birth stories among the Mayans, Columbians, Nicaraguans, and many other cultures.

So what shall we make of all this information? Should we consider all these stories as literal historic fact? Or shall we say that only the Christian versions are historically true and all the others are false?

Suppose we accept the stories for their symbolic truth: finding similar stories in so many cultures might be an indication that something very, very important is seeking expression through the stories.

Truth that is indescribable often clothes itself in outrageous stories, designed to startle us and make us pay attention. Once the Virgin Birth stories get our attention, then we are ready to ask, "What in the world do they mean?"

Virgin Birth stories are packed with meaning regarding who Jesus is. A human mother is impregnated by the Holy Spirit. Thus one of the things the stories are saying is that the divine is manifesting fully in a human being. Might the stories be expressing deep human yearning to connect and become fully aware of the divine, the Holy Mystery in whom we live and move and have our being?

Exploring the Inner Meaning of Virgin Birth Stories: Sermon Ideas?

Virgin Birth stories also offer insight into the depths of our own spiritual lives. The Christmas carol, "O Little Town of Bethlehem," written by Bishop Phillips Brooks says it all in one line: "Be born in us today!" Consider the Virgin birth stories as a symbolic description of our own inner rebirth.

Start with the place of birth: What might the three symbols of the stable, the house, and the cave suggest?

A stable is a very earthy, natural place. Do you have places in nature where God is especially real and present to you: a mountaintop, a forest, a desert, a waterfall, a tranquil lake, a special beach, or somewhere else?

Do you experience something of God's presence in your home, in your marriage, in your family, in a close friendship, with your lover? As you think about your significant relationships, now or at another time in your life, are there moments when you feel very deeply that the Divine is Present and alive?

Consider the third symbol, a cave: a natural womb of the earth. There is within every human being that inner cave-like place where the Divine seeks to be born.

And where does this spiritual birth happen for us — in Nature, in our Relationships, in the depths of our Souls, or in all of these?

The Nativity stories provide us with the symbolic clues we need. Have you ever looked at the stories and considered the possibility that all the characters might represent parts of ourselves?

Just as Mary is viewed as a virgin, there is also a virginal part within each of us. And what might that virgin part be? The untouched part? The part that wants to be open to receive the Holy Spirit? The part that is wanting new life to be created from within? Might it even be the void within? Is there an emptiness yearning to be filled?

Such a place actually exists within us. Of course, we may be like Mary who asks, "How can this be?" We may question, we may doubt, and that questioning and doubting are a natural part of the process. When we are ready to hear it, the Truth remains, quite simply and amazingly, that the Divine is seeking to be born within us. You may know what this experience is all about. You may have received the Baptism in the Holy Spirit. You may have experienced your own rebirth. There may be other ways in which the Divine is real to you.

If so, I suspect your experience may have come when you were especially vulnerable, receptive, and able to say, "Let it be!" The New Birth can occur somewhere out in Nature, or when we are very open and vulnerable to another person, or whenever we let go and allow God to enter us and touch our hearts.

Once the new birth has been conceived in us, then there is a time of inner growth. Women who have become pregnant, carried a child for nine months, and given birth have a distinct advantage in understanding the process: conception, pregnancy, and birth are an incredible Mystery and can be a deep spiritual experience for a woman.

In addition, this nine month growth period is a symbol of the rebirth process that is possible for all of us, males as well as females. For example, both sexes can experience something new struggling to be born in the midst of a mid-life crisis But the newness is not restricted to mid-life. It can happen at any age.

When we experience in ourselves something of the union with the divine and the new birth has occurred, then it is time for the friends to see the Child: the relatives come and so do the shepherds and the wise ones. In this realization of new life there is a feeling of amazement and great exultation, a song in the heart. It is time to rejoice.

And what might these figures represent? Joseph symbolizes that part of ourselves that serves as the protector of the mother and the New Life that has just been born. Joseph is attentive to what is going on and who is coming in and out of the place. Even at night he is alert because he pays attention to his dreams; he knows that they may contain the very information he needs for carrying out his task of protecting the new life from danger.

Shepherds live close to the earth. Symbolically, they care for our animal, instinctual nature. So bring your naturalness, your instincts and desires to be with the New Life. Look for those which are lost and are crying out to be found. They could be transformed with new power and energy.

Symbolically, the wise ones bring the treasures of the mind: your intellect, and all your rational faculties. Let them come into relationship with the New Life. Bring both your Shepherds and Your Wise Ones to that new Holy Center of your life and you may discover you are beginning to feel and think differently.

There is one character who is not usually portrayed in Nativity Scenes but is hidden away, King Herod. Consider what he might represent. A king has power, authority, and control. So why would a king be afraid of a baby? Maybe this baby will grow up and threaten the king. Nip the problem in the bud: kill the infant now if necessary.

There is no historical evidence of any king actually killing all these babies during the time when Jesus was born. But the symbolic truth remains: change in the soul can be a threat to our inner power structure, the parts of ourselves that want to remain in control, the standard operating procedures that do not want to yield. Change is difficult; we resist and fight against it.

Anyone who has a spiritual breakthrough, can anticipate an initial feeling of resolution and peace. Often this feeling is followed by a second reaction. For example, the person with a problem of drinking, drugs, gambling, or debt who has turned his life over to a Higher Power may first experience a feeling of great peace. Before long, however, the old forces and habits may come charging back and put up a fight. These forces, old patterns constellated in the symbol of Herod, do not want to be displaced.

The part of ourselves that provides inner law and order is necessary, but needs to be transformed. Otherwise it becomes dangerous to ourselves and to others. When the inner king lets go of his fears and comes to the Child, the New Life, not to kill it but to see what he might learn, then there is real movement toward wholeness.

Consider an example of spiritual rebirth: an unenlightened chief executive officer of a corporation for whom the bottom line is all that matters. A CEO can do some very unethical and destructive things, like manipulating excessive salaries for himself and a few others while putting large numbers of people out of work and destroying any sense of loyalty to and from employees. Through decisions made by this CEO, the company might also exploit workers in other countries and cause serious ecological damage. Yet there is hope. An unethical CEO could have an experience of enlightenment and come to realize that besides the bottom line there are other considerations: trust, loyalty, consideration for employees, suppliers, and the environment, just to mention a few factors. After coming into a new consciousness, will the CEO's old king, old standard operating procedures, adjust easily or are they likely to put up a fight first?

So is the Virgin Birth story true? Yes, it is very true! It describes our own inner spiritual process of Rebirth. It illustrates our potential and the process toward enlightenment.

Stop for a moment and consider each of the characters in the story as parts of yourself: Is there a virginal Mary within you ready for something new? Is there a child waiting to be born? Might there be Joseph, the protector, with his dreams? Are you in touch with your shepherds who have responsibility for guiding your instinctual animal energies? Are you acknowledging your wise ones with their treasures of the mind and intellect? Are there angels within carrying messages for you? Does your hidden King Herod have something to say? Is one of these characters in the story summoning your attention now?

I hope I have illustrated something of the tremendous value of the Nativity Stories. They carry at least two levels of mythic meaning: one presents, in symbolic language, the mystery of Jesus in whom the human and divine are fully integrated. The other provides the dynamics of our own spiritual rebirth.

It is my conviction that the Nativity stories, the Resurrection stories, and most stories in Holy Scripture contain both symbolic truth and historic truth. The two kinds of truth are woven together like the warp and woof in cloth. If the vertical strands in cloth are removed from the horizontal ones, the cloth falls apart and is lost. Instead of attempting to separate them from each other, why not enjoy the beauty of the whole cloth Mystery is wearing?

Note 1. Joseph Campbell defined myth as "a tale told to tell the truth" in a lecture given at the first Unitarian-Universalist Church, San Francisco, California, April 28, 1978.

Ninth Sunday Before Christmas

Reading *1 Samuel 1:1–7a, Tanakh*

There was a man from Ramathaim of the Zuphites, in the hill country of Ephraim, whose name was Elkanah son of Jeroham son of Elihu son of Tohu son of Zuph, an Ephraimite. He had two wives, one named Hannah and the other Peninnah; Peninnah had children, but Hannah was childless. This man used to go up from his town every year to worship and to offer sacrifice to the LORD of Hosts at Shiloh.—Hophni and Phinehas, the two sons of Eli, were priests of the LORD there.

One such day, Elkanah offered a sacrifice. He used to give portions to his wife Peninnah and to all her sons and daughters; but to Hannah he would give one portion only—though Hannah was his favorite—for the LORD had closed her womb. Moreover, her rival, to make her miserable, would taunt her that the LORD had closed her womb. This happened year after year.

Psalm *Ode 37*

I extend my hands to You, O Lord*
I lift my voice toward You, Most High.

I speak through the lips of my heart*
You hear me when my voice goes to You.
Your Word comes to me with fruit of my labor.*
You give me rest through Your grace, O Lord. Hallelujah!

Gospel *Infancy Gospel of James 1–2, SV*

According to the records of the twelve tribes of Israel, there once was a very rich man named Joachim. He always doubled the gifts he offered to the Lord, and would say to himself, "One gift, representing my prosperity, will be for all the people; the other, offered for forgiveness, will be my sin-offering to the Lord God."

Now the great day of the Lord was approaching, and the people of Israel were offering their gifts. And Reubel confronted Joachim and said, "You're not allowed to offer your gifts first because you haven't produced an Israelite child."

And Joachim became very upset and went to the book of the twelve tribes of the people, saying to himself, "I'm going to check the book of the twelve tribes of Israel to see whether I'm the only one in Israel who hasn't produced a child." And he searched the records and found that all the righteous people in Israel did indeed have children. And he remembered the patriarch because in his last days the Lord God had given a son, Isaac.

And so he continued to be very upset and did not see his wife but banished himself to the wilderness and pitched his tent there. And Joachim fasted 'forty days and forty nights.' He would say to himself, "I will not go back for food or drink until the Lord my God visits me. Prayer will be my food and drink."

Now his wife Anna was mourning and lamenting on two counts: "I lament my widowhood and I lament my childlessness."

The great day of the Lord approached, however, and Juthine her slave said to her, "How long are you going to humble yourself? Look, the great day of the Lord has arrived, and you're not supposed to mourn. Rather, take this headband which the mistress of the workshop gave to me, but which I'm not allowed to wear because I'm your slave and because it bears a royal insignia."

And Anna said, "Get away from me! I won't take it. The Lord God has greatly shamed me. Maybe a trickster has given you this, and you've come to make me share in your sin."

And Juthine the slave replied, "Should I curse you just because you haven't paid any attention to me? The Lord God has made your womb sterile so you won't bear any children for Israel."

Anna, too, became very upset. She took off her mourning clothes, washed her face, and put on her wedding dress. Then, in the middle of the afternoon, she went down to her garden to take a walk. She spied a laurel tree and sat down under it. After resting, she prayed to the Lord: "O God of my ancestors, bless me and hear my prayer, just as you blessed our mother Sarah and gave her a son, Isaac."

Eighth Sunday Before Christmas

Reading *1 Samuel 1:7b–19a, Tanakh*

Every time Hannah went up to the House of the LORD, Peninnah would taunt her, so that she wept and would not eat. Her husband Elkanah said to her, "Hannah, why are you crying and why aren't you eating? Why are you so sad? Am I not more devoted to you than ten sons?"

After they had eaten and drunk at Shiloh, Hannah rose and stood before the LORD. The priest Eli was sitting on the seat near the doorposts of the temple of the Lord. In her wretchedness, she prayed to the LORD, weeping all the while. And she made this vow: "O LORD of Hosts, if You will look upon the suffering of Your maidservant and will remember me and not forget Your maidservant, and if You will grant your maidservant a male child, I will dedicate him to the LORD for all the days of his life; and no razor shall ever touch his head."

As she kept on praying before the LORD, Eli watched her mouth. Now Hannah was praying in her heart; only her lips moved, but her voice could not be heard. So Eli thought she was drunk. Eli said to her, "How long will you make a drunken spectacle of yourself? Sober up!"

And Hannah replied, "Oh no, my lord! I am a very unhappy woman, I have drunk no wine or other strong drink, but I have been pouring out my heart to the LORD. Do not take your maidservant for a worthless woman; I have only been speaking all this time out of my anguish and distress."

"Then go in peace," said Eli, "and may the God of Israel grant you what you have asked of Him." She answered, "You are most kind to your handmaid." So the woman left, and she ate, and was no longer downcast. Early next morning they bowed low before the LORD, and they went back to Ramah.

Psalm *Ode 29*

Lord, You are my hope. With You I shall not be lost.*
    Through Your Praise You make me.
Through Your Goodness You give me common things.*
    Through Your Mercy You raise me up.
Through Your Beauty You set me on high.*
    You lead me out of the depths of Sheol, out of the mouth of
      death.
My enemies are laid low*
    and You justify me through Your Grace.
I believe in You, I believe in the Anointed One.*
    You come to me, show me Your sign, and lead me by Way of
      Your light.
You give me the rod of power*
    to subdue the dreams of others, to bring down the mighty,
to make war through Your Word*
    and come to victory through Your power.
Through Your Word You overthrow my enemy*
    who is like stubble blown away in the wind.
I praise You. You are Most High and You exalt me, Your ser-
    vant.*
    You exalt the son of Your handmaid. Hallelujah!

Gospel *Infancy Gospel of James 3–4, SV*

And Anna looked up toward the sky and saw a nest of sparrows in the laurel tree. And immediately Anna began to lament, saying to herself: "Poor me! Who gave birth to me? What sort of womb bore me? For I was born under a curse in the eyes of the people of Israel. And I've been reviled and mocked and banished from the temple of the Lord my God.

"Poor me! What am I like? I am not like the birds of the sky, because even the birds of the sky reproduce in your presence, O Lord.

"Poor me! What am I like? I am not like the domestic animals, because even domestic animals bear young in your presence, O Lord.

"Poor me! What am I like? I am not like the wild animals of the earth, because even the animals of the earth reproduce in your presence, O Lord.

"Poor me! I am not like these waters, because even these waters are productive in your presence, O Lord.

"Poor me! What am I like? I am not like this earth, because even the earth produces its crops in season and blesses you, O Lord."

Suddenly a messenger of the Lord appeared to her and said: "Anna, Anna, the Lord God has heard your prayer. You will conceive and give birth, and your child will be talked all over the world."

And Anna said, "As the Lord God lives, whether I give birth to a boy or a girl, I'll offer it as a gift to the Lord my God, and it will serve him its whole life."

And right then two messengers reported to her: "Look, your husband Joachim is coming back with his flocks." You see, a messenger of the Lord had come down to Joachim and said, "Joachim, Joachim, the Lord God has heard your prayer. Get down from there. Look, your wife Anna is pregnant."

And Joachim went down right away and summoned his shepherds with these instructions: "Bring me ten lambs without spot or blemish, and the ten lambs will be for the Lord God. Also, bring me twelve tender calves, and the twelve calves will be for the priests and the council of elders. Also, one hundred goats, and the one hundred goats will be for the whole people."

And so Joachim came with his flocks, while Anna stood at the gate. Then she spotted Joachim approaching with his flocks and rushed out and threw her arms around his neck: "Now I know that the Lord God has blessed me greatly. This widow is no longer a widow, and I, once childless, am now pregnant!"

And Joachim rested the first day at home.

Seventh Sunday Before Christmas

Reading *1 Samuel 1:19b–28, Tanakh*

Elkanah knew his wife Hannah and the LORD remembered her. Hannah conceived, and at the turn of the year bore a son. She named him Samuel, meaning, "I asked the LORD for him." And when the man Elkanah and all his household were going up to offer to the LORD the annual sacrifice and his votive sacrifice, Hannah did not go up. She said to her husband, "When the child is weaned, I will bring him. For when he had appeared before the LORD, he must remain there for good." Her husband Elkanah said to her, "Do as you think best. Stay home until you have weaned him. May the LORD fulfill the utterance of your mouth. May the LORD fulfill His word." So the woman stayed home and nursed her son until she weaned him.

When she had weaned him, she took him up with her, along with three bulls, one ephah of flour, and a jar of wine. And though the boy was still very young, she brought him to the House of the LORD at Shiloh. After slaughtering the bull, they brought the boy to Eli. She said, "Please, my lord! As you live, my lord, I am a woman who stood here beside you and prayed to the LORD. It was this boy I prayed for; and the LORD granted me what I asked of Him. I, in turn, hereby lend him to the LORD. For as long as he lives he is lent to the LORD." And they bowed low there before the LORD.

Psalm *1 Samuel 2:1–11*

And Hannah prayed:
My heart exults in the LORD;*
    I have triumphed through the LORD.
I gloat over my enemies;*
    I rejoice in your deliverance.
There is no holy one like the LORD,*
    Truly, there is none beside You;
There is no rock like our God.*
    Talk no more with lofty pride,
Let no arrogance cross your lips!*
    For the LORD is an all knowing God;

By him actions are measured.*
    The bows of the mighty are broken,
    And the faltering are girded with strength.
Men once sated must hire out for bread;*
    Men once hungry hunger no more.
While the barren woman bears seven,*
    The mother of many is forlorn.
The LORD deals death and gives life,*
    casts down Sheol and raises up.
The LORD makes poor and makes rich;*
    He casts down, He also lifts high.
He raises the poor from the dust,*
    Lifts up the needy from the dunghill,
Setting them with nobles,*
    Granting them seats of honor.
For the pillars of the earth are the LORD'S;*
    He has set the world upon them.
He guards the steps of His faithful,*
    But the wicked perish in darkness —
    For not by strength shall man prevail.
The foes of the LORD shall be shattered;*
    He will thunder against them in the heavens.
The LORD will judge the ends of the earth.*
    He will give power to His King,
    And triumph to his anointed one.
    Then Elkanah and Hannah went home to Ramah; and the boy entered the service of the LORD under the priest Eli.

Gospel *Infancy Gospel of James 5–6, SV*

But on the next day, as he was presenting his gifts, he thought to himself, "If the Lord God has really been merciful to me, the polished disc on the priest's headband will make it clear to me." And so Joachim was presenting his gifts and paying attention to the priest's headband until he went up to the altar of the Lord. And he saw no sin in it. And Joachim said, "Now I know that the Lord God has been merciful to me and has forgiven me all my sins." And he came down from the temple of the Lord acquitted and went back home.

And so her pregnancy came to term, and in the ninth month Anna gave birth. And she said, "Is it a boy or a girl?"

And her midwife said, "I have been greatly honored this day." Then the midwife put the child to bed.

When, however, the prescribed days were completed, Anna cleansed herself of the flow of blood. And she offered her breast to the infant and gave her the name Mary.

Day by day the infant grew stronger. When she was six months old, her mother put her on the ground to see if she could stand. She walked seven steps and went to her mother's arms. Then her mother picked her up again and said, "As the Lord my God lives, you will never walk on this ground again until I take you into the temple of the Lord."

And so she turned her bedroom into a sanctuary and did not permit anything profane or unclean to pass the child's lips. She sent for the undefiled daughters of the Hebrews, and they kept her amused.

Now the child has her first birthday, and Joachim gave a great banquet and invited the high priests, priests, scholars, council of elders, and all the people of Israel. Joachim presented the child to the priests and they blessed her: God of our fathers, bless this child and give her a name which will be on the lips of future generations forever."

And everyone said, "So be it. Amen."

He presented her to the high priests, and they blessed her: "Most high God, look on this child and bless her with the ultimate blessing, one which cannot be surpassed."

Her mother then took her up to the sanctuary — the bedroom—and gave her breast to the child. And Anna composed a song for the Lord God:

"I will sing a sacred song to the Lord my God because he has visited me and taken away the disgrace attributed to me by my enemies. The Lord my God has given me the fruit of his righteousness, single yet manifold before him.

Who will announce to the sons of Reubel that Anna has a child at her breast?

'Listen, listen, you twelve tribes of Israel: Anna has a child at her breast!'"

Anna made her rest in the bedroom — the sanctuary — and

then went out and began serving her guests. When the banquet was over, they left in good spirits and praised the God of Israel.

Sixth Sunday Before Christmas

Reading *Genesis 28:10–17, Tanakh*

Jacob left Beersheba, and set out for Haran. He came upon a certain place and stopped there for the night, for the sun had set. Taking one of the stones of that place, he put it under his head and lay down in that place. He had a dream; a ladder was set on the ground and its top reached to the sky, and angels of God were going up and down on it. And the LORD was standing beside him and He said, "I am the LORD, the God of your father Abraham and the God of Isaac: the ground on which you are lying I will assign to you and to your offspring. Your descendants shall be as the dust of the earth; you shall spread out to the west and to the east, to the north and to the south. All the families of the earth shall bless themselves by you and your descendants. Remember, I am with you: I will protect you wherever you go and will bring you back to this land. I will not leave you until I have done what I have promised you."

Jacob woke from his sleep and said, "Surely the LORD is present in this place, and I did not know it!" Shaken, he said, "How awesome is this place! This is none other than the abode of God, and that is the gateway to heaven."

Psalm *Psalm 87, BCP 1979*

On the holy mountain stands the city he has founded;*
    the LORD loves the gates of Zion more than all the dwellings
      of Jacob.
Glorious things are spoken of you,*
    O city of our God.
I count Egypt and Babylon among those who know me;*
    behold Philistia, Tyre, and Ethiopia: in Zion were they born.
Of Zion it shall be said, "Everyone was born in her,*
    and the Most High himself shall sustain her."
The LORD will record as he enrolls the peoples,*
    "These also were born there."

The singers and the dancers will say,*
"All my fresh springs are in you."

Gospel *Infancy Gospel of James 7–8, SV*

Many months passed, but when the child reached two years of age, Joachim said, "Let's take her up to the temple of the Lord, so that we can keep the promise we made, or else the Lord will be angry with us and our gift will be unacceptable."

And Anna said, "Let's wait until she is three, so she won't miss her father or mother."

And Joachim agreed: "Let's wait."

When the child turned three years of age, Joachim said, "Let's send for the undefiled Hebrew daughters. Let them each take a lamp and light it, so the child won't turn back and have her heart captivated by things outside the Lord's temple." And this is what they did until the time they ascended to the Lord's temple.

The priest welcomed her, kissed her, and blessed her: "The Lord God has exalted your name among all generations. In you the Lord will disclose his redemption to the people of Israel during the last days."

And he sat her down on the third step of the altar, and the Lord showered favor on her. And she danced, and the whole house of Israel loved her.

Her parents left for home marveling and praising and glorifying the Lord God because the child did not look back at them. And Mary lived in the temple of the Lord. She was fed there like a dove, receiving her food from the hand of a heavenly messenger.

When she turned twelve, however, there was a meeting of the priests. "Look," they said, "Mary has turned twelve in the temple of the Lord. What should we do with her so she won't pollute the sanctuary of the Lord our God?" And they said to the high priest, "You stand at the altar of the Lord. Enter and pray about her, and we'll do whatever the Lord God discloses to you."

And so the high priest took the vestment with the twelve bells, entered the Holy of Holies, and began to pray about her. And suddenly a messenger of the Lord appeared: "Zechariah,

Zechariah, go out and assemble the widowers of the people and have them each bring a staff. She will become the wife of the one to whom the Lord God shows a sign." And so heralds covered the surrounding territory of Judea. The trumpet of the Lord sounded and all the widowers came running.

Fifth Sunday Before Christmas

Reading *Ladder of Jacob 7:1–35, OTP*

And as for the angels you saw descending and ascending the ladder, in the last years there will be a man from the Most High, and he will desire to join the upper (things) with the lower. And before his coming your sons and daughters will tell about him and your young men will have visions about him.

Such will be the signs at the time of his coming.

A tree cut with an ax will bleed, three-month-old babes will speak understanding; a baby in the womb of his mother will speak this way; a youth will be like an old man. And then the unexpected will come, whose path will not be noticed by anyone.

Then the earth will be glorified, receiving heavenly glory. What was above will be below also. And from your seed will bloom a root of kings; it will emerge and overthrow the power of Eve. And he himself will be the Savior for every land and rest for those who toil, and a cloud shading the whole world from the burning heat. For otherwise the uncontrolled will not be controlled. If he does not come, the lower (things) cannot be joined with the upper.

At his coming the idols of brass, stone, and any sort of carving will give voice for three days. They will give wise men news of him and let them know what will be on earth. By a star, those who wish to see on earth him whom the angels do not see above will find the way to him.

Then the Almighty will be on earth in body, and embraced by corporeal arms, he will restore human nature. And he will revive Eve, who died by the fruit of the tree. Then the deceit of the impious will be exposed and all the idols will fall face down. For they will be put to shame by a dignitary. For because (they were) lying by means of hallucinations, henceforth they will not be able to rule or prophesy. Honor will be taken from them and they will remain without glory.

For he who comes will take power and might and will give Abraham the truth which he previously told him. Everything sharp he will make dull, and the rough will be smooth. And he will cast all the iniquitous into the depths of the sea. He will work wonders in heaven and on earth. And he will be wounded in the midst of his beloved house. And when he is wounded, then salvation will be ready, and the end to all perdition. For those who have wounded him will themselves receive a wound which will not be cured in them forever. And all creation will bow to him who was wounded, and many will trust in him. And he will become known everywhere in all lands, and those who acknowledge his name will not be ashamed. His own dominion and years will be unending forever.

Psalm *Ode 33*

Grace raced away from the Corrupter,*
    then turned her back on him to denounce him.
He left utter havoc around him and spoiled his constructions.*
    He stood on a summit and screamed from one end of the
    earth to the other.
He drew near those who obeyed him. He did not look evil.*
    Yet a perfect Virgin stood near and cried,
"Sons and daughters, come back, leave the Corrupter.*
    Do not destroy yourself. Do not perish. Come to me.
I will enter you and lead you out of devastation.*
    I will make you wise in the Way of truth.
Hear me and be saved. I tell you of God's grace.*
    By me you will be redeemed and blessed.
I am your judge. Those who help me will not be injured.*
    They will possess purity in a fresh world.
My chosen walks in me. I will inform those who seek me.*
    I will make them trust my name." Hallelujah!

Gospel *Infancy Gospel of James 9–10, SV*

And Joseph, too, threw down his carpenter's axe and left for the meeting. When they had all gathered, they went to the high priest with their staffs. After the high priest had collected everyone's staff, he entered the temple and began to pray. When he had finished his prayer, he took the staffs and went out and began to give them back to each man. But there was no sign on any of them. Joseph got the last staff. Suddenly a dove came out of his staff and perched on Joseph's head, "Joseph, Joseph," the high priest said, "you've been chosen by lot to take the virgin of the Lord into your care and protection."

But Joseph objected: "I already have sons and I'm an old man; she's only a young woman. I'm afraid that I'll become the butt of jokes among the people of Israel."

And the high priest responded, "Joseph, fear the Lord your God and remember what God did to Dathan, Abiron,. and Kore: the earth was split open and they were all swallowed up because of their objection. So now, Joseph, you ought to take heed so that the same thing won't happen to your family."

And so out of fear Joseph took her into his care and protection. He said to her, "Mary, I've gotten you from the temple of the Lord, but now I'm leaving you at home. I'm going to build houses, but I'll come back to you. The Lord will protect you."

Meanwhile, there was a council of the priests, who agreed: "Let's make a veil for the temple of the Lord."

And the high priest said, "Summon the true virgins from the tribe of David." And so the temple assistants left and searched everywhere and found seven. And the high priest then remembered the girl Mary, that she, too, was from the tribe of David and was pure in God's eyes. And so the temple assistants went out and got her.

And they took the maidens into the temple of the Lord. And the high priest said, "Cast lots for me to decide who'll spin which threads for the veil: the gold, the white, the linen, the silk, the violet, the scarlet, and the true purple."

And the true purple and scarlet threads fell to Mary. And she took them and returned home. Now it was at this time that Zechariah became mute, and Samuel took his place until Zechariah regained his speech. Meanwhile, Mary had taken up the scarlet thread and was spinning it.

Commentary Mary is given the work of making the veil (curtain) for the Temple which, at the death of her son, Jesus, will be

"torn in two, from top to bottom" Mark 15:38 thus opening the
Way into the Holy of Holies. Note Hebrews 9:1–10

First Sunday of Advent
(Fourth Sunday Before Christmas)

Reading *Testament of Adam 3, OTP*

Adam said to his son, Seth, "You have heard, my son, that
God is going to come into the world after a long time, he will
be conceived of a virgin and put on a body, be born like a
human being, and grow up as a child. He will perform signs
and wonders on the earth, will walk on the waves of the sea.
He will rebuke the winds and they will be silenced. He will
motion to the waves and they will stand still. He will open the
eyes of the blind and cleanse the lepers.

He will cause the deaf to hear, and the mute to speak. He
will straighten the hunchbacked, strengthen the paralyzed, find
the lost, drive out evil spirits, and cast out demons.

"He spoke to me about this in Paradise after I picked some
of the fruit in which death was hiding: 'Adam, Adam do not
fear. You wanted to be a god; I will make you a god, not right
now, but after a space of many years. I am consigning you to
death, and the maggot and the worm will eat your body.'

"And I answered and said to him, 'Why, my Lord?' And he
said to me, 'Because you listened to the words of the serpent,
you and your posterity will be food for the serpent. But after a
short time there will be mercy on you because you were created
in my image, and I will not leave you to waste away in Sheol.

For your sake I will be born of the Virgin Mary. For your
sake I will taste death and enter the house of the dead. For your
sake I will make a new heaven, and I will be established over
your posterity. And after three days, while I am in the tomb, I
will raise up the body I received from you. And I will set you at
the right hand of my divinity. And I will make you a god just
like you wanted. And I will receive favor from God and I will
restore to you and to your posterity that which is the justice of
heaven.' . . ."

And I, Seth, wrote this testament. And my father died, and
they buried him at the east of Paradise opposite the first city

built on the earth, which was named after Enoch. And Adam was borne to his grave by the angels and powers of heaven because he had been created in the image of God. And the sun and the moon were darkened, and there was thick darkness for seven days.

And we sealed the testament and we put it in the cave with the treasures with the offerings Adam had taken out of Paradise, gold and myrrh and frankincense. And the sons of kings, the magi, will come and get them, and they will take them to the son of God, to Bethlehem of Judea, to the cave.

Psalm *Ode 14*

As the eyes of a child turn toward father, so my eyes turn to
>   You, Lord,*
>   at all times You are my consolation and joy.
Do not turn Your mercy from me, O Lord, nor Your kindness,*
>   but stretch out Your right hand and be my guide to the end.
Care for me, save me from evil,*
>   and let Your serenity and love be with me.
Teach me to sing of truth*
>   that I may produce fruit in You.
Open to me the harp of Your Holy Spirit*
>   so I may praise You, Lord, with all its notes.
From Your sea of mercy help me;*
>   help me in the hour of my need. Hallelujah!

Gospel *Infancy Gospel of James 11–12, SV*

And she took her water jar and went out to fill it with water. Suddenly there was a voice saying to her, "Greetings, favored one! The Lord is with you. Blessed are you among women." Mary began looking around, both right and left, to see where the voice was coming from. She became terrified and went home. After putting the water jar down and taking up the purple thread, she sat down on her chair and began to spin.

A heavenly messenger suddenly stood before her: "Don't be afraid, Mary. You see, you've found favor in the sight of the Lord of all. You will conceive by means of his word."

But as she listened, Mary was doubtful and said, "If I actually conceive by the Lord, the living God, will I also give birth the way women usually do?"

And the messenger of the Lord replied, "No, Mary, because the power of God will overshadow you. Therefore, the child to be born will be called holy, son of the Most High. And you will name him Jesus — the name means 'he will save his people from their sins.'"

And Mary said, "Here I am, the Lord's slave before him. I pray that all you've told me comes true."

And she finished spinning the purple and the scarlet thread and took her work up to the high priest. The high priest accepted them and praised her and said, "Mary, the Lord God has extolled your name, and so you will be blessed by all the generations of the earth."

Mary rejoiced and left to visit her relative Elizabeth. She knocked at the door. Elizabeth heard her, tossed aside the scarlet thread, ran to the door, and opened it for her. And she blessed her and said, "Who am I that the mother of my Lord should visit me? You see, the baby inside me has jumped for joy and blessed you."

But Mary forgot the mysteries which the heavenly messenger Gabriel had spoken, and she looked up to the sky and said, "Who am I that every generation on earth will congratulate me now?"

She spent three months with Elizabeth. Day by day her womb kept swelling. And so Mary became frightened, returned home, and hid from the people of Israel. She was just sixteen years old when these mysterious things happened to her.

Second Sunday of Advent
(Third Sunday Before Christmas)

Reading *Deuteronomy 22:23–24, Tanakh*

In the case of a virgin who is engaged to a man — if a man comes upon her in town and lies with her, you shall take the two of them out to the gate of that town and stone them to death: the girl because she did not cry out for help in the town, and the man because he violated another man's wife. Thus you will sweep away evil from your midst.

Psalm *Ode 38:1–6*

> I move up into the light of Truth as into a chariot*
>> and Truth takes me and causes me to come.
> Truth causes me to pass across canyons and ravines*
>> and preserves me against waves smashing against cliffs.
> Truth is my haven of salvation*
>> and puts me in the arms of Eternal life.
> Truth goes with me, soothes me, keeps me from error,*
>> because You were and are the Truth.
> There is no danger for me because I constantly walk with You.*
>> When I obey You, I am not in error.
> Error flees from You and never meets You.*
>> Truth proceeds on the upright Way.

Gospel *Infancy Gospel of James 13–14, SV*

Mary was in her sixth month when one day Joseph came home from his building projects, entered his house, and found her pregnant. He struck himself in the face, threw himself to the ground on sackcloth, and began to cry bitterly: "What sort of face should I present to the Lord God? What prayer can I say on her behalf since I received her as a virgin from the temple of the Lord God and didn't protect her? Who has set this trap for me? Who has done this evil deed in my house? Who has lured this virgin away from me and violated her? The story of Adam has been repeated in my case, hasn't it? For just as Adam was praying when the serpent came and found Eve alone, deceived her, and corrupted her, so the same thing has happened to me."

So Joseph got up from the sackcloth and summoned Mary and said to her, "God has taken a special interest in you — how could you have done this? Have you forgotten the Lord your God? Why have you brought shame on yourself, you who were raised in the Holy of Holies and fed by a heavenly messenger?"

But she began to cry bitter tears: "I'm innocent. I haven't had sex with any man."

And Joseph said to her, "Then where did the child you're carrying come from?"

And she replied, "As the Lord my God lives, I don't know where it came from."

And Joseph became very frightened and no longer spoke with

her as he pondered what he was going to do with her. And Joseph said to himself, "If I try to cover up her sin, I'll end up going against the law of the Lord. And if I disclose her condition to the people of Israel, I'm afraid that the child inside her might be heaven-sent and I'll end up handing innocent blood over to a death sentence. So what should I do with her? I know, I'll divorce her quietly."

But when night came a messenger of the Lord suddenly appeared to him in a dream and said: "Don't be afraid of this girl, because the child in her is the Holy Spirit's doing. She will have a son and you will name him Jesus — the name means 'he will save his people from their sins.'" And Joseph got up from his sleep and praised the God of Israel, who had given him this favor. And so he began to protect the girl.

Commentary Joseph is aware of the unfairness in which he would "end up handing innocent blood over to a death sentence." This terrible law blames the victim who is raped! Because she is so frightened that she does not cry out, she is stoned along with the one who raped her. This mythic story challenges an unfair portion of the Deuteronomic law.

Third Sunday of Advent
(Second Sunday Before Christmas)

Reading *Isaiah 7:10–14, Tanakh*

The Lord spoke further to Ahaz: "Ask for a sign from the LORD your God, anywhere down to Sheol or up to the sky." But Ahaz replied, "I will not ask, and I will not test the LORD." "Listen, House of David," Isaiah retorted, "is it not enough for you to treat men as helpless that you also treat my God as helpless? Assuredly, my Lord sill give you a sign of His own accord! Look the woman is with child and about to give birth to a son. Let her name him Immanuel.

Psalm *Ode 38:7–14*

Whatever I do not understand, You make clear to me.*
> You warn me of all the drugs of error and pains of death which some consider sweetness.

You expose the corrupting of the Corrupter,*
    the corrupting Bride and corrupting Bridegroom.
When I ask Truth, "Who are these?"*
    You respond, "This is the Deceiver and the Error."
They imitate the Beloved and his Bride*
    They cause the world to err and be corrupted.
They invite many to an imitation wedding feast*
    and allow them to drink wine of their intoxication.
They cause many to vomit up their wisdom and their knowl-
    edge,*
    make them senseless, and abandon them.
Those invited stumble about mad and corrupted*
    with no understanding and no desire to seek it.
You make me wise so as not to fall into the hands of deceivers,*
    I rejoice when Truth goes with me.
You plant me and I am established and live and am saved*
    Your hands lay my foundation and I am secure.

Gospel *Infancy Gospel of James 15–16, SV*

Then Annas the scholar came to him and said to him, "Joseph, why haven't you attended our assembly?" And he replied to him, "Because I was worn out from the trip and rested my first day home."

Then Annas turned and saw that Mary was pregnant.

He left in a hurry for the high priest and said to him, "You remember Joseph, don't you — the man you yourself vouched for? Well, he has committed a serious offense."

And the high priest asked, "In what way?"

Joseph has violated the virgin he received from the temple of the Lord," he replied. "He had his way with her and hasn't disclosed his action to the people of Israel."

And the high priest asked him, "Has Joseph really done this?"

And he replied, "Send temple assistants and you'll find the virgin pregnant."

And so the temple assistants went and found her just as Annas had reported, and then they brought her, along with Joseph, to the court.

"Mary, why have you done this?" the high priest asked her.

"Why have you humiliated yourself? Have you forgotten the Lord your God, you who were raised in the Holy of Holies and were fed by the heavenly messengers? You of all people, who heard their hymns and danced for them — why have you done this?"

And she wept bitterly: "As the Lord God lives, I stand innocent before him. Believe me, I've not had sex with any man."

And the high priest said, "Joseph, why have you done this?"

And Joseph said, "As the Lord lives, I am innocent where she is concerned."

And the high priest said, "Don't perjure yourself, but tell the truth. You've had your way with her and haven't disclosed this action to the people of Israel. And you haven't humbled yourself under God's mighty hand, so that your offspring might be blessed."

But Joseph was silent.

Then the high priest said, "Return the virgin you received from the temple of the Lord."

And Joseph, bursting into tears . . .

And the high priest said, "I'm going to give you the Lord's drink test, and it will disclose your sin clearly to both of you."

And the high priest took the water and made Joseph drink it and sent him into the wilderness, but he returned unharmed. And he made the girl drink it, too, and sent her into the wilderness. She also came back unharmed. And everybody was surprised because their sin had not been revealed. And so the high priest said, "If the Lord God had not exposed your sin, then neither do I condemn you." And he dismissed them. Joseph took Mary and returned home celebrating and praising the God of Israel.

Commentary The primitive drink test is found in Num 5:12ff

Fourth Sunday of Advent
(Sunday Next Before Christmas)
Reading *Genesis 25:19–26, Tanakh*

This is the story of Isaac, son of Abraham. Abraham begot Isaac. Isaac was forty years old when he took to wife Rebekah, daughter of Bethuel, the Aramean of Paddan-aram, sister of Laban the Aramean. Isaac pleaded with the LORD on behalf of his wife, because she was barren; and the LORD responded to his plea, and his wife Rebekah conceived.

But the children struggled inside her womb, and she said, "If so, why do I exist?" She went to inquire of the LORD, and the LORD answered her,

"Two nations are in your womb,
Two separate people shall be mightier than the other,
And the older shall serve the younger."

When her time to give birth was at hand, there were twins in her womb. The first one emerged red, like a hairy mantle all over; so they named him Esau. Then his brother emerged, holding on to the heel of Esau; so they named him Jacob. Isaac was sixty years old when they were born.

Psalm *Ode 38:15–19*

You plant me and I am established and live and am saved*
    Your hands lay my foundation and I am secure.
Truth sets the root, waters, adapts, and blesses*
    Truth yields fruits forever.
Truth penetrates deeply, springs up, and spreads out.*
    Truth is full and growing.
I praise You, Lord, in Your planting and cultivation,*
    in Your care and the blessing of Your lips.
I praise You in the beautiful planting of Your right hand,*
    in the fruition of Your planting in the understanding of the
        mind.

Gospel *Infancy Gospel of James 17*

Now an order came from Emperor Augustus that everybody in Bethlehem of Judea be enrolled in the census. And Joseph wondered, "I'll enroll my sons, but what am I going to do with this girl? How will I enroll her? As my wife? I'm ashamed to do that. As my daughter? The people of Israel know she's not my daughter. How this is to be decided depends on the Lord."

And so he saddled his donkey and had her get on it. His son led it and Samuel brought up the rear. As they neared the three mile marker, Joseph turned around and saw that she was sulking. And he said to himself, "Perhaps the baby she is carrying is causing her discomfort." Joseph turned around again and saw her laughing and said to her, "Mary, what's going on with you? One minute I see you laughing and the next minute you're sulking."

And she replied, "Joseph, it's because I imagine two peoples in front of me, one weeping and mourning and the other celebrating and jumping for joy."

Halfway through the trip Mary said to him, "Joseph, help me down from the donkey — the child inside me is about to be born."

And he helped her down and said to her, "Where will I take you to give you some privacy, since this place is out in the open?"

Christmas Season

In order to give a taste for the richness of symbolic material that surrounds the Holy Birth, readings are provided for the Twelve Days of Christmas, December 25 through January 6.

Many congregations will assemble as a body for worship only on Christmas Eve and Christmas Day along with the Sundays between Christmas and Epiphany on January 6. Creative liturgists may wish to review the stories in the entire twelve days and decide which sets to use on Sundays after Christmas. The remainder of the material may be useful in sermons or in study groups.

During the Christmas Season this lectionary features the Infancy Gospel of Thomas with its fanciful tales of Jesus' childhood.

Christmas Day, December 25

Reading *Sibylline Oracles, Book 10, lines 456–479, OTP*

In the last times God changed the earth and, coming late as a new light, he rose from the womb of the Virgin Mary. Coming from heaven, he put on a mortal form. First, then Gabriel was revealed in his strong and holy person. Second, the archangel also addressed the maiden in speech:

"Receive God, Virgin, in your immaculate bosom." Thus speaking, he breathed in the grace of God, even to one who was always a maiden. Fear, and at the same time, wonder seized her as she listened. She stood trembling. Her mind fluttered while her heart was shaken by the unfamiliar things she heard.

But again she rejoiced, and her heart was healed by the voice. The maiden laughed and reddened her cheek, rejoicing with joy and enchanted in her heart with awe. Courage also came over her.

A word flew to her womb. In time it was made flesh and came to life in the womb, and was fashioned in mortal form and became a boy by virgin birth.

For this is a great wonder to men, but nothing is a great wonder for God the Father and God the Son. The joyful earth fluttered to the child at its birth. The heavenly throne laughed and the world rejoiced. A wondrous, new shining star was venerated by Magi. The newborn child was revealed in a manger to those who obey God: cowherds and goatherds and shepherd of sheep. And Bethlehem was said to be the divinely named homeland of the Word.

Psalm *Ode 19*

A cup of milk is offered to me*
    and I drink its sweetness as the delight of the Lord.
The Son is the cup and the Father is the one Who is milked.*
    The Holy Spirit is she who milks him.
His breasts are full*
    and his milk should not drip out wastefully.
The Holy Spirit opens the Father's bosom*
    and mingles the milk from the Father's two breasts.
She gives that mingling to the world, which is unknowing.*
    Those who drink it are near the Father's right hand.
The Spirit opens the Virgin's womb and she receives the milk.*
    The Virgin becomes a mother of great mercy;
She labors and bears a Son without pain.*
    No midwife comes.
She bears him strongly, openly, with dignity, with kindness.*
    She loves him, swaddles him, and reveals his majesty.

Gospel *Infancy Gospel of James 18–19, SV*

Joseph found a cave nearby and took Mary inside. He stationed his sons to guard her and went to look for a Hebrew midwife in the country around Bethlehem.

"Now I, Joseph, was walking along and yet not going anywhere. I looked up at the vault of the sky and saw it standing still, and then at the clouds and saw them paused in amazement, and at the birds of the sky suspended in midair. As I looked on the earth, I saw a bowl lying there and workers reclining around it with their hands in the bowl; some were chewing and yet did not chew; some were picking up something to eat and yet did not pick it up; and some were putting food in their mouths and yet did not do so. Instead, they were all looking upward.

"I saw sheep being driven along and yet the sheep stood still; the shepherd was lifting his hand to strike them, and yet his hand remained raised. And I observed the current of the river and saw goats with their mouths in the water and yet they were not drinking. Then all of a sudden everything and everybody went on with what they had been doing.

"Then I saw a woman coming down from the hill country, and she asked, 'Where are you going, sir?'

"I replied, 'I am looking for a Hebrew midwife.'

"She inquired, 'Are you an Israelite?'

"I told her, 'Yes.'

"And she said, 'And who's the one having a baby in the cave?'

"I replied, 'My fiancee.'

"And she continued, 'She isn't your wife?'

"I said to her, 'She is Mary, who was raised in the temple of the Lord; I obtained her by lot as my wife. But she's not really my wife; she's pregnant by the Holy Spirit.'

"The midwife said, 'Really?'"

Joseph responded, "Come and see."

And the midwife went with him. As they stood in front of the cave, a dark cloud overshadowed it. The midwife said, "I've really been privileged, because today my eyes have seen a miracle in that salvation has come to Israel."

Suddenly the cloud withdrew from the cave and an intense light appeared inside the cave, so that their eyes could not bear to look. And a little later that light receded until an infant became visible; he took the breast of his mother Mary.

Then the midwife shouted: "What a great day this is for me because I've seen this new miracle!"

And the midwife left the cave and met Salome and said to

her, "Salome, Salome, let me tell you about a new marvel: a virgin has given birth, and you know that's impossible!"

And Salome replied, "As the Lord my God lives, unless I insert my finger and examine her, I will never believe that a virgin has given birth."

December 26

Reading *Exodus 1:15–21, Tanakh*

The king of Egypt spoke to the Hebrew midwives, one of whom was named Shiphrah and the other Puah, saying, "When you deliver the Hebrew women, look at the birthstool: if it is a boy, kill him; if it is a girl, let her live." The midwives, fearing God, did not do as the king of Egypt had told them; they let the boys live. So the king of Egypt summoned the midwives and said to them, "'Why have you done this thing, letting the boys live?" The midwives said to Pharaoh, "Because the Hebrew women are not like the Egyptian women: they are vigorous. Before the midwife can come to them, they have given birth."

And God dealt well with the midwives; and the people multiplied and increased greatly.

Psalm *Select a Christmas Carol*

Gospel *Infancy Gospel of James 20, SV*

The midwife entered and said, "Mary, position yourself for an examination. You are facing a serious test."

And so Mary, when she heard these instructions, positioned herself, and Salome inserted her finger into Mary. And then Salome cried aloud and said, "I'll be damned because of my transgression and my disbelief; I have put the living God on trial. Look! My hand is disappearing! It's being consumed by the flames!"

Then Salome fell on her knees in the presence of the Lord, with these words: "God of my ancestors, remember me because I am a descendant of Abraham, Isaac, and Jacob. Do not make an example of me for the people of Israel, but give me a place among the poor again. You yourself know, Lord, that I've been healing people in your name and have been receiving payment from you."

And suddenly a messenger of the Lord appeared, saying to her, "Salome, Salome, the Lord of all has heard your prayer. Hold out your hand to the child and pick him up, and then you'll have salvation and joy."

Salome approached the child and picked him up with these words: "I'll worship him because he's been born to be king of Israel." And Salome was instantly healed and left the cave vindicated.

Then a voice said, abruptly, "Salome, Salome, don't report the marvels you've seen until the child goes to Jerusalem."

Commentary The midwife story is built upon its predecessor in the story of the birth of Moses. In both, the child is born before the midwife comes.

Salome inserting her finger is similar to the story of Thomas saying he would not believe unless he put his finger into the print of the nails. (John 20:25)

December 27

First Reading *Isaiah 1:1–4, Tanakh*

Hear, O heavens, and give ear, O earth,
For the LORD has spoken:
I reared children and brought them up —
And they have rebelled against Me!
An ox knows its owner,
An ass its master's crib:
Israel does not know,
My people takes no thought."
Ah, sinful nation!
People laden with iniquity!
Brood of evildoers!
Depraved children!
They have forsaken the LORD,
Spurned the Holy One of Israel,
Turned their backs on Him.

Christmas

Second Reading *Sibylline Oracles, Book I, lines 324–355, OTP*

Then indeed the son of the great God will come, incarnate, likened to mortal men on earth . . . Consider in your heart Christ, the son of the most high, immortal God. He will fulfill the law of God — not destroy it — bearing a likeness which corresponds to types, and he will teach everything.

Priests will bring gifts to him, bringing forward gold, myrrh, and incense.

For he will also do all these things.

But when a certain voice will come through the desert land bringing tidings to mortals, and will cry out to all to make the paths straight and cast away evils from the heart, and that every human person may be illumined by waters, so that being born from above they may no longer in any respect at all transgress justice — but a man with barbarous mind, enslaved to dances will cut out this voice and give it as a reward — then there will suddenly be a sign to mortals when a beautiful stone which has been preserved will come from the land of Egypt. Against this the people of the Hebrews will stumble. But the gentiles will be gathered under his leadership. For they will also recognize God who rules on high on account of this man's path in common light.

For he will show eternal life to chosen men but will bring fire upon the lawless for all ages. Then indeed he will cure the sick and all who are blemished, as many as put faith in him. The blind will see, the lame will walk. The deaf will hear. Those who cannot speak will speak. He will drive out demons. There will be a resurrection of the dead. He will walk the waves, and in a desert place he will satisfy five thousand from five loaves and a fish of the sea, and the leftovers of these will fill twelve baskets for the hope of the peoples.

Psalm *Select a Christmas Carol*

Gospel *The Gospel of Pseudo Matthew 14, NTA*

On the third day after the birth of our Lord Jesus Christ holy Mary went out from the cave, and went into a stable and put her child in a manger, and an ox and an ass worshiped him. Then was fulfilled that which was said through the prophet Isaiah, "The ox knows his owner and the ass his mother's crib."

Thus the beasts, ox and ass, with him between them, unceasingly worshipped him. Then was fulfilled what was said through the prophet Habakkuk, "Between two beasts are you known." And Joseph remained in the same place with Mary for three days.

Commentary Most nativity scenes include animals, not only the sheep, but also "the ox and the ass." These animals are also featured in Christmas carols. Yet they are not mentioned in any of the first or second century nativity stories. In written form, they arrive late on the scene in the Gospel of Pseudo Matthew which originated in the eighth or ninth century.

December 28

Reading *Infancy Gospel of James 21–22, NTA*

There took place a great tumult in Bethlehem of Judea. For there came wise men saying, "Where is the newborn king of the Jews? For we have seen his star in the east and have come to worship him." When Herod heard this he was troubled and sent officers to the wise men, and sent for them and they told him about the star.

Herod also sent for the high priests and questioned them: "How is it written concerning the Messiah? Where is he born?" They said to him, "In Bethlehem of Judea; for so it is written." And he let them go.

And Herod questioned the wise men and said to them, "What sign did you see concerning the newborn king?" And the wise men said, "We saw how an indescribably greater star shone among those stars and dimmed them, so that they no longer shone; and so we knew that a king was born for Israel. And we have come to worship him." And Herod said, "Go and seek, and when you have found him, tell me, that I also may come to worship him."

And the wise men went forth. And behold, the star which they had seen in the east, went before them until they came to the cave. And the star stood over the head of the child (the cave). And the wise men saw the young child with Mary his mother, and they took out of their bags gifts, gold, and frankincense and myrrh.

Christmas

And being warned by the angel that they should not go to Judea, they went to their own country by another way.

But when Herod perceived that he had been tricked by the wise men he was angry and sent his murderers and commanded them to kill all the children who were two years old and under. When Mary heard that the children were to be killed, she was afraid and took the child and wrapped him in swaddling clothes and laid him in a manger.

But Elizabeth, when she heard that John was sought for, took him and went into the hill country. And she looked around to see where she could hide him, and there was no hiding place. And Elizabeth groaned aloud and said, "O mountain of God, receive me, a mother, with my child." For Elizabeth could not go up further for fear. And immediately the mountain was rent asunder and received her. And that mountain made a light to gleam for her; for an angel of the Lord was with them and protected them.

Psalm *Select a Christmas Carol*

Gospel *Gospel of Matthew 2:13–15, SV*

After (the astrologers) had departed, a messenger of the Lord appeared in a dream to Joseph, saying, "Get ready, take the child and his mother and flee to Egypt. Stay there until I give you instructions. You see, Herod is determined to hunt the child down and destroy him."

So Joseph got ready and took the child and his mother under cover of night and set out for Egypt. There they remained until Herod's death. This happened so the Lord's prediction spoken by the prophet would come true: "Out of Egypt I have called my son."

December 29

Reading *Pseudo Matthew 18–20, NTA*

On their journey to Egypt, when they came to a cave and wished to rest in it, holy Mary dismounted and sat down the child Jesus in her lap. And on the journey there were with Joseph three boys and with Mary some maidens. And behold, suddenly many dragons came out of the cave. When the boys saw them they cried out in terror. Then Jesus got down from his mother's lap, and stood on his feet before the dragons; thereupon they worshipped Jesus, and then went back from them. Then was fulfilled that which was spoken through the prophet David, "Praise the Lord, you dragons from the earth, you dragons and all deeps." And the child Jesus himself went before the dragons and commanded them not to harm anyone.

But Mary and Joseph had great fear lest the child should be hurt by the dragons. And Jesus said to them, "Have no fear, and do not think that I am a child; for I have always been and even now am perfect; all wild beasts must be docile before me."

Likewise lions and leopards worshipped him and accompanied them in the desert. Wherever Joseph and holy Mary went, they went before them, showing them the way and lowering their heads in worship; they showed their servitude by wagging their tails and honored him with great reverence. But when Mary saw the lions and leopards and all kinds of wild beasts surrounding them, she was at first gripped by violent fear.

But the child Jesus looked at her face with a happy countenance, and said, "Do not fear, Mother; for they do not come to harm you, but they hasten to obey you and me." With these words he removed all fear from her heart. And the lions went along with them, and with the oxen and asses and the beasts of burden which carried what they needed, and they harmed no one, although they remained with them. Rather they were docile among the sheep and rams which they had brought with them from Judea and had with them. They walked among the wolves without fear, and neither was harmed by the other. Then was fulfilled that which was said by the prophet, "The wolves pasture with the lambs; lions and oxen eat straw together." And the lions guided on their journey the two oxen and the wagon in which they carried what they needed.

Now on the third day of their journey, as they went on, it happened that blessed Mary was wearied by too great heat of the sun in the desert, and seeing a palm tree, she said to Joseph, "I should like to rest a little in the shade of this tree." And Joseph led her quickly to the palm and let her dismount from her animal. And when blessed Mary had sat down, she looked

Christmas

up at the top of the palm tree and saw that it was full of fruits, and said to Joseph, "I wish someone would fetch some of these fruits of the palm tree." And Joseph said to her, "I wonder that you say this; for you see how high this palm tree is, and I wonder that you even think about eating of the fruits of the palm. I think rather of the lack of water, which already fails us in the skins, and we have nothing with which we can refresh ourselves and the animals."

Then the child Jesus, who was sitting with a happy countenance in his mother's lap, said to the palm, "Bend down your branches, O tree, and refresh my mother with your fruit." And immediately at this command the palm bent its head down to the feet of blessed Mary, and they gathered from it fruits with which they all refreshed themselves. But after they had gathered all its fruits, it remained bent down and waited to raise itself again at the command of him at whose command it had bent down. Then Jesus said to it, "Raise yourself, O palm, and be strong and join my trees which are in the paradise of my Father. And open beneath your roots a vein of water which is hidden in the earth, and let the waters flow so that we may quench our thirst from it." And immediately it raised itself, and there began to gush out by its root a fountain of water very clear, fresh, and completely bright. And when they saw the fountain of water, they rejoiced greatly, and quenched their thirst, and also all the beasts of burden and all the animals, and gave thanks to God.

Psalm *Select a Christmas Carol*

Gospel *Matthew 2:19–23, SV*

After Herod's death, a messenger of the Lord suddenly appeared in a dream to Joseph in Egypt: "Get ready, take the child and his mother, and return to the land of Israel; those who were seeking the child's life are dead."

So he got ready, took the child and his mother, and returned to the land of Israel. He heard that Archelaus was the king of Judea in place of his father Herod; as a consequence, he was afraid to go there.

He was instructed in a dream to go to Galilee; so he went there and settled in a town called Nazareth. So the prophecy uttered by the prophets came true: "He will be called a Nazorean."

December 30

Reading *Gospel of Luke 2:22–28, SV*

Now when the time came for their purification according to the Law of Moses, they brought him up to Jerusalem to present him to the Lord — as it is written in the Law of the Lord, "Every male that opens the womb is to be considered holy to the Lord" — and to offer sacrifice according to what is dictated in the Law of the Lord: "A pair of turtledoves or two young pigeons."

Now there was a man in Jerusalem, named Simeon, a decent and devout man who was waiting for the consolation of Israel, and the holy spirit was with him. It had been disclosed to him by the holy spirit that he would not see death before he had laid eyes on the Lord's Anointed. And so he was guided by the spirit to the temple area. When the parents brought in the child Jesus, to perform for him what was customary according to the Law he took him in his arms and blessed God:

Psalm *Luke 2:29–32, SV*

Now, Lord, you can dismiss your slave in peace,*
    according to your word
now that my eyes have seen your salvation,*
    which you have prepared in the sight of all peoples —
a revelatory light for foreigners,*
    and glory for your people Israel.

Gospel *Luke 2:33–38, SV*

His father and mother were astonished at what was being said about him. Then Simeon blessed them and said to Mary his mother, "This child is linked to the fall and rise of many in Israel, and is destined to be a sign that is rejected. You too will have your heart broken — and the schemes of many minds will be exposed."

A prophetess was also there, Anna, daughter of Phanuel, of the tribe of Asher. She was well along in years, since she had

Christmas

married as a young girl and lived with her husband for seven years, and then alone as a widow until she was eighty-four. She never left the temple area, and she worshiped day and night with fasting and prayer. Coming on the scene at that very moment, she gave thanks to God, and began to speak about the child to all who were waiting for the liberation of Jerusalem.

December 31

First Reading *The Infancy Gospel of Thomas 1–2, SV*

I, Thomas the Israelite, am reporting to you, all my non-Jewish brothers and sisters, to make known the extraordinary childhood deeds of our Lord Jesus Christ — what he did after his birth in my region. This is how it all started.

When this boy, Jesus, was five years old, he was playing at the ford of a rushing stream. He was collecting the flowing water into ponds and made the water instantly pure. He did this with a single command. He then made soft clay and shaped into into twelve sparrows. He did this on the sabbath day, and many other boys were playing with him.

But when a Jew saw what Jesus was doing while playing on the sabbath day, he immediately went off and told Joseph, Jesus' father: "See here, your boy is at the ford and has taken mud and fashioned twelve birds with it, and has so violated the sabbath."

So Joseph went there, and as soon as he spotted him he shouted, "Why are you doing what's not permitted on the sabbath?"

But Jesus simply clapped his hands and shouted to the sparrows: "Be off, fly away, and remember me, you who are now alive!" And the sparrows took off and flew away noisily.

The Jews watched with amazement, then left the scene to report to their leaders what they had seen Jesus doing.

Second Reading *The Infancy Gospel of Thomas 3, SV*

The son of Annas the scholar, standing there with Jesus, took a willow branch and drained the water Jesus had collected. Jesus, however, saw what had happened and became angry, saying to him, "Damn you, you irreverent fool! What harm did the ponds of water do to you? From this moment you, too, will dry up like a tree, and you'll never produce leaves or root or bear fruit."

In an instant the boy had completely withered away. Then Jesus departed and left for the house of Joseph. The parents of the boy who had withered away picked him up and were carrying him out, sad because he was so young. And they came to Joseph and accused him: "It's your fault — your boy did all this."

Psalm *Select a Christmas Carol*

Gospel *The Infancy Gospel of Thomas 5, SV*

So Joseph summoned his child and admonished him in private, saying, "Why are you doing all this? These people are suffering and so they hate and harass us." Jesus said, "I know that the words I spoke are not my words. Still, I'll keep quiet for your sake. But those people must take their punishment." There and then his accusers became blind.

Those who saw this became very fearful and at a loss. All they could say was, "Every word he says, whether good or bad, has become a deed — a miracle, even!" When Joseph saw that Jesus had done such a thing, he got angry and grabbed his ear and pulled very hard. The boy became infuriated with him and replied, "It's one thing for you to seek and not find; it's quite another for you to act unwisely. Don't you know that I don't really belong to you? Don't make me upset."

January 1

First Reading *The Infancy Gospel of Thomas 6:1–8, SV*

A teacher by the name of Zacchaeus was listening to everything Jesus was saying to Joseph, and was astonished, saying to himself, "He is just a child, and saying this!" And so he summoned Joseph and said to him, "You have a bright child, and he has a good mind. Hand him over to me so he can learn his letters. I'll teach him everything he needs to know so as not to be unruly."

Joseph replied, "No one is able to rule this child except God alone. Don't consider him to be a small cross, brother."

When Jesus heard Joseph saying this he laughed and said to

Zacchaeus, "Believe me, teacher, what my father told you is true. I am the Lord of these people and I'm present with you and have been born among you and am with you. I know where you've come from and how many years you'll live. I swear to you, teacher, I existed when you were born. If you wish to be a perfect teacher, listen to me and I'll teach you a wisdom no one else knows except for me and the one who sent me to you. It's you who happen to be my student, and I know how old you are and how long you have to live. When you see the cross that my father mentioned, then you'll believe that everything I've told you is true."

Second Reading *The Infancy Gospel of Thomas 6:9–12, SV*

The Jews who were standing by and heard Jesus marveled and said, "How strange and paradoxical! This child is barely five years old and yet he says such things. In fact, we've never heard anyone say the kind of things this child does."

Jesus said to them in reply, "Are you really so amazed? Rather, consider what I've said to you. The truth is that I also know when you were born, and your parents, and I announce this paradox to you: when the world was created, I existed along with the one who sent me to you."

The Jews, once they heard that the child was speaking like this, became angry but were unable to say anything in reply. But the child skipped forward and said to them, "I've made fun of you because I know that your tiny minds marvel at trifles."

Psalm *Select a Christmas Carol*

Gospel *The Infancy Gospel of Thomas 6:13–23, SV*

When, therefore, they thought that they were being comforted by the child's exhortation, the teacher said to Joseph, "Bring him to the classroom and I'll teach him the alphabet."

Joseph took him by the hand and led him to the classroom. the teacher wrote the alphabet for him and began the instruction by repeating the letter alpha many times. But the child clammed up and did not answer him for a long time. No wonder, then, that the teacher got angry and struck him on the head.

The child took the blow calmly and replied to him, "I'm teaching you rather than being taught by you: I already know the letters you're teaching me, and your condemnation is great. To you these letters are like a bronze pitcher or a clashing cymbal, which can't produce glory or wisdom because it's all just noise. Nor does anyone understand the extent of my wisdom." When he got over being angry he recited the letters from alpha to omega very quickly.

Then he looked at the teacher and told him, "Since you don't know the real nature of the letter alpha, how are you going to teach me the letter beta." He began to quiz the teacher about the first letter, but he was unable to say anything.

Then while many were listening, he said to Zacchaeus, "Listen, teacher, and observe the arrangement of the first letter: How it has two straight lines or strokes proceeding to a point in the middle, gathered together, elevated, dancing, three-cornered, two-cornered, not antagonistic, of the same family, providing the alpha has lines of equal measure."

January 2

First Reading *The Infancy Gospel of Thomas 7, SV*

After Zacchaeus the teacher had heard the child expressing such intricate allegories regarding the first letter, he despaired of defending his teaching. He spoke to those who were present: "Poor me, I'm utterly bewildered, wretch that I am. I've heaped shame on myself because I took on this child. So take him away, I beg you, brother Joseph. I can't endure the severity of his look or his lucid speech. This child is no ordinary mortal; he can even tame fire! Perhaps he was born before the creation of the world. What sort of womb bore him, what sort of mother nourished him? — I don't know. Poor me, friend, I've lost my mind. I've deceived myself, I who am wholly wretched. I strove to get a student, and I've been found to have a teacher. Friends, I think of the shame, because, although I'm an old man, I've been defeated by a mere child. And so I can only despair and die on account of this child; right now I can't look him in the face. When everybody says that I have been defeated by a small child, what can I say? And what can I report about the lines of the first letter which he told me about? I just don't know, friends. For I don't know its beginning or its end. Therefore, I ask you, brother Joseph, take him back toy our house. What great thing he is — god or angel or whatever else I might call him — I don't know.

Second Reading *The Infancy Gospel of Thomas 8, SV*

While the Jews were advising Zacchaeus, the child laughed loudly and said, "Now let the infertile bear fruit and the blind see and the deaf in the understanding of their hearts hear: I've come from above so that I might save those who are below and summon them to higher things, just as the one who sent me to you commanded me."

Commentary For the blind to receive sight is characteristic of the activity of Jesus as an adult. See Mark 20:46; Matt 11:5; 21:14; Luke 7:21–22; John 9

Psalm *Select a Christmas Carol*

Gospel *The Infancy Gospel of Thomas 9, SV*

A few days later Jesus was playing on the roof of a house when one of the children playing with him fell off the roof and died. When the other children saw what had happened, they fled, leaving Jesus standing all by himself.

The parents of the dead child came and accused Jesus: "You troublemaker you, you're the one who threw him down."

Jesus responded, "I didn't throw him down — he threw himself down. He just wasn't being careful and leaped down from the roof and died."

Then Jesus himself leaped down from the roof and stood by the body of the child and shouted in a loud voice: "Zeno!" that was his name — "Get up and tell me: Did I push you?"

He got up immediately and said, "No, Lord, you didn't push me, you raised me up."

Those who saw this were astonished, and the child's parents praised God for the miracle that had happened and worshiped Jesus.

January 3

First Reading *The Infancy Gospel of Thomas 10–11, SV*

A few days later a young man was splitting wood in the neighborhood when his axe slipped and cut off the bottom of his foot. He was dying from loss of blood.

The crowd rushed there in an uproar, and the boy Jesus ran up, too. He forced his way through the crowd and grabbed hold of the young man's wounded foot. It was instantly healed.

He said to the youth, "Get up now, split your wood, and remember me."

When Jesus was six years old, his mother sent him to draw water and bring it back to the house. But he lost his grip on the pitcher in the jostling crowd, and it fell and broke. So Jesus spread out the cloak he was wearing and filled it with water and carried it back to his mother.

His mother, once she saw the miracle that had occurred, kissed him; but she kept to herself the mysteries that she had seen him do.

Commentary The episode about the wood splitting may echo the saying preserved in the Gospel of Thomas 77, "Split a piece of wood: I am there."

Jesus using his cloak (mantle) to carry water is reminiscent of the activities of the prophets, Elijah and Elisha in I Kgs 19:18ff and 2 Kgs 2:1–15. In this story the child Jesus is identified with the prophetic tradition.

Second Reading *The Infancy Gospel of Thomas 12, SV*

Again, during the sowing season, the child went out with his father to sow their field with grain. While his father was sowing, the child Jesus sowed one measure of grain. When he had harvested and threshed it, it yielded one hundred measures. Then he summoned all the poor in the village to the threshing floor and gave them grain. Joseph carried back what was left of the grain. Jesus was eight years old when he did this miracle.

Note The yield is perhaps inspired by Mark 4:8; Matt 13:8; Luke 8:8

Psalm *Select a Christmas Carol*

Gospel *The Infancy Gospel of Thomas 13, SV*

Now Jesus' father was a carpenter, making ploughs and yokes at that time. He received an order from a rich man to make a bed for him. When one board of what is called the crossbeam turned out shorter than the other, and Joseph didn't know what to do, the child Jesus said to his father, "Put the two boards down and line them up at one end."

Joseph did as the child told him. Jesus stood at the other end and grabbed hold of the shorter board and, by stretching it, made it the same length as the other.

His father Joseph looked on and marveled, and he hugged and kissed the child, saying, "How fortunate I am that God has given this child to me."

January 4

First Reading *The Infancy Gospel of Thomas 16, SV*

Joseph sent his son James to tie up some wood and carry it back to the house, and the child Jesus followed. While James was gathering the firewood, a viper bit his hand. And as he lay sprawled out on the ground, dying, Jesus came and blew on the bite. Immediately the pain stopped, the animal burst apart, and James got better on the spot.

Commentary Compare this story with the one of Paul and the viper on Malta in Acts 28:1–6.

Second Reading *The Infancy Gospel of Thomas 17, SV*

After this incident an infant in Joseph's neighborhood became sick and died, and his mother grieved terribly. Jesus heard the loud wailing and the uproar that was going on and quickly ran there.

When he found the child dead, he touched its chest and said, "I say to you, infant, don't die but live, and be with your mother."

And immediately the infant looked up and laughed. Jesus then said to the woman, "Take it, give it your breast, and remember me."

The crowd of onlookers marveled at this: "Truly this child was a god or a heavenly messenger of God — whatever he says instantly happens." But Jesus left and went on playing with the other children.

Psalm *Select a Christmas Carol*

Gospel *The Infancy Gospel of Thomas 18, SV*

A year later, while a building was under construction, a man fell from the top of it and died. There was quite a commotion, so Jesus got up and went there. When he saw the man lying dead, he took his hand and said, "I say to you, sir, get up and go back to work." And he immediately got up and worshiped him.

The crowd saw this and marveled: "This child's from heaven — he must be, because he has saved many souls from death, and he can go on saving all his life."

Commentary Jesus' command to take someone by the hand and raise from the dead, is also in Mark 5:41 and Luke 7:14

January 5

First Reading *The Infancy Gospel of Thomas 14, SV*

When Joseph saw the child's aptitude, and his great intelligence for his age, he again resolved that Jesus should not remain illiterate. So he took him and handed him over to another teacher. The teacher said to Joseph. First I'll teach him Greek, then Hebrew." This teacher, of course, knew of the child's previous experience with a teacher and was afraid of him. Still, he wrote out the alphabet and instructed him for quite a while, though Jesus was unresponsive.

Then Jesus spoke: "If you're really a teacher, and if you know the letters well, tell me the meaning of the letter alpha, and I'll tell you the meaning of beta."

The teacher became exasperated and hit him on the head. Jesus got angry and cursed him, and the teacher immediately lost consciousness and fell face down on the ground.

Christmas

The child returned to Joseph's house. But Joseph was upset and gave this instruction to his mother: Don't let him go outside, because those who annoy him end up dead."

Second Reading *The Infancy Gospel of Thomas 15, SV*

After some time another teacher, a close friend of Joseph, said to him, Send the child to my schoolroom. Perhaps with some flattery I can teach him his letters."

Joseph replied, if you can muster the courage, brother, take him with you.

And so he took him along with much fear and trepidation, but the child was happy to go.

Jesus strode boldly into the schoolroom and found a book lying on the desk. He took the book but did not read the letters in it. Rather, he opened his mouth and spoke by the power of the Holy Spirit and taught the law to those standing there.

A large crowd gathered and stood listening to him, and they marveled at the maturity of his teaching and his readiness of speech — a mere child able to say such things.

When Joseph heard about this he feared the worst and ran to the schoolroom, imagining that this teacher was having trouble with Jesus.

But the teacher said to Joseph, "Brother, please know that I accepted this child as a student, but already he's full of grace and wisdom. So I'm asking you, brother, to take him back home."

When the child heard this, he immediately smiled at him and said, "Because you have spoken and testified rightly, that other teacher who was struck down will be healed." And right away he was. Joseph took his child and went home.

Psalm *Select a Christmas Carol*

Gospel *Infancy Gospel of Thomas 19, SV*

When Jesus was twelve years old his parents went to Jerusalem as usual, for the Passover Festival, along with their fellow travelers. After passover they began the journey home. But while on their way, the child Jesus went back up to Jerusalem. His parents, of course, assumed he was in the traveling party. After they had traveled one day, they began to look for him among their relatives. When they did not find him, they were worried and returned again to the city to search for him.

After three days they found him in the temple area, sitting among the teachers, listening to the law and asking them questions. All eyes were on him, and everyone was astounded that he, a mere child, could interrogate the elders and teachers of the people and explain the main points of the law and the parables of the prophets.

His mother Mary came up and said to him, "Child, why have you done this to us? Don't you see, we've been worried sick looking for you."

"Why are you looking for me?" Jesus asked them. "Don't you know that I have to be in my father's house?"

Then the scholars and the Pharisees said, "Are you the mother of this child?" She said, "I am."

And they said to her, "You more than any woman are to be congratulated, for God has blessed the fruit of your womb! For we've never seen nor heard such glory and such virtue and wisdom."

Jesus got up and went with his mother, and was obedient to his parents. His mother took careful note of all that had happened. And Jesus continued to excel in learning and gain respect.

To him be glory for ever and ever. Amen.

Christmas

Eucharistic Prayers

The Eucharistic Prayers that follow are given in approximate chronological order:

The Didache (first edition)	60–80 CE
Justin Martyr	early second century
Apostolic Tradition of Hippolytus	ca. 217 CE
Apostolic Constitutions	second or third century
Nag Hammadi Library	second or third century
Acts of John	second century
Acts of Thomas	third century

1. A Eucharistic Prayer from the Didache

On every Lord's Day — his special day — come together and break bread and give thanks, first confessing your sins so that your sacrifice may be pure. Anyone at variance with his neighbor must not join you, until they are reconciled, lest your sacrifice be defiled. For it was of this sacrifice that the Lord said, "Always and everywhere offer me a pure sacrifice; for I am a great King, says the Lord, and my name is marveled at by the nations."

Now about the Eucharist: this is how to give thanks: First in connection with the cup: We thank you, our Father, for the holy vine of David, your child, which you have revealed through Jesus, your child. To you be glory forever.

Then in connection with the piece broken off the loaf:
We thank you our Father for the life and knowledge which you have revealed through Jesus, your child. To you be glory forever.

As this piece of bread was scattered over the hills and then was brought together and made one, so let your Church be brought together from the ends of the earth into your Kingdom. For yours is the glory and the power through Jesus Christ forever.

After you have finished your meal, say grace in this way:
We thank you, holy Father, for your sacred name which you have lodged in our hearts, and for the knowledge and faith and immortality which you have revealed through Jesus, your child. To you be glory forever.

Almighty Master, you have created everything for the sake of your name, and have given human beings food and drink to enjoy that they may thank you. But to us you have given spiritual food and drink and eternal life through Jesus, your child.

Above all, we thank you that you are mighty. To you be glory forever.

Remember, Lord, your Church, to save it from all evil and to make it perfect by your love. Make it holy, 'and gather it together from the four winds', into your Kingdom which you have made ready for it. For yours is the power and the glory forever.'

Let Grace come and let this world pass away.
Hosanna to the Son of David!
If anyone is holy, let him come. If not, let him repent.
Our Lord come!
Amen.
In the case of prophets, however, you should let them give thanks in their own way.

Early Christian Fathers, Cyril C. Richardson, trans., Westminster 1963, p. 178, 175–176

2. An Order for Eucharistic Celebrations from Justin Martyr

In the passage which follows, Justin Martyr does not give us the actual words used for a Eucharistic Prayer, but he provides the elements and the usual sequence which is given spontaneous expression. His description which follows is in the context of baptism which precedes the eucharistic rite:

But we, after we have thus washed him who has been convinced and has assented to our teaching, bring him to the place where those who are called brethren are assembled, in order that we may offer hearty prayers in common for ourselves and the baptized (illuminated) person, and for all others in every place, that we may be counted worthy, now that we have learned the truth, by our works also to be found good citizens and keepers of the commandments, so that we may be saved with an everlasting salvation.

Having ended the prayers, we salute one another with a kiss.

There is then brought to the president of the brethren bread and a cup of wine mixed with water; and he taking them gives praise and glory to the Father of the universe, through the name of the Son and of the Holy Spirit, and offers thanks at considerable length for our being counted worthy to receive these things at His hands.

And when he has concluded the prayers and thanksgivings, all the people express their assent by saying Amen. This word Amen answers in the Hebrew language to (so be it).

And when the president has given thanks, and all the people have expressed their assent, those who are called by us deacons give to each of those present to partake of the bread and wine mixed with water over which the thanksgiving was pronounced, and to those who are absent they carry away a portion.

And this food is called among us (the Eucharist), of which no one is allowed to partake but the person who believes that the things which we teach are true, and who has been washed with the washing that is for the remission of sins, and unto regeneration, and who is so living as Christ has enjoined.

For not as common bread and common drink do we receive these; but in like manner as Jesus Christ our Savior, having been made flesh by the Word of God, had both flesh and blood for our salvation, so likewise have we been taught that the food which is blessed by the prayer of His word, and from which our blood and flesh by transmutation are nourished, is the flesh and blood of that Jesus who was made flesh. For the apostles, in the memoirs composed by them, which are called Gospels, have thus delivered unto us what was enjoined upon them; that Jesus took bread, and when he had given thanks, said, "This do in remembrance of Me, this is My body;" and that, after the same manner, having taken the cup and given thanks, he said, "This is my blood;" and gave it to them alone . . .

And we afterwards continually remind each other of these things. And the wealthy among us help the needy; and we always keep together; and for all things wherewith we are supplied, we bless the Maker of all through His Son Jesus Christ and through the Holy Spirit. And on the day called Sunday, all who live in cities or in the country gather together in one place, and the memoirs of the apostles or the writings of the prophets are read, as long as time permits; then when the reader has ceased, the president verbally instructs, and exhorts to the imitation of these good things.

Then we all rise together and pray, and, as we before said, when our prayer is ended, bread and wine and water are brought, and the president in like manner offers prayers and thanksgivings, according to his ability, and the people assent, saying Amen; and there is a distribution to each, and a participation of that over which thanks have been given, and to those who are absent a portion is taken by the deacons.

And they who are well to do, and willing, give what each thinks fit; and what is collected is deposited with the president, who succours the orphans and widows, and those who through sickness or any other cause, are in want, and those who are in bonds, and the strangers sojourning among us, and in a word takes care of all who are in need.

But Sunday is the day on which we all hold our common assembly, because it is the first day on which God, having wrought a change in the darkness and matter, made the world; and Jesus Christ our Saviour on the same day rose from the dead. For He was crucified on the day before that of Saturn (Saturday); and on the day after that of Saturn, which is the day of the Sun, having appeared to his apostles and disciples, he taught them these things, which we have submitted to you also for your consideration.

The First Apology of Justin, LXV–LXVII as found in the *Ante Nicene Fathers*, Volume I, Grand Rapids, Eerdmans Publishing 1981

Commentary Justin Martyr can serve as a guide for those today who choose to offer the Eucharist following his sequence and their own Spirit filled wording.

Here is the basic outline, the Order for the Eucharist:
> The Faithful gather in the name of the Lord
> Readings from the Holy Scriptures
> Teaching given by the Presider
> Prayers
> Kiss of Peace
> Bread and Cup of Wine mixed with Water brought to the Presider
> Praise and Thanksgiving
> AMEN!
> Partaking of Bread and Cup
> Offerings for the needy are given to the Presider
> Deacons take blessed Bread and Wine to those who are absent

3. A Eucharistic Prayer from the Apostolic Tradition of Hippolytus

And then the offering is immediately brought by the deacons to the bishop, and by thanksgiving he shall make the bread into an image[1] of the body of Christ, and the cup of wine mixed with water according to the likeness of the blood, which is shed for all who believe in him. And milk and honey mixed together for the fulfillment of the promise to the fathers, which spoke of a land flowing with milk and honey; namely Christ's flesh which he gave, by which they who believe are nourished like babes, he making sweet the bitter things of the heart by the gentleness of his word. And the water into an offering in a token of the laver, in order that the inner part of man, which is a living soul, may receive the same as the body.

The Bishop shall explain the reason of all these things to those who partake.

The Deacons shall bring the offering to the Bishop and he, laying his hand upon it, with all the presbytery, shall say as the thanksgiving:

	The Lord be with you.
And all shall say	And with your spirit.
	Lift up your hearts
And all reply	We lift them up unto the Lord
	It is meet and right.

And then he shall proceed immediately:

We give thanks, O God, through thy beloved Servant Jesus Christ, whom at the end of time You sent to us a Saviour and Redeemer and the Messenger of Your counsel. Who is Your Word, inseparable from You; through whom You make all things and in whom You are well pleased. Whom You sent from heaven into the womb of the Virgin, and who, dwelling within her, was made flesh, and was manifested as Your Son, being born of the Holy Spirit and the Virgin. Who, fulfilling Your will, and winning for himself a holy people, spread out his hands when he came to suffer, that by his death he might set free them who believed on You Who, when he was betrayed to his willing death, that he might bring to nought death, and break the bonds of the devil, and tread hell under foot, and give light to the righteous, and set up a boundary post, and manifest his resurrection, taking bread and giving thanks to You said, "Take, eat: this is my body, which is broken for you." And likewise also the cup, saying, "This is my blood, which is shed for you. As often as you perform this, perform my memorial."

Having in memory, therefore, his death and resurrection, we offer to You the bread and the cup, yielding You thanks, because You have counted us worthy to stand before You and to minister to You.

And we pray that You would send Your Holy Spirit upon the offerings of Your holy church; that, gathering them into one, You would grant to all Your saints who partake to be filled with Holy Spirit, that their faith may be confirmed in truth, that we may praise and glorify You. Through Your Servant Jesus Christ, through whom be to You glory and honour, with the Holy Spirit in the holy church, both now and always and world without end. Amen.

And when the Bishop breaks the Bread and distributes the fragments he shall say: The heavenly Bread in Christ Jesus. *And the recipient shall say,* Amen

And the presbyters — or if there are not enough presbyters, the deacons — shall hold the cups, and shall stand by with reverence and modesty; first he who holds the water, then the milk, thirdly the wine. And the recipients shall taste of each three times, he who gives the cup saying,

In God the Father Almighty;
and the recipient shall say, Amen.
Then: In the Lord Jesus Christ;
and he shall say, Amen.
Then: In the Holy Spirit and the holy church;
And he shall say, Amen.
So it shall be done to each.

And when these things are completed, let each one hasten to do good works, and to please God and to live aright, devoting himself to the church, practising the things he has learned, advancing in the service of God.

Note 1. Image, in Greek "Antitypos", an impression answering to a die. Likewise, a type or symbol of Christ.

Apostolic Tradition of Hippolytus translated into English by Burton Scott Easton, Archon, 1962

4. A Eucharistic Prayer from the Apostolic Constitutions

Be ye always thankful as faithful and honest servants; and concerning the eucharistical thanksgiving say thus:

We Thank You, our Father, for that life which You have made known to us by Jesus Your Son, by whom You make all things, and take care of the whole world; whom You have sent to become human for our salvation; whom You have raised up, and been pleased to glorify, and have set Him down on Your right hand; by whom You have promised us the resurrection of the dead. Do You, O Lord, Almighty, everlasting God, so gather together Your Church from the ends of the earth into Your

Kingdom, as this corn was once scattered, and is now become one loaf. We also, our Father, thank You for the precious blood of Jesus Christ, which was shed for us, and for his precious body, whereof we celebrate this representation, as Himself appointed us, "to show forth His death." For through Him glory is to be given to You for ever. Amen.

After the participation, give thanks in this manner:
We thank You, O God and Father of Jesus our Savior, for thy holy name, which You have made to inhabit among us; and that knowledge, faith, love, and immortality which You have given us through Your Son Jesus.

You, O Almighty Lord, the God of the universe, have created the world, and the things that are therein, by Him; and have planted a law in our souls, and beforehand prepared things for the convenience of people. O God of our holy and blameless father, Abraham, and Isaac, and Jacob, Your faithful servants; You, O God are powerful, faithful, and true, and without deceit in Your promises; You send upon earth Jesus Your Christ to live with people, as a human being, when He was God the Word, and human being, to take away error by the roots: even now, through Him be mindful of this Your holy Church, which You have purchased with the precious blood of Your Christ, and deliver it from all evil, and perfect it in Your love and Your Truth, and gather us all together into Your kingdom which You have prepared.

Let this your kingdom come.

"Hosanna to the Son of David. Blessed be He who comes in the name of the Lord." — God the Lord, who was manifested to us in the flesh.

Apostolic Constitutions Book VI, xxv, xxvi

5. A Prayer of Thanksgiving in the Nag Hammadi Library

This is the prayer they spoke:
"We give thanks to You! Every soul and heart is is lifted up to You, undisturbed name, honored with the name 'God" and praised with the name 'Father,' for to everyone and everything

comes the fatherly kindness and affection and love, and any teaching there may be that is sweet and plain, giving us mind, speech, and knowledge: mind, so that we may understand You, speech, so that we may expound You, knowledge so that we may know You. We rejoice, having been illumined by Your knowledge. We rejoice because You have shown us Yourself. We rejoice because while we were in the body, You have made us divine through Your knowledge.

The thanksgiving of the one who attains to You is one thing: that we know You. We have known You, intellectual light. Life of life, we have known You. Womb of every creature, we have known You. Womb pregnant with the nature of the Father, we have known You. Eternal permanence of the begetting Father, thus have we worshipped your goodness. There is one petition that we ask: we would be preserved in knowledge. And there is one protection that we desire: that we not stumble in this kind of life.

When they had said these things in the prayer, they embraced each other and they went to eat their holy food, which has no blood in it.

The Nag Hammadi Library, Third Edition, 1988, p. 329

6. A Eucharistic Prayer to Jesus from the Acts of John

John asked for bread, and gave thanks with these words:
Jesus, what praise or what offering or what thanksgiving shall we name as we break this bread, but yours? We glorify the name Father which you reveal. We glorify the name Son which you reveal. We glorify your entering of the door. We glorify your Resurrection which you reveal. We glorify your Way. We glorify your Seed, the Word, Grace, Faith, the Salt, the Pearl of great value, the Treasure, the Plough, the Net, the Greatness, the Diadem. You for our sake are called the Son of Man, *the Truly Human Being.* In you is the truth, repose, knowledge, power, commandment, confidence, freedom, and refuge.

For you alone, O Lord, are the eternal root and the inexhaustible fountain, the source of all powers. You are called all these things for our sake, so that calling on you through them we may know your greatness, which at present is invisible to us, but visible only to the pure in heart.

Then John took the bread and gave it to the people, praying over each of the brothers and sisters to be aware of the Lord's grace and of the most holy Eucharist. And he took bread himself and said, "May there be for me also a part with you," and "Peace be with you, my beloved."

Acts of John 109, Seers Version

7. A Eucharistic Prayer to Jesus from the Acts of Thomas

Jesus, the hidden mystery that has been revealed to us, you are the one who makes many mysteries known to us. You set us apart from all our companions and speak to us three words which set our hearts on fire, yet are beyond our speaking to others.

Jesus, slain, corpse, buried God of God, who revives the dead and heals the sick. Jesus, you were in need like a poor man and you save us as one who has no need of anything; you caught fish for breakfast and the dinner, and you make all satisfied with a little bread;

Jesus, you rest from the weariness of the journey like a man and walk upon the waves like a God;

Jesus most high, voice rising like the sun from the perfect mercy,

Savior of all, right hand of the light which overthrows the evil one by his own nature, you who gather all nature into one place; you of many forms, who are the only begotten, the first born of many brethren; God from God Most high, man despised until now, Jesus Christ, who does not neglect us when we call upon you; you have become an occasion of life to all humankind.

For our sakes you were judges and shut up in prison, and you set free all who are in bondage. You, who was called a deceiver, deliver your own from deception;

I pray for all these who stand here and believe in you. For they crave to obtain your gifts, having good hope in your help, and having their refuge in your greatness. They have their ears open to hear from us the words which are spoken to them. Let your peace come and dwell in them, and let it renew them from their former deeds, and let them put off the old man with his deeds and put on the new who is proclaimed to them by me. . . .

Jesus, you make us worthy to partake of the Eucharist of your holy body and blood, behold we make bold to approach your Eucharist, and to call upon your holy name; come and have fellowship with us!
Come, gift of the Most High;
Come, perfect Compassion;
Come fellowship of the male *and female*;
Come, Holy Spirit;
Come, You who know the mysteries of the Chosen;
Come, You who have part in all the combats of the noble Athlete;
Come, treasure of glory;
Come, darling of the compassion of the Most High;
Come, silence, that reveals the great deeds of the whole greatness;
Come, You who show forth the hidden things and make the ineffable manifest;
Holy Dove that bears the twin young;
Come, hidden Mother;
Come, You who manifest in your actions and furnish us with joy and rest for all that are joined with You;
Come and partake with us in this Eucharist which we celebrate in your name,
And in the love-feast in which we are gathered together at Your call.

Acts of Thomas 50, Seers Version

A Prayer after all have received communion:
Glory be to the only begotten of the Father, glory to the first-born of many brothers and sisters, glory to you, the defender and helper of those who come to your refuge, the sleepless and the one who awakens those in sleep, who lives and gives life to

those who are in death, O God Jesus Christ, Son of the living God, redeemer and helper, refuge and rest of all who labor in your work, giver of healing to those who for your name's sake endure the burden and heat of the day:

We thank you for the gifts given to us by you, and the help given to us by you, and the provision that comes to us from you. Bring to completion these things in us even to the end, that we may have the confidence that is in you.

Look upon us, because for your sake we have left our homes and our fathers' goods, and for your sake we have gladly and willingly become strangers.

Look upon us, Lord, because we have left our own possessions for your sake, that we may obtain you, the possession that cannot be taken away.

Look upon us, Lord, because we have left those things that belong to us by race, that we may be united with your kindred.

Look upon us, Lord, who have left our fathers and mothers, our foster parents, that we may behold our Father and be satisfied with his divine nourishment.

Look upon us, Lord, for your sake we have left our bodily consorts and our earthly fruits, that we may share in that true and abiding fellowship and bring forth true fruits, whose nature is from above, which none can take away from us, with whom we abide and they abide in us. Amen!

Acts of Thomas 60, Seers Version

8. Another Eucharistic Prayer to Jesus from the Acts of Thomas

Jesus: companion and friend, hope of the weak, and confidence of the poor, refuge and lodging of the weary, voice that comes from farthest out, comforter who dwells within us, lodging and haven of those who pass through times of darkness, physician who heals without payment, who among people was crucified for many, who descended into Hades with great power, the sight of whom the princes of death could not endure, and who ascends with great glory and gathering all who take refuge in you!

You prepare a way and in your footsteps will journey those whom you are redeeming, You bring them to your own flock and unite them with your sheep.

You are the son of compassion, the son sent to us out of love for people from the perfect land of our Father *and Mother.*

Lord of possessions, you serve your servants that they may live. You fill creation with your riches You were in need and hungry for forty days. Now you satisfy thirsty souls with your own good things. Be with us, gather us into your fold and unite us with your number. Be our guide in a land of error. Be our physician in a land of sickness. Be our rest in a land of the weary. Sanctify us in a polluted land. Be the physician of our bodies and souls and make us your holy temples and let your Holy Spirit dwell fully in us! . . .

Take bread and a cup in hand, bless God and say:

Your Holy Body which was crucified for us we eat. Your Blood which was poured out for us for salvation we drink. Let Your Body become our salvation, Let Your Blood be for the remission of sins!

For the gall which you drank for our sakes, let the gall of the devil be taken away for us. For the vinegar which you have drunk for us, let our weakness be made strong. For the spitting which you received for our sakes, let us receive the dew of Your Goodness. And for the reed with which they struck you for our sakes, let us receive the perfect house!

Because You received a crown of thorns for our sakes, let us who have loved you put on a crown that does not fade away; and for the linen cloth in which You were wrapped, let us be wrapped with Your unconquerable power; and for the new grave and burial let us receive renewal of soul and body!

Because you rose and came to life again, let us come to life again and live and stand before You in righteous judgment!

Break the bread of the Eucharist and say:

Let this Eucharist be to you for salvation and joy and health for your souls!

And the people reply, Amen.

Acts of Thomas 156–158, Seers Version

Eucharistic Prayers

Prayers

An Extended Lord's Prayer from the Acts of Thomas

Our Father who art in heaven, hallowed be thy name; thy kingdom come; thy will be done, as in heaven so on earth; give us constantly our daily bread and forgive us our debts, as we also have forgiven our debtors; and lead us not into temptation, but deliver us from evil.

My Lord and my God, hope and confidence and teacher and my comforter, you have taught me to pray this way. Behold, I pray this prayer and fulfill your command. Be with me until the end. You are the One who from childhood has sown life in me, and preserved me from corruption. You are The One who brought me out of the poverty of the world and invited me to true riches. You are the One who made yourself known to me, and showed me that I am yours . . .

My mouth is incapable of rendering thanks to you. My understanding cannot ponder in your zeal for me. When I wished to be rich and possess everything, you showed me that for many on earth riches are a loss. But I believed your revelation and remained in the poverty of the world, until you, the true riches, appeared and filled with riches both me and those worthy of you, and you freed us from want and care and avarice.

Look, therefore, I have fulfilled your work and accomplished your command; and I have become poor and needy and a stranger and a slave, despised and a prisoner and hungry and thirsty and naked and weary.

Do not let my trust, then, come short of its fulfillment, and let not my hope in you be put to shame! Do not let my labors become vain! Let not my continual prayer and fastings perish, and do not let my works toward you be diminished!

Do not let the devil snatch away the seed of wheat from the land, and do not let his tares be found upon it; for your land cannot receive his tares, neither can they be laid in the barns of your managers.

Your vine have I planted in the land; may it send its roots into the depths, and spread its branches up to heaven! And may its fruits be seen on earth, and may they delight in it who are worthy of you, and whom you have acquired!

Look, the money which you have given I have laid on the table of the bankers; demand it and return it to me with interest, as you promised! With each dollar you gave me I have gained another ten; may they be added to my account as you ordained! I remitted the dollars to the bankers; may that not be demanded from me which I have remitted!

When called to dinner, I have come, released from field and partner; may I not then be thrown out, but freely taste your food.

To the wedding I have been invited, and have put on white robes; may I be worthy of wearing them and not be bound hand and foot and thrown into outer darkness!

My lamp shines with its light; may its Lord keep it burning until he leaves the bridal chamber and I receive him; may my light not be extinguished for lack of oil! Let my eyes behold you and my heart rejoice, because I have fulfilled your will and accomplished your command! Let me be like the wise and God-fearing servant, who with careful diligence did not neglect his vigilance! Watching all night long I have wearied myself, to guard my house from the robbers, that they might not break in.

I have dressed myself with truth and I have bound my shoes to my feet, that I may not see their thongs loosened. My hands I have put to the yoked plough, and I have not turned around backward, that the furrows may not be crooked. The field is become white and the harvest is at hand, that I may receive my reward.

My garment that has grown old I have worn out, and the laborious work that leads to rest I have accomplished. I have kept the first watch and the second and the third, that I behold your face and worship your holy radiance.

I have pulled down the barns and left them desolate on earth, that I may be filled from your treasures. The abundant spring within me I have dried up, that I may find thy living spring.

I have slain the prisoner whom you committed to me that the freed man in me may not lose his trust.

The inside I have made outside, and the outside inside, and your wholeness has been fulfilled in me. I have not turned back to what is behind, but have advanced to what is before, that I may not become a reproach.

The dead I have brought to life and the living I have put to death, and what was lacking I have filled up, that I may receive the crown of victory and the power of Christ become complete in me.

Reproach have I received on earth, but give me recompense and requital in heaven!

Acts of Thomas 144–147, Seers Version

Prayer of the Apostle Paul NHL

My redeemer, redeem me, for I am yours: from you have I come forth.

You are my mind: bring me forth!

You are my treasure house: open for me!

You are my fullness: take me to you!

You are my repose; give me the perfection that cannot be grasped!

I invoke you, the one who is and preexisted, by the name which is called above every name, through Jesus Christ the Lord of Lords, the king of the ages: give me your gifts which you do not regret through the Son of Man, the Spirit, the Paraclete of truth.

Give me authority when I ask you; give healing for my body when I ask you through the Evangelist, and redeem my eternal light-soul and my spirit.

And the First-born of the Pleroma of grace — reveal him to my mind!

Grant what no angel eye has seen, and no archon ear has heard and what has not entered into the human heart, which came to be angelic and came to be after the image of the psychic God when it was formed in the beginning, since I have faith and hope. And place upon me your beloved, elect, and blessed greatness, the First-born, the First-begotten, and the wonderful mystery of your house; for yours is the power and the glory and the praise and the greatness forever and ever. Amen.

Commentary The title of this prayer means it is in honor of Paul, but it was written by another person sometime toward the end of the second century or the beginning of the third. This prayer is on the front flyleaf of the first book in the Nag Hammadi Library, and thus serves as an introductory prayer to the entire volume and possibly to the entire library. This intense prayer of seeking to know the Eternal One through Jesus Christ is in response to Jesus who says "I will give you what no eye has seen, no ear has heard, no hand has touched, and what has never occurred to the human mind." Gospel of Thomas 17 References to First-Born and First-begotten are to Christ. Archons are cosmic powers. Pleroma means "Fullness." Here is deep desire to know All that IS!

A Table of Major Moveable Days in the Liturgical Year

Year	Sundays after Epiphany	Ash Wednesday	Easter	Pentecost
2003	Seven & the Last	March 5	April 20	June 8
2004*	Six & the Last	February 25	April 11	May 30
2005	Four & the Last	February 9	March 27	May 15
2006	Seven & the Last	March 1	April 16	June 4
2007	Six & the Last	February 21	April 8	May 27
2008*	Three & the Last	February 6	March 23	May 11
2009	Six & the Last	February 25	April 12	May 31
2010	Five & the Last	February 17	April 4	May 23
2011	Eight & the Last	March 9	April 24	June 12
2012*	Six & the Last	February 22	April 8	May 27
2013	Four & the Last	February 13	March 31	May 19
2014	Seven & the Last	March 5	April 20	June 8
2015	Six & the Last	February 18	April 5	May 24
2016*	Four & the Last	February 10	March 27	May 15
2017	Seven & the Last	March 1	April 16	June 4
2018	Five & the Last	February 14	April 1	May 20
2019	Seven & the Last	March 6	April 21	June 9
2020*	Six & the Last	February 26	April 12	May 31
2021	Five & the Last	February 17	April 4	May 23
2022	Seven & the Last	March 2	April 17	June 5
2023	Six & the Last	February 22	April 9	May 28
2024*	Five & the Last	February 14	March 31	May 19
2025	Seven & the Last	March 5	April 20	June 8
2026	Six & the Last	February 18	April 5	May 24

A Chart of Readings for the Liturgical Year

Epiphany

	First	Second	Psalm	Gospel
1	Isa 40:1–8	Mark 1:1–6, Q 3	Ode 24	Mark 1:9–13, Q 4
2	Deut 30:11–14	GPhil 70:34–71:4, 74:29–31, 77:8–15	Sir 51:13–18	GThom Prol, 1–5
3	Isa 64:1–3,	GHeb 3	Ode 11:1–8	GThom 8–11, 17
4	SongSol 1:1–4	SongSol 2:1–6	Ode 3	Luke 8:1–3 and GPhil 59:7–11, 63:32–64:5
5	Dan 10:1–14	GPhil 73:2–8, 75:22–24, 56:26–32, 57:19–22	Ode 30	SecMark 1–2,
6	Rev 22:12–17	GPhil 63:12–21	Ode 1	POxy 840
7	Sir 38:1–15	GPhil 77:35–78:11	Ode 32	EgerG 1–3,
8	Gen 35:22b–26	GPhil 61:12–20, 63:25–30	Bar 3:29–32	GEbi 2
Last	GPhil 53:24–54:18, 56:3–15, 59:12–17	GPhil 57:28–58:10,	Ode 4	GThom 13, 61

Lent

	First	Second	Psalm	Gospel
Ash Wed	Isa 58:1–8	Job 42:1–6	Ps 102:1–12	GThom 6,7,14, 27,104
1	Eccl 3:1–8	GPhil 67:27–35, 70:13–17	Ode 41:1–7	GThom 21–23,
2	Prov 1:20–31	Job 28:1–12	Ode 13	GThom 24–26, 28–30
3	Gen 2:18–25	Job 28:12–20	Ode 2–6	GThom 32–38
4	Archons & Origins	Job 28:20–28	Ode 7:7–13	GThom 39–46
5	Isa 2:2–4	GPhil 82:30–84:13	Ode 7:14–18	GThom 47–53

Holy Week

	First	Second	Psalm	Gospel
Passion	Job 1:1–12	Job 1:13–22	Ode 5	GThom 54–60, 62–63
Mon	Job 2:1–6	Job 2:7–13	Ode 20	POxy 1224
Tues	Job 3:1, 11–12, 16, 20–28	Job 4:1–9, 5:17–19, 27	Ode 31	DialSav
Wed	Job 6:1–4, 8–17, 7:11–21	Job 8:1–10, 20–22	Ode 41:8–15	DialSav
Thurs	Job 9:1–2, 14–24	Job 11:1–6, 13–18, 13:1–5	AcJohn 94	GThom 12, 15, 16, 18, 19, 31
Fri	Zech 14:1, 4–9	GPhil 69:14–25, 70:1–4, 85:10–21	Ode 27 Ode 28:7–12	GPet 1–6
Sat	Zech 12:9–12a.	WisSol 2:1–5	Ode 42	GPet 7–8

Easter

Easter	Job 14:1–2, 7–14a,	GPet 9–11	Ode 17:1–5	GPet 12–13
2	Exod 12:16–19	GPet 14	Ode 17:6–9	John 21:1–14
3	Gen 1:1–15	GPhil 53:14–23	Ode 8:1–12	GMary 2–3
4	Ezek 1:28b–3:3	GPhil 79:18–33	Ode 8:13–22	GMary 4–5
5	AcPet & 12	Resurrection 48:4–49:8	Ode 9	GMary 6–7
6	AcPet & 12	GPhil 67:9–27	Ode 10	GMary 9
7	AcPet & 12	GPhil 63:32–64:5, 59:2–6	Ode 11:9–19	GMary 10

Pentecost

	First	Second	Psalm	Gospel
Pentecost	Ezek 37:1–14	Acts 2:1–15	Ode 6	Sophia Jesus X
2	SecJas 2	Deut 20:5–9	Ode 16	GThom 64
3	SecJas 3	Sylvanus 106:22–107:4, 109:11–25	WisSol 7:24–30	GThom 65–71
4	SecJas 4	Sylvanus 86:17–24, 88:16–21, 89:17–23	Ode 35	GThom 72–79
5	SecJas 5	Sylvanus 90:29–91:1–33	Sir 51:18–27	GThom 80–88
6	SecJas 6:1–18	Sylvanus 96:19–20, 32–97:3, 98:21–28, 99:13–20, 100:24–29	Sir 6:23–31	GThom 89–95
7	SecJas 6:19–40	Sylvanus 100:32–101:21	Ode 12	GThom 96–100
8	SecJas 7	Sylvanus 103:11–30, 104:18–19, 106:14–15	Ode 23	GThom 101–107
9	SecJas 8	Sylvanus 110:14–111:5, 116:27–117:9	Sir 48:4–14	GThom 108–113
10	SecJas 9	Isa 61:1–3	Ode 32	Beatitudes
11	SecJas 10	Prov 19:11, 20:22, 24:29, 25:21	Sir 22:16–18	Q 6:20–23, 27–28
12	SecJas 11	SecJohn 1:4–25, 30–32, 2:1–25	Ode 15	Q 6:39–49
13	Did 1	ThomCont 138:4–27, 139:13–21	Ode 18	Q 7:1–10
14	Did 2	Mal 3:1–3	Ode 21	Q 7:18–19, 22–35
15	Did 3	1Kgs 19:19–21	Ode 39	Q 9:57, 10:2–4
16	Did 4	2Kgs 4:29–37	Ode 36	Q 10:5–22
17	Did 5 & 6	Ezek 36:22–28	Sir 28:2–7	Q 10:23–24, 11:2–13
18	Did 7–8	2 Esdr 7:78–87	Ode 40	Q 11:14–32
19	Did 9	2 Sam 12:1–12	Mic 6:6–9	Q 11:33–51, 12:2–3
20	Did 10	GPhil 63:21, 55:6–14, 57:6–9, 75:14–24	WisSol 1:1–7	Q 12:4–21

21	Did 11	Tob 4:5–11	Ode 22	Q 12:33–34, 22b-31, 39–40
22	Did 12	Mic 7:1–7	Ode 25	Q 12:42–46, 49–59
23	Did 13	Ezek 17:22–23	Ode 26	Q 13:18–35, 14:11
24	Did 14	Prov 9:1–6	Ode 28:1–6	Q 14:16–23
25	Did 15	2Esdr 13:51–56	Ode 34	Q 17:3–4, 6, 22–35
26	Did 16	ApocPaul 18:3–19:20	WisSol 4:11–18	Q 19:12–26, 22:28–30

Pre-Christmas

9 Before	1Sam 1:1–7a		Ode 37	InJas 1–2
8 Before	1Sam 1:7b–19a		Ode 29	InJas 3–4
7 Before	1Sam 1:19b–28		1Sam 2:1–11	InJas 5–6
6 Before	Gen 28:10–17		Ps 87	InJas 7–8
5 Before	LadJac 7:1–35		Ode 33	InJas 9–10
1 Advent	Adam 3		Ode 14	InJas 11–12
2 Advent	Deut 22:23–24		Ode 38:1–6	InJas 13–14
3 Advent	Isa 7:10–14		Ode 38:7–14	InJas 15–16
4 Advent	Gen 25:19–26		Ode 38:15–19	InJas 17

Christmas Season

Christmas	SibOr 10:456–479		Ode 19	InJas 18–19
Dec 26	Exod 1:15–21		Carol	InJas 20
Dec 27	Isa 1:1–4	SibOr 1:324–355	Carol	Pseudo Matt 14
Dec 28	InJas 21–22		Carol	Matt 2:13–15
Dec 29	Pseudo Matt 18–20		Carol	Matt 2:19–23
Dec 30	Luke 2:22–28		Luke 2:29–32	Luke 2:33–38
Dec 31	InThom 1–2	InThom 3	Carol	InThom 5
Jan 1	InThom 6:1–8	InThom 6:9–12	Carol	InThom 6:13–23
Jan 2	InThom 7	InThom 8	Carol	InThom 9
Jan 3	InThom 10–11	InThom 12	Carol	InThom 13
Jan 4	InThom 16	InThom 17	Carol	InThom 18
Jan 5	InThom 14	InThom 15	Carol	InThom 19

Eucharistic Prayers

The Didache
Justin Martyr
Apostolic Tradition of Hippolytus
Apostolic Constitutions
Nag Hammadi Library
Acts of John
Acts of Thomas

Prayers

Acts of Thomas
Prayer of the Apostle Paul

Abbreviations

AcJohn	Acts of John	NHL	Nag Hammadi Library
AcPet	Acts of Peter	NJB	New Jerusalem Bible
Acts	Acts of the Apostles	NRSV	New Revised Standard
Adam	Testament of Adam		Version
ApocPaul	Apocalypse of Paul	NTA	New Testament
Archons	Hypostasis of the		Apocrypha
	Archons	Num	Numbers
Barn	Barnabas	Ode	Odes of Solomon
Bar	Baruch	Origins	On the Origin of the
BCP	Book of Common		World
	Prayer	OTP	Old Testament
1,2 Cor	1,2 Corinthians		Pseudepigrapha
Dan	Daniel	1,2 Pet	1,2 Peter
Deut	Deuteronomy	POxy 840	Oxyrhynchus Papyrus
Did	Didache		840
DialSav	Dialogue of Savior	POxy 1224	Oxyrhynchus Papyrus
Eccl	Ecclesiastes		1224
EgerG	Egerton Gospel	Prov	Proverbs
1,2 Esdr	1,2 Esdras	Ps(s)	Psalm(s)
Exod	Exodus	Pseudo Matt	Pseudo Matthew
Ezek	Ezekiel	Q	Q Gospel
Gal	Galatians	Resurrection	Treatise on the
GEbi	Gospel of the Ebionites		Resurrection
Gen	Genesis	Rev	Revelation
GHeb	Gospel of the Hebrews	Rom	Romans
GMary	Gospel of Mary	RSV	Revised Standard
GPet	Gospel of Peter		Version
GPhil	Gospel of Philip	1,2 Sam	1,2 Samuel
GThom	Gospel of Thomas	SecJas	Secret Book of James
Heb	Hebrews	SecMark	Secret Mark
InJas	Infancy James	SibOr	Sibylline Oracles
InThom	Infancy Thomas	Sir	Sirach
Isa	Isaiah	SongSol	Song of Solomon
Job		SophiaJesus	Sophia of Jesus Christ
1,2 Kgs	1,2 Kings	SV	Scholars Version
LadJac	Ladder of Jacob	Sylvanus	Teachings of Sylvanus
Lev	Leviticus	1,2 Thess	1,2 Thessalonians
Luke		Thomas	Gospel of Thomas
1,2,3,4, Macc	1,2,3,4, Maccabees	ThomCont	Thomas the Contender
Mal	Malachi	Tob	Tobit
Mark		WisSol	Wisdom of Solomon
Matt	Matthew	Zech	Zechariah
Mic	Micah	Zeph	Zephaniah

Glossary

Acts of the Apostles: A continuation of the Gospel of Luke providing stories of the Holy Spirit empowering Peter, Paul, and the other apostles in proclaiming the Gospel and forming congregations along the eastern shore of the Mediterranean, Asia Minor, and Rome. Not included is the spread of the church into other areas such as Egypt, Syria, and India. Written about 90 C.E.

Acts of John: Usually placed in the second half of the second century, Acts of John presupposes the tradition of John's activity in Ephesus and Asia Minor. Highlights include the Dance of Christ and a meditation on the Mystery of the Cross.

Acts of Peter and the Twelve Apostles: A second century NHL composite text of four originally independent accounts of resurrection experiences brought together by an editor.

Acts of Thomas: Originally composed in East Syria at the beginning of the third century includes the legendary story of Thomas taking the Gospel to India. Highlights include the Hymn of the Pearl, intense prayers, baptism, and eucharistic liturgies.

Advent and Pre-Christmas: The liturgical year has had several 'beginnings' in the course of its development in the Western Church. The original one, still maintained in the Eastern Churches, was Easter Day. At Rome the old custom of beginning the civil year with the month of March was combined with the Church's practice of preparing candidates for Easter baptism. When Christmas was instituted in the fourth century it became the beginning of the church year. The season of Advent meaning "Coming" was first inaugurated in the Gallican churches of France and Spain, exactly when is not known, but it was probably the fourth century. Celtic Christianity, rooted in the festival of Samhain, begins the year with All Saints Day on November 1 followed by Sundays before Christmas.

Apocalypse of Paul: The date and provenance of the Apocalypse of Paul cannot be determined with any certainty, but the second century is most likely. Highly symbolic resurrection stories centering in Paul and his journey through the heavens may refer to the movement of spiritual energy through the body.

Apostolic Constitutions: A compilation of early church canons and church order derived from sources differing in age. The entire work is not later than the fourth century.

Apostolic Tradition of Hippolytus: Writing from Rome ca. 217 C.E., Hippolytus describes baptism, eucharist, and other liturgies. As a conservative in his time, his descriptions reflect much earlier practices.

Ash Wednesday: Late medieval liturgies provide for imposition of ashes as a sign of penitence and mortality, but the practice has deeper roots as illustrated in the book of Job. The words normally given with the ashes are "Remember that you are dust and to dust you shall return." In today's context, this ritual may also invoke a sense of deep connection with the Earth and a focus on environmental and ecological concerns.

Baruch: More than likely composed in Hebrew in Palestine sometime during the second to first centuries B.C.E., Baruch provides valuable insight into the wisdom and everyday piety of Jews of that time.

Bridal Chamber Liturgies are individual and corporate rites in which souls experience mystical union. The Bridal Chamber is most notable in the Gospel of Philip, the Exegesis of the Soul, the Teachings of Sylvanus, and other NHL texts.

Canon: An authoritative list or collection of books accepted as holy scripture. The canon was determined for Roman Catholics at the Council of Trent (1546), which formally ratified the list of books in use since the fourth century. Orthodox churches follow a canon that does not include the Book of Revelation. The canon has never been determined for Protestants, except by common consent.

C.E., B.C.E.: C.E. stands for Common Era; B.C.E. for Before the Common Era. These designations are used rather than the earlier forms out of deference to those for whom the birth of Christ marks the beginning of a new era only in a secular sense.

Christmas: The feasts of Christmas and Epiphany developed as means to oppose or transform pagan festivals related to the winter solstice. The *dies natalis Solis Invicti*, the birthday of the Unconquerable Sun (Saturn), was celebrated at Rome beginning about December 21 and lasting for more than a week. Probably by 336 C.E. Christians had appropriated December 25 as the day to celebrate the incarnation. Note Epiphany below.

Coptic: The form of the Egyptian language in use at the time of the introduction of Christianity in Egypt. Coptic uses the Greek alphabet.

Dialogue of the Savior: This highly fragmentary Gospel found in the NHL is a series of dialogues between the Lord and several disciples. The instructions are probably addressed to those in the author's community who are preparing for baptism. This text of traditional sayings of Jesus most likely reached its final form around 150 C.E.

Didache, also known as the Teachings of the Twelve Apostles, is a compact handbook of ethics, liturgy, and church leadership. The final form of the Didache, which was discovered in 1875, dates from the early second century. However, its main selections go back to the first century with numerous quotations from the Gospels.

Egerton Gospel: This unknown gospel is named after the Englishman who funded the purchase of fragments from the a papyrus codex which can be dated to the second century C.E., perhaps as early as 125 C.E.

Epiphany: An English cognate term for the Greek *epiphaneia* meaning, "Manifestation." In Egypt, January 6 was celebrated as the winter solstice when the sun god made his appearance (epiphany) and was honored with light, water, and wine. The Christians chose this time as the feast of the incarnation and connected it with three Gospel stories: the coming of the Magi, the baptism of Jesus, and the wedding at Cana. Of these, baptism was the primary event. Since Vatican II and the liturgical renewal in Roman, Anglican, Protestant, and other liturgical churches, the Sunday after January 6 has become the day to celebrate the Baptism of Jesus.

Easter: Originally the name of a goddess and her spring festival, Easter became the principal festival of the liturgical year in celebrating the Resurrection of Jesus. Rooted in Sunday as a weekly celebration of the Resurrection, Easter goes back to the beginnings of Christianity.

2 Esdras: Written in Hebrew by a Jew from Judea about 100 C.E., 2 Esdras is a composite book containing three works of different origins. It gives expression to a crisis of faith for Jews which occurred after the destruction of the Second Temple in Jerusalem in 70 C.E.

Gospel of the Ebionites: A Jewish-Christian gospel preserved only in passages cited by Epiphanius, a fourth century Christian theologian. The original title is unknown. The "Ebionim" are the poor. They were Greek-speaking Jewish Christians who flourished in the second and third centuries. Their gospel probably dates to the mid-second century C.E.

Gospel of the Hebrews: Probably composed in Egypt sometime between the mid first century and the mid-second century. Several early Christian theologians knew and quoted this gospel, but it did not survive as an independent text.

Gospel of Mary: The only Gospel named for a woman, Mary provides conversations between the Risen Savior, Mary Magdalene, and other disciples. It reveals the leadership of women in the early church and resistance from some males. Nothing is known about the author or provenance of the original text, although both Egypt and Syria have been suggested. Dating is also highly tentative, but the Gospel of Mary arguably may have been written sometime in the late first or early second century.

Gospel of Peter: Preserved only as a fragment discovered in a monk's grave at Akhmim, located along the Nile in Upper Egypt, about 50 miles north of Nag Hammadi. In its original form, the Gospel of Peter may have arisen in the second half of the first century C.E. It contains a passion narrative and a resurrection-ascension story which may be earlier than those in the Synoptics. It became known as the Gospel of Peter due to the fact that Simon Peter is presented as its author.

Gospel of Philip: Named in honor of Philip the apostle, this gospel contains occasional words or deeds of Jesus and his companion, Mary Magdalene. Most of the book reflects later development of faith and practice including the intriguing Bridal Chamber liturgy. There are indications to suggest a Syrian origin, probably in Antioch or its neighborhood. Discovered in a Coptic translation in the NHL, this gospel probably goes back to a Greek original dating from the second half of the second century.

Gospel of Thomas: A Gospel of sayings attributed to Jesus. Its first edition and the Q Gospel, ca. 50 C.E, are earlier than the Synoptics. Matthew and Luke used some of the sayings in Thomas when creating their gospels. A complete Gospel of Thomas survives in Coptic in the NHL. Fragments of a Greek version of Thomas were discovered at Oxyrhynchus, Egypt, ca. 1900 C.E.

Infancy Gospel of James: Probably written in the middle of the second century C.E., Infancy James expands upon the birth stories in Matthew and Luke. It adds stories about the parents of Mary, her birth and childhood. It's highly symbolic imagery features the birth of Jesus in a cave with a profound moment of silence and stillness in all of creation.

Infancy Gospel of Thomas: The legendary childhood stories in this gospel fill the gap between Jesus birth and his visit to Jerusalem at the age of twelve. Evidence from Irenaeus shows that it was in circulation in the second century. Nothing certain can be said about the place or circumstances of its composition. Infancy Thomas survives in various forms in a number of languages including Syriac, Greek, Latin, and Slavonic.

Hypostasis of the Archons, meaning "Reality of the Powers," is an anonymous tractate presenting a third century interpretation of the Genesis creation story in which the serpent serves as instructor opening the eyes of Adam and Eve to consciousness. Hypostasis has a clear literary relationship with another NHL document, On the Origin of the World.

Judeans: The religion of the first Jerusalem temple (959-597 B.C.E.) was practiced by the Israelites. The religion of the second temple (520 B.C.E.-70 C.E.) was practiced by Judeans. The religion of the rabbis and synagogue (90 C.E. and continuing) was and is practiced by Jews. The Fellows of the Jesus Seminar have adopted this nomenclature in order to be historically accurate and to avoid confusing the three major periods of Jewish history.

Justin Martyr: Justin was a Christian apologist who was martyred between 163 and 167 C.E. He composed the First and Second Apologies and the Dialogue with Trypho. These books were produced shortly after 150 C.E. Justin provides a description of how the Eucharist was celebrated in early communities of faith.

Ladder of Jacob expands the story of Jacob's ladder dream in Gen. 28:10-17. Greek may be the original language of the Ladder but its date and provenance are unknown. A first century C.E. date has been suggested.

Lent: The origins of Lent go back to at least as early as the second century, and may be traced as the development of a time of prayer, fasting, and instruction of candidates preparing for Baptism at Easter. The length of the pre-Easter fast varied in different churches, but in the beginning of the fourth century we first hear of a forty-day period of fasting in the famous Festal Letters of St. Athanasius. Association of the forty days with Jesus' time in the wilderness was an afterthought; it did not directly affect the early development of the Lenten season. The word, 'Lent' derives from an old Anglo-Saxon word meaning 'spring.'

LXX: The Greek translation of the Hebrew Bible, together with other works, some of which were composed in Greek. According to legend, seventy (or seventy-two) translators were involved in the work.

Nag Hammadi Library (NHL): A collection of 13 leather bound books discovered inside a large earthenware jar in December, 1945, by the farmer Muhammad Ali when he was digging for nitrates at the base of a cliff just outside Nag Hammadi, a town in Egypt located at the northern beginning of the big bend of the Nile River. The library, buried for safe keeping at the beginning of the fourth century, contains 52 documents (6 being duplicates) including the Gospel of Thomas and other early Christian writings. The documents are Coptic translations from earlier Greek originals.

Odes of Solomon: Sometime around 100 C.E., a Christian living in Syria and heavily influenced by Jewish thought composed 42 odes. Their thought is similar to that found in the Jewish apocalypses and within some of the Dead Sea Scrolls. As with other books in the wisdom tradition, the Odes are named in honor of King Solomon who lived one thousand years earlier. The Odes of Solomon is the oldest song book of the early church other than the Hebrew Book of Psalms.

On the Origin of the World: An expansion and symbolic development of the Genesis creation stories, this NHL tractate is most likely to have originated in Alexandria during the third century.

Passion: This term traditionally refers to the last two days of Jesus' life, beginning with the last supper and including his agony in Gethsemane, his arrest, trials, crucifixion, death, and burial. Liturgically, Holy Week begins with Passion Sunday when normally the entire passion narrative is read.

Pentecost is the fiftieth day after Passover, the popular Feast of Weeks of early harvest (Exod 23:26, 34:22; Lev. 23:15-21; Deut 16:9-12.) Midrashic Jewish interpretation made Pentecost a celebration of the giving of the Law to Moses on Sinai. Acts adds one more layer of midrash by centering attention on the outpouring of the Holy Spirit writing the law on hearts and releasing tremendous energy in the gathered assembly.

POxy 840 and POxy 1240: see Oxyrynchus below.

Oxyrhynchus: An ancient village in Egypt where numerous papyri have been discovered. Among its most important treasures are Oxyrhunchus Gospels 840 and 1224, fragments of otherwise unknown gospels, and POxy 1, 654, 655, Greek fragments of the Gospel of Thomas.

Papyrus: The predecessor to modern paper. Ancient works were written on animal skins, called parchment or vellum, or on papyrus, made from Egyptian reeds.

Q Gospel: "Q" is an abbreviation of the German word Quelle, meaning "source." It is used to designate a document which most scholars believe the authors of Matthew and Luke used in writing their gospels. Likewise, it is believed that these gospel writers used the Gospel of Mark. While Mark is an extant text, Q is a hypothetical construct. No independent copy of it exists. But it is widely believed that the passages in Matthew and Luke that are almost the same, and that did not come from Mark, must have come from this lost source. Q is a collection of the sayings attributed to Jesus, similar in form to the Gospel of Thomas.Unlike the sayings in Thomas, however, most of the sayings in Q are gathered into discourses. Originating in Galilee or Syria, the first edition of Q is dated ca. 50 C.E.

Pseudo Matthew: Written in the eighth or ninth century, Pseudo Matthew continues the expansion of the birth stories by adding new symbolic details including the ox and the ass so familiar in Christmas nativity scenes.

Secret Book of James, also known as the Apocryphon of James, consists primarily of conversations between James and his Resurrected brother, Jesus. It concludes with a rare ascension story. Discovered in its Coptic version in the NHL, Secret James may well have been written in the first half of the second century and contains much earlier oral tradition.

Secret Book of John, also known as the Apocryphon of John, is a highly symbolic development of the creation myths. God is known as both Mother and Father. Christ and Sophia are one. Reports from the early church fathers indicate that this book was known in the second century. A coptic copy is in the NHL.

Secret Gospel of Mark: Fragments of an early edition of the Gospel of Mark were found in a letter of Clement of Alexandria (second century C.E.). One fragment continues the story of the rich young man. Its discovery poses the question: Why was this material deleted from the Gospel of Mark? Might now be the time to restore the missing pieces to their rightful place?

Sibylline Oracles: The dates of the various Sibylline books range from the middle of the second century B.C.E. to the seventh century C.E. Approximately half the collection can be ascribed to Egypt and the other half, with varying degrees of probability, to Syria. Among the prophecies and teachings can be found highly energized hymns and poems.

Sirach: Jesus ben Sira taught in Jerusalem ca. 200-175 B.C.E. His teachings were collected into a book called Sirach or Ecclesiasticus, which is preserved in the LXX. It belongs to the wisdom tradition of the Judeans.

Sophia: Greek for "wisdom." Wisdom is often personified in early Judean literature. She is Consort of the Lord, the feminine in the Holy Mystery.

Sophia of Jesus Christ: A discourse between the Risen Redeemer and his disciples: twelve men and seven women. Found at Nag Hammadi, this tractate was probably composed in Egypt in the second half of the first century. It is a Christianized version of an earlier treatise known as Eugnostos the Blessed.

Synoptic: A term from the Greek synoptikos, "seeing together," meaning "having a common view of," referring to the Gospels of Mark, Matthew, and Luke, which are similar in form, outline, and contents.

Tanakh: Hebrew Bible, The Jewish "Old Testament."

Teachings of Sylvanus: This NHL book is a rare example of Hellenistic Christian wisdom literature displaying a remarkable synthesis of biblical and late Jewish ideas with Middle Platonic and late Stoic anthropological, ethical, and theological concepts. This synthesis has a clear purpose: to impart the Wisdom of Christ toward union with God. Dating is late second to early third century C.E.

Testament of Adam: Beginning with a Jewish text, the Testament acquired Christian additions and grew in length during the second to fifth centuries C.E. Three languages have been proposed as the originals of the Testament of Adam: Hebrew, Greek, and Syriac. While it is most likely to have been written in Syria or Palestine, its precise location is unknown. This is a theological work focusing on the cosmos, creation, and angelology. Genesis does not say what kind of fruit was offered by the serpent to Adam and Eve in the Garden of Eden but the Testament of Adam identifies it as a fig.

Thomas the Contender (Thomas the Athlete) is a conversation between the resurrected Jesus and his twin brother Judas Thomas. Thinking of Jesus and Thomas as literal twins may be quite startling. The writers in the Thomas tradition are speaking symbolically. They are also inviting the reader to come into a close relationship with Jesus experiencing him not only as a brother, but also as a twin. Thomas the Athlete is likely to have been composed in eastern Syria between Edessa and Messene in the first half of the third century.

Tobit is a three part novel about Tobit and his future daughter in law, Sarah, written in Hebrew or Aramaic for a Jewish audience during the Greco-Roman period, ca. third to second century B.C.E. It contains many references to Persian lands, and though it may not have been written in the east, it has an eastern orientation.

Treatise on Resurrection focuses attention on the meaning of death and resurrection. A dating of late second century is likely. The book is part of the NHL but as to its original provenance, neither internal nor external evidence provide any clues.

Wisdom of Solomon was originally composed in Greek by a Hellenized Jew who almost certainly lived in Alexandria, Egypt, somewhere around the turn of the first century, C.E. The book is one of many works of wisdom literature written in honor of King Solomon but composed by someone else. It is written in a poetic style.

Index of Scripture

Christian Texts

*Please note that this lectionary follows the usual definition of a gospel as being material related to the life and teachings of Jesus. Since the Gospel of Philip does not meet this definition of a Gospel it is included here.

Indexes

Jewish Texts

Indexes